Contemporary Applied Management:
Behavioral Science Techniques for Managers and Professionals

Contemporary Applied Management:
Behavioral Science Techniques for Managers and Professionals

ANDREW J. DuBRIN
Rochester Institute of Technology

1985

Second Edition

BUSINESS PUBLICATIONS, INC.   Plano, Texas 75075

To Doug

©BUSINESS PUBLICATIONS, INC., 1982 and 1985

ISBN 0-256-03258-0

Library of Congress Catalog Card No. 84-72741

Printed in the United States of America.

1 2 3 4 5 6 7 8 9 0 ML 2 1 0 9 8 7 6 5

Preface

In recent years, management thought and action has been influenced by the work of behavioral scientists. Many students of organizational behavior, management, and personnel/human resource management have been exposed to general information about behaviorally based techniques and concepts (such as team building, methods of conflict resolution, and career development programs). Students could also benefit from information about the specific application of these approaches. The purpose of this book is to provide managers, aspiring managers, and staff professionals with a look at the practical value of a current selection of behavioral science techniques, methods, and strategies. Toward this purpose, each chapter begins with a hands-on demonstration—in a job setting—of the technique, method, or strategy under consideration. The demonstration, or illustrative case history, is preceded by a statement of why the technique was chosen or what problem it was designed to solve.

The underlying theme of this book is that applied management techniques serve useful ends (such as increased performance and morale) despite some of their disadvantages and shortcomings. In order to realize the advantages of these methods, certain guidelines should be followed. In support of this theme, each chapter considers both the advantages and disadvantages, or strengths and weaknesses, of the technique or method. In addition, guidelines are presented for the appropriate application of each technique, method, or concept.

This book is written for two audiences. One is managers and individual contributors (nonmanagers) seeking professional development on their own, or within the context of internal management development programs. The other audience is students of organizational behavior, human relations, organizational psychology, management, or personnel/human resource management. The book is designed to be used either as a supplement to a formal text, or alone in applied courses, or in management development programs.

Generally the user of this book will have some understanding of, or will have completed some reading in organizational behavior, human relations, management, or personnel/human resource management. *Contemporary Applied Management* intentionally does not duplicate the vital background theory contained in various readings on behavioral science applications to management practice. Following this preface is a representative list of text books that would serve as appropriate theoretical background for the mate-

material contained in this book. Most current texts in the organizational behavior, management, and personnel/human resource management fields would provide the student an adequate theoretical background and research orientation to the field of applied management.

In addition to providing a concise look at the application of current applied management techniques and methods, this book has several other objectives. A major objective is to provide an explanation of techniques which can be applied by managers acting alone with some assistance from a specialist in the applied behavioral science area. Two examples would be a career development specialist and an organization development specialist (both workers are usually found within the human resource management department). Some of the techniques described (such as negotiating with others or improving work habits and time management) do not require an organization-wide program in order to be implemented.

Another objective is to offer a balanced presentation of the methods described, looking at both strengths and potential pitfalls. However, if a particular technique is considered of neutral or negative value, it is not included here.

Still another objective is to provide readers an opportunity to enhance their managerial skills. One approach to this objective is to include discussions of managerial skill development at various places in the manuscript. Another approach is to provide the reader with concrete guidelines for the effective use of the techniques described. We therefore include a Guidelines for Action and Skill Development section at the end of each chapter. The guidelines can also be regarded as generalizations for applying the technique or method under disscussion. A final objective is to increase the self-awareness of the reader in relation to such key aspects of job behavior as assertiveness, negotiating skill, creativity, teamwork, and burnout. To accomplish this purpose, self-examination questionnaires are included as appendixes to appropriate chapters. Although these instruments are not scientifically validated, they can serve as potent launching points for personalized discussions about the technique under examination.

CHANGES IN THE NEW EDITION

The revised edition has several major changes in content and structure and updates research evidence and opinion about the methods and techniques described in the book. The new part structure is designed to fit more closely the design of courses in which the book is used both in educational and businss settings.

Part I, *Improving Individual Effectiveness*, describes four techniques individuals can use to improve personal productivity and enhance their careers. Part II, *Improving Interpersonal Relationships*, deals with four techniques and methods designed to overcome or prevent problems among people in organizations. Part III, *Improving the Functioning of Work Groups*, describes four methods designed to enhance both productivity and morale.

Part IV, *Improving Productivity and Quality at the Organizational Level*, describes four popular methods for boosting productivity, and sometimes morale. Part V, *Human Resource Management Programs*, describes four well-structured human resource programs typically administered through the personnel (human resource management) department.

Exhibit I

Representative list of texts that provide appropriate theoretical and conceptual background for techniques and methods described in *Contemporary Applied Management: Behavioral Science Techniques for Managers and Professionals.*

Organizational behavior:

DuBrin, Andrew J. *Foundations of Organizational Behavior: An Applied perspective.* Englewood Cliffs, N. J.: Prentice-Hall, 1984.
Gibson, James L., John M. Ivancevich, and James H. Donnelly, Jr. *Organizations: Behavior, Structure, Process,* 5th ed. Plano, Tex.: Business Publications, 1985.
Hamner, W. Clay, and Dennis W. Organ. *Organizational Behavior: An Applied Psychological Approach,* rev. ed. Plano, Tex.: Business Publications, 1982.
Luthans, Fred. *Organizational Behavior,* 4th ed. New York: McGraw-Hill, 1985.
Szilagyi, Andrew, and Marc Wallace. *Organizational Behavior and Performance,* 3rd ed. Glenview, Ill.: Scott, Foresman, 1983.

Management:

Albanese, Robert. *Managing: Toward Accountability for Performance,* 3rd. ed. Homewood, Ill.: Richard D. Irwin, 1981.
Donnelly, James H., Jr., James L. Gibson, and John M. Ivancevich, *Fundamentals of Management,* 5th ed. Plano, Tex.: Business Publications, 1984.
Kreitner, Robert. *Management,* 2nd ed. Boston: Houghton Mifflin, 1983.
Robbins, Stephen P. *Management: Concepts and Practices.* Englewood Cliffs, N. J.: Prentice-Hall, 1984.
Stoner, James A. F. *Management,* 2nd ed. Englewood Cliffs, N.J.: Prentice–Hall, 1982.
Williams, J. Clifton, Andrew J. DuBrin, and Henry J. Sisk, *Management and Organization,* 5th ed. Cincinnati: South–Western, 1985.

Personnel/Human Resource Management:

Chruden, Herbert J., and Arthur W. Sherman. *Managing Human Resources,* 7th ed. Cincinnati: South-Western, 1984.
Dessler, Gary. *Personnel Management: Modern Concepts and Techniques,* 3rd ed. Reston, Va.: Reston Publishing, 1984.
French, Wendell L., *The Personnel Management Process,* 5th ed. Boston: Houghton Mifflin, 1982.
Heneman, Herbert G., III, Donald P. Schwab, John A. Fossum, and Lee D. Dyer, *Personnel/Human Resource Management,* rev. ed. Homewood, Ill.: Richard D. Irwin, 1983.
Glueck William F. and Milkovich, George T. *Personnel: A Diagnostic Approach,* 3rd, ed. Plano, Tex.: Business Publications, 1984.
Schuler, Randall S. *Effective Personnel Management,* 2nd. ed. St. Paul, Minn.: West Publishing, 1984.

Another change in this new edition is an enlarged and expanded instructor's manual. It now contains approximately 475 test questions, answers to discussion questions, many role-playing activities, comments about the use of the self-examination questionnaires, and a section on how *Contemporary Applied Management* can be used to supplement several current texts.

ACKNOWLEDGMENTS

Producing a book of this nature is a team effort. Among the key contributors to this project was the late Donald A. Kolbe, Jr., the editor at Business Publications, Inc., who authorized this revised edition. Professor John M. Ivancevich receives my appreciation for presenting me with the basic concept for the first edition of this book. The outside reviewers for this project provided major suggestions for improving the structure and the content of the book. In alphabetical order they are M. K. Badawy, Cleveland State University; John D. Blair, Texas Tech University; Angelo S. DeNisi, University of South Carolina; Bill Fannin, University of Houston; and Mary Van Sell, Michigan State University. Nancy Johnson, my secretary, made an important contribution to this project.

The many professors, trainers, and students who had kind words about the first edition of this book also receive my appreciation. Thanks also to Maria Jeremias for her love and support, and her belief in the contribution of my writing. My children, Drew, Doug, and Melanie receive credit for collectively giving me one more external reason for preparing another book.

Andrew J. DuBrin

Contents

The Argument against Assessment Centers. Guidelines for Action and Skill Development. *Questions and Activities. Notes. Some Additional References.*

Part 1

Improving Individual Effectiveness

The four chapters in this section concentrate on developing skills, techniques, and attitudes that can help the individual perform more effectively on the job. Frequently these same skills, techniques, and attitudes can be applied to improving effectiveness in personal life. These four chapters provide insight into overcoming problems that face many managers and staff specialists. The four major problems covered here are low personal productivity, insufficient job creativity, shyness, and burnout.

Chapter 1, Work Habits and Time Management, covers the always current topic of improving personal productivity. The goal of improving organizational productivity often can be met partially by improving efficiency and effectiveness among organizational members. Improvement of work habits and time management results in control of time and work and often prevents stress caused by feeling overwhelmed by the job.

Chapter 2, Improving Your Creativity, presents several do-it-yourself techniques for making better use of creative potential. A case description of how brainstorming works in practice is included. The chapter concludes with a scientifically validated instrument for measuring creative potential.

Chapter 3, Assertiveness Training, provides some specific tips for helping people attain their goals by expressing their feelings and taking action. Assertiveness training (AT) is an offshoot of principles of behavior therapy, which itself is based on principles of behavior modification. It is often used in contemporary organizations to encourage women and minorities to assert themselves and thus improve their chances for advancement. Assertiveness is also a valuable managerial behavior.

Chapter 4, Preventing and Overcoming Job Burnout, deals with a topic of great current concern—the problem of burnout in managerial work. During the past several years, much attention has been paid to this topic in relation to the helping professions, particularly teaching and mental health care. Recently, behavioral scientists have come to recognize that sometimes managerial workers also suffer from a gap between the rewards they receive and those they hope to receive. Large numbers of workers at every level may suffer from burnout when two organizational conditions are present: the firm is in decline while, at the same time, workers are given limited recognition from management for their efforts. The theory underlying the burnout prescriptions described in the chapter comes from literature on stress. Some of the remedial suggestions are based on direct experience in helping individuals and organizations cope with burnout.

Chapter 1

Work Habits and Time Management

A social agency executive faced the typical managerial challenge of having too much to accomplish in too little time. He also began to feel he was losing control of his job. To learn how to cope with these problems, he chose to attend a time management workshop.

It is a windswept Saturday morning in El Paso, Texas. Miguel Ramirez clutches his tightly stuffed attache case as he climbs into his VW Rabbit. He heads toward his office downtown and thinks to himself:

There goes a Saturday morning of paneling the basement. I'm two months behind schedule on that project. I've promised Melinda and the children I would cut down my Saturdays at the agency. I guess I've blown that too, at least for the next two or three weeks.

But it's all for the good. Things are going to be better from this point on. I'm going to somehow untangle the mess at Mountainview Family Services. I think I can get a good return on investment from my two days at Lucy Clark's time management workshop. The things she told us weren't too far removed from common sense. I've known about them for years. I have to admit, though, the woman is right. Knowing about good time management and doing something about it are two different things. I've been running around stamping out fires for too long. I've got to learn to control events rather than let them control me.

Maybe Lucy Clark is right. I'm too nice a guy. I let everybody else determine what I should be doing even though I'm supposed to be in charge. Whatever they want, I give them. I listen to all their emergencies. In the meantime, my in-basket is the most fully stuffed one in the agency. And I'm the one who suffers the most. I start early, I stay late, and still I'm way behind. I'm listening to my marriage counselors tell me about the problems in their own marriage while I should be working on the budget. I'm filling out federal government forms when I should be coaching my people.

I've never been a workaholic. I take my scheduled vacations and I get penalized for it when I return. Loads of letters, memos, and phone calls have piled up in my absence. It takes me two weeks to catch up.

Miguel waved hello to the security guard as he entered the modest building in which Mountainview Family Services is located. Upon entering his office, he placed his lunch box on top of a file cabinet. He thought to himself, "It's 8:55. I'm five minutes ahead of schedule. I'll work until 4:30 with only a 30-minute lunch break. No phone calls except for one at midday to check how things are going at home. No trips to the photocopying machine. A 30-minute break for lunch; no 90 minutes down the tubes for a lunch with another agency head."

Miguel sat down at his desk and pulled out a yellow writing tablet and a pen from his desk. Out of his briefcase came his notes from the time management seminar. "Let's see, Lucy Clark said that really to improve your time management you have to begin with a clean-up campaign. Grab a shovel, dig in, and get rid of everything in your desk and personal files that you don't need. I'll start right here with my small desk drawer."

Miguel began to sort through the miscellany accumulated in his desk. With a determined look on his face he thought to himself, "No need for these bent paper clips; out with these dried up pens. Here's an address book so old that some of the addresses don't even have zip codes. It must have belonged to the founder of Mountainview. Who needs a cocktail stirrer? Why keep these appointment calendars from more than five years ago? Who needs three packs of dental floss in the office? I'll take two home. Here are some copy masters for a machine we stopped using two years ago. Why do I have this broken ruler?"

Already feeling that he was on the road to improvement, Miguel next tackled the files in his private office with similar zeal. "Why am I holding on to travel vouchers for trips I took three years ago?" As he picked through his files, Miguel continued his rhetorical questioning: "What's the purpose of keeping rough notes for a presentation to the United Way I made last year? Why hold on to this manual for implementing a performance appraisal system we discarded two years ago? Why keep copies of correspondence to job candidates who've been hired or rejected in the past?"

Within two hours of concentrated action, Miguel had discarded two cardboard cartons and two wastebaskets of forms, memos, and miscellaneous files of no apparent value to him or the agency. Miguel thought:

> I must watch myself. I'm not going to improve my time management by just getting rid of useless files and cleaning up my office. I've also got to tackle the major demands of my job. The first step in this direction according to Lucy Clark's manual is to find out what my job really is. My job description and my goals and objectives are a good starting point. I'll put that on the agenda for the next board meeting. I'll ask them to put in specific terms what they think my job encompasses. I suspect the board and I will both be in for some surprises.

I know they think my department heads should be ironing out all the difficult problems with community leaders. But as executive director, I know I have to spend a lot of time putting out those kinds of fires. When a heavyweight in the community wants action, they want to see the executive director. Even if we have a few healthy disagreements over the scope of my job, I know things can be worked out.

Another idea that hit me in the workshop was the importance of eliminating some of the work I'm currently doing. Maybe the board and I could agree on eliminating a couple of the major reports I prepare each year. Maybe that six-month summary of activities could be converted into an annual report. Why do I have to attend the national conference of family service executives? Maybe I should just attend the regional conference given every two years. I think that if I could eliminate about 15 percent of the things I do, I'd have the time to do a better job as executive director.

Enough on that topic, for now. It's time to tackle another biggie—establishing priorities for my job responsibilities. Once I get the list done, I'll touch base with the board of directors and my department heads. I'd be curious to know if they share my priorities. Of course, I won't modify all my priorities to meet their demands. Let's see, according to this system, you list all the tasks to be done and rate them A, B, or C. A is the most urgent; C the least; B is in the middle. Here goes my first try (Miguel spends 20 minutes working and reworking his list.)

Tasks to Be Done within 30 Days

1. Meet with my four department heads individually to discuss their objectives for the upcoming year. I'll give that an A. I'll meet with them in inverse order of their ability to prepare objectives. In order, I will meet with heads of drug counseling, marriage and family counseling, the day-care center, and youth activities.

2. Prepare budget for the next year. No doubt, this is a clear A.

3. Get temporary replacement for my secretary Juanita. Definitely an A item. She is seven months pregnant and will be out for two months. (Miguel thought to himself as he prepared this objective, "This really shows me we have to get organized around here. I wonder if we're in shape to run this agency without Juanita.")

4. Plan for refurbishing the offices; painting some new file cabinets; replace the worst furniture; hang a few decent prints on the wall. Maybe a B. It might improve morale, but we've suffered along for many years with this same drab setting.

5. Get project started for developing new brochure for our agency. A C rating is OK here. A brochure would be nice but we have more business than we can handle using the same outdated brochure.

After lunch Miguel spent a couple of hours further cleaning out the files and dictating six overdue letters. At 4 P.M. he reminded himself that he must try a sample time log one day this week. He reflected, "Monday would not be a good day to try a time log. It's just too hectic. The other days are more normal. Maybe I'll try a time log some other Monday. Tuesday will be my first attempt." Miguel left the office feeling a greater sense of accomplishment than he had in many months.

Dutifully, he filled in his time log on Tuesday. Miguel divided two sheets of lined paper into 15-minute intervals and made a notation of at least one activity he was performing at each interval. Following is a sample from his log:

8:30   Greet Juanita; sign authorization for her typewriter repair.
9:15   Conference with Randy to discuss his objectives for upcoming year.
10:00   Spend 10 minutes reading mail.
10:30   Telephone call to new board member of United Way, offering my congratulations.
11:15   Telephone call to two contractors about getting bids for repainting the agency.
11:45   Interview with Ellsworth Barnes, job candidate for marriage counselor position in our agency.
12:30   Wait 10 minutes in line at bank to cash check.
1:00   Review of quarterly report of our income and expenses.
1:30   Return call from social services executive who has some questions about financial arrangements with our day-care center.
2:00   Tour agency to get general feel for ongoing activities.
2:45   Listen to social worker complaint that director of marriage and family counseling services is playing favorites.
4:00   Dictate thank-you letter to donor of $3,000 gift to Mountainview.

Tuesday evening, after the children had gone to bed, Miguel scrutinized his diary. Trying to be as detached as possible he said to himself:

"Okay, where are my time wasters? What am I doing wrong? How could I be more productive?" Among Miguel's candid self-criticisms were these:

You goofed right off the bat. You forgot to spend a few minutes planning before you jumped into the day's activities. Why didn't you group your telephone calls together as much as possible? You scattered them too much throughout the day. You would be better off trying to do them in one block of time. The same goes for your letter writing. Why didn't you bring some mail to read while you were waiting in line? Then you wouldn't have minded the wait. It was dead time that didn't even relax you.

Old boy, I think you're making a lot of progress. I can already feel the improvement and I've just been under this program of time management for a few days.

STRATEGIES FOR PERSONAL PRODUCTIVITY

Why improve your work habits and time management? The major justification is to increase your personal productivity by making you both more efficient and more effective. *Efficiency* means that you accomplish tasks with a minimum of wasted time, material, and fanfare. This ratio of output to input represents the traditional concept of productivity. *Effectiveness* refers to the importance and quality of what you actually accomplish. As the popular management cliche states, "Efficiency is doing things right, while effectiveness is doing the right things." Nevertheless, efficiency and effectiveness are not unrelated. Being efficient often clears the way for being effective. If you are on top of your job, it gives you time to work on the major tasks facing you. To be productive in the contemporary meaning of the term, you must be both efficient and effective.[1]

There are other significant reasons for improving your work habits and time management. People with good work habits and time management practices tend to be more successful in their careers than poorly organized individuals. In addition, good work habits and time management allow you to have more time to spend on your personal life. You will also enjoy your personal life more if you are not preoccupied with unfinished tasks.

Our discussion of suggestions for improved personal productivity is divided into two major categories: productive attitudes and values, and productive skills and techniques. All together, 27 suggestions are offered. If practiced, they should lead to improved productivity as a manager or individual contributor.[2] Readers with work experience will be familiar with many of these attitudes, skills, and techniques. In that case, the discussion can serve as a reminder to put into practice familiar ideas.

Productive Attitudes and Values

Be Aware of the Dangers of Procrastination. Beyond question, procrastination is the major way in which employees at all levels waste time. People procrastinate for many different reasons. One reason is that they perceive the task to be done as unpleasant—such as conducting a performance appraisal with a problem employee. We procrastinate also when we perceive the job to be overwhelming, such as preparing a strategic plan for the department.[3] Procrastination also takes place when we fear the consequences of our actions. One possible negative consequence is a poor evaluation of your work. Bad news is another uncomfortable consequence of action that procrastination can sometimes delay. For example, if an executive thinks that a budget analysis will reveal a deficit, he or she may delay preparing the report.

Procrastination is a major hindrance to personal productivity; these four suggestions can help in dealing with the problem. First, calculate the price of procrastination.[4] For example, by not having your resume prepared and printed on time, you may miss out on a high-paying job opportunity. The cost of procrastination includes the difference in salary between the job you find and the one you really want. Another cost is the loss of potential job satisfaction. You may overcome procrastination by creating momentum to get you moving. A useful tactic is to find a leading task (an easy, warm-up activity) to perform.[5] If you have to prepare a strategic plan, it is helpful to get momentum going by performing such tasks as getting a new file folder, sharpening a few pencils, cleaning your desk, and reaching for a text dealing with the subject.

You can also fight procrastination by rewarding yourself for progress you make toward not delaying activity.[6] If you do go ahead and schedule the performance appraisal with the problem employee, treat yourself to a new sweater or a pair of athletic shoes. Finally, making a commitment to other people that you will accomplish something by a certain date *may* help you curb procrastination. If you fail to meet the deadline, you are likely to experience embarrassment or guilt.

Try to Discover Your Mental Blocks. Some forms of low productivity are caused by personal problems or mental blocks. If you can figure out the nature of the block(s), you may be able to increase your productivity. Ronald Ashkenas and Robert Schaffer have discovered, for example, that many managers engage in busy work to help them deal with the anxiety caused by the major tasks facing them. By observing managers in a large assortment of industries, these two consultants have identified three job characteristics common to almost all management levels that create anxiety. All of them lead to busy work:

1. Modifying one's daily work patterns and routines.
2. Responding to heavy pressure from above to improve performance.
3. Obtaining improved results from subordinates.[7]

An example of a retreat to a relatively unproductive task is a quality control director who scans the detailed results of every quality trial but cannot find the time to organize a much-needed quality improvement project. By asking himself or herself, "What is blocking me?" the director may recognize the problem and begin to tackle the major project. The anxiety-related block is only one of hundreds. Another block to getting an important project completed is fear of success. If you perform well on the project, you may be given additional responsibilities in the future.

Avoid Perfectionism. Thoroughness is a virtue on most jobs until it reaches the point of diminishing returns. Two time-management specialists, Peter A. Turla and Kathleen L. Hawkins, note that it is worthwhile to be interested in quality, but you must also be fair with yourself. "Compulsive striving for unrealistic goals can impair your creativity, cause tension between you and others, and waste valuable time. Is it worth the price? Or is this the time to break these self-defeating patterns?"[8]

Sir Simon Marks, who was chairman of the consistently profitable Marks & Spencer retailing chain in Great Britain, maintained that those who make a fetish of perfection are wasting time and money that could be allocated elsewhere. Hence his system of "sensible approximation" in inventory procedures. His motto: "The price of perfection is prohibitive."[9]

Appreciate the Value of Rest and Relaxation. In your zeal to multiply your productivity, watch out for work's becoming an addiction. True workaholism sets in when nonwork activities no longer yield pleasure, making rest and relaxation difficult to achieve. The workaholic sets up a work schedule devoid of family and personal responsibilities. The link to low productivity is that many workaholics lose perspective and creativity. However, some workaholics find so much pleasure in their jobs that work becomes a form of relaxation. Nonwork, in contrast, is a source of stress. A case in point is author Dennis E. Hensley who is only content when he puts in an 18-hour workday. When asked if workaholism is hazardous to health, he replied:

> Positive workaholism is very good for your health. The myth we've always heard that you can work youself to death is only true when you are working laboriously and without exitement. Lack of work is far more deadly than too much work. I truly believe that it's not stress that kills these people; it's boredom.[10]

Value Cleanliness and Orderliness. An orderly desk, file cabinet, or attache case does not inevitably indicate an orderly mind, but it does help most people become more productive. Less time is wasted, and less energy is expended if you do not have to hunt for information that you thought you had on hand. Knowing where information is and what information you have available is a way of being in control of your job. When your job gets out of control, you are probably working at less than peak efficiency.

Miguel Ramirez launched his much needed work habit improvement program with this technique. Even the most orderly career person should clean out his or her work area every six months. Two hours devoted to office housekeeping may give you some hints as to whether or not you are taking care of all the things that you should on your job. You might be surprised as to what has filtered down to the bottom of your in-basket.

Learn to Say No. "Of all the time-saving techniques ever developed, perhaps the most effective is the frequent use of the word *no* ," points out one time-management consultant.[11] You cannot take care of your own priorities unless you learn tactfully to decline requests from other people that interfere with your work.

If your boss interrupts your work with an added assignment, "Point out to your boss how the new task will conflict with higher-priority ones and suggest alternatives."[8] When your boss recognizes that you are motivated to get your major tasks accomplished and not to avoid work, you'll have a good chance of avoiding unproductive tasks.

A word of caution. Do not turn down your boss too frequently. Much discretion and tact is needed in using this approach to work efficiency.

Appreciate the Importance of Paperwork. Although it is fashionable to decry the necessity of having to do paperwork in responsible jobs, the effective career person does not neglect paperwork. Unless paperwork is efficiently attended to, a person's job may get out of control. Once a job is out of control, it may lead to a stress reaction for the jobholder. Ideally, a small amount of time should be invested in paperwork every day. Nonprime time (when you are at less than your peak of efficiency, but not overfatigued) is the best time to take care of routine paperwork. (Paperwork in this context refers essentially to taking care of minor administrative details, such as correspondence, expense reports, and inventory forms.)

Many people who do a slipshod job of handling their paperwork offer rationalizations for their actions. A sales representative may say, "I can't be bothered with paperwork. I'm paid to sell." Not taking care of paperwork usually creates problems for others in the organization. In the sales example just cited, the accounting and market research departments may have a critical need for the information generated by sales representatives.

Challenge Your Use of Time. A major tool for improving your efficiency and effectiveness is to ask Lakein's question: "What is the best use of my time right now?"[12] This question helps you to justify your every action. Lakein notes that a particularly good time to ask this question is when you have been interrupted by a visitor or phone call. When it's over, he advises to check whether you should go back to what you were doing or on to something new.

Your answer to Lakein's question may be different when asked about what seems to be a comparable situation. One day you are waiting for an elevator in your office building. You ask, "What is the best possible use of my time right now?" Your answer is "Certainly not waiting for an elevator. I'll jog up the stairs and get some needed exercise."

One week later you are again waiting for the elevator. You ask the same question. This time your answer is, "Waiting for the elevator is a good use of my time right now. It's about time I touched base with a few employees from different departments in the company."

Be Decisive. A good deal of time is wasted by managers who vacillate too long before choosing among the alternative solutions to a problem facing them. If you value decisiveness, you should learn the skill of being decisive, assuming you have a reasonable degree of self-confidence. If a person has too little self-confidence, he or she may never become a rapid decision maker. Business school graduates are often criticized for being so analytical that they are indecisive. The productive individual will invest a reasonable amount of time in weighing alternatives, but then will make a decision.

Dru Scott has developed a technique for helping people become more decisive. In general, it follows the logic of the steps involved in problem solving and decision making. Its unique thrust is that it asks you to define what you most want to accomplish before you begin comparing alternatives.[13] To illustrate, if you were trying to decide which office automation system to purchase, you should define precisely what you want the system to accomplish. One such answer could be, "We want a system that will take care of the computing demands of our managerial, professional, and clerical employees without having to purchase a variety of equipment." You would then narrow down your choice to office automation systems with software and hardware capable of satisfying these three sets of demands simultaneously.

Productive Skills and Techniques

Clarify Your Own Objectives. Knowing what you want to accomplish can improve your work habits and time management in additional ways. A basic starting point in improving your work habits and time management is to know what it is you are supposed to accomplish.[14] A careful review of your job description and objectives with your boss is of fundamental importance. Some people are accused of being ineffective simply because they do not know what is really expected of them. A manager in a computer software firm was chastised by the owner for being ineffective. Asked why he was considered ineffective, the owner replied "You have failed to keep the systems analysts off my back." The manager rightfully replied, "This must have been some hidden purpose of my job. You never told me that before." From that point on, the manager increased his effectiveness by dealing with the complaints and concerns of the systems analysts.

Establish Weighted Priorities. Few people are so innately well organized that they can make good use of time without preparing a list of activities that need doing. The executive planners commercially available are basically orderly systems of allocating your time among various activities. Some of these planners suggest apportioning your time into 30-minute chunks. In addition to time allocation, such planners serve as convenient record-keeping devices for luncheon engagements, expense account items, and important dates.

Alan Lakein advocates assigning an A, B, or C rating to each item on your list (Miguel attempted this approach). A items have the highest value; B items have medium value; and C items have the lowest value.[15]

Find Some Uninterrupted Time for Planning. As implied in the techniques of establishing priorities and clarifying your job objectives, planning is part of time management. In order to plan—or do any other tough mental task—you need some periods of uninterrupted time. Some people point out justifiably that their job is concerned mostly with taking care of emergencies. Uninterrupted time is, therefore, virtually impossible to achieve. Under these extreme circumstances it might be necessary to spend the first 15 minutes of each workday in seclusion in order to plan and think. Fifteen minutes of unavailability after lunch can serve the same purpose. After a while, other people in the organization with whom you are in contact will learn to accept the fact that thinking is a form of work. You will then receive some uninterrupted time.

Concentrate on High-Output Tasks. To become more effective in your job, you have to concentrate on tasks where superior performance could have a big payoff for your department or company. This is the familiar distinction between breakthrough versus routine or trivial tasks, maintenance but not productive activities, or necessary but insufficient tasks. For example, no matter how diligent you are in paying your bills on time, it will not make your store an outstanding sucess. However, concentrating your efforts on bringing unique and desirable merchandise into the store could have a big impact on your business success. Looking for high-output items for your effort is akin to looking for a good return on your investment for your money.[16]

In following the A-B-C system, you should devote ample time to the A items. You should not pay more attention than absolutely necessary to the C items. However, if you find that working on C items is tension-reducing, proceed, but recognize that you must return to A items as soon as you feel relaxed. When the suggestion of working on high-output items is offered, many managers respond, "I don't think that concentrating on important tasks applies to me. My job is so filled with routine, I have no chance to work on breakthrough ideas." True, most jobs are filled with routine requirements. What a person can do is spend some time—even one hour per week—concentrating on tasks that may prove to have high output.

Eliminate or Minimize Low-Output Tasks. Miguel tried to follow this principle as he questioned the practice of attending the national conference of executive directors. It is critical to your job success to avoid doing work that has no real payoff to the organization. Consultant John Humble says, "The major opportunities for elimination lie in stopping meetings that no longer serve a useful purpose and in cutting out time-consuming, needless paperwork. For some international managers the elimination of regular trips is usually possible."[17]

Eliminating or minimizing low-output items is tied in with most of the suggestions presented in this chapter. Michael LeBoeuf notes that once you know what is important to you, you can use the entire gamut of time-management techniques to take care of external time wasters such as interruptions, unnecessary meetings, and excessive telephone calls and paperwork.[18]

Work at a Steady Pace. In most jobs, working at a steady pace pays dividends in efficiency. The spurt worker creates many problems for superiors, co-workers, and subordinates. An important advantage of the steady-pace approach is that you accomplish much more than someone who puts out extra effort just once in a while. Trying to catch up for lost time may result in a high error rate even in managerial work.

In the steady-pace approach, you strive for a constant expenditure of energy every working day. (As one person describes this strategy, "Every day is Monday.") The payoff is that you develop a precious supply of bonus time that you can use for planning and thinking creatively about your job. If you find yourself with an afternoon of discretionary time, you can figure out ways of doing your job more effectively. Such improvements should ultimately enhance your reputation wherever you work. Despite the advantages of maintaining a steady pace, some peaks and valleys in your work may be inevitable. The seasonal demands placed on employees in public accounting firms are a prime example.

Keep an Accurate Time Log. Another good starting point in improving your work habits and time management is to analyze how you are currently spending your time. If you are privileged to have a secretary or assistant, that person might help compile the log. A time analysis of this nature often reveals some surprises because we tend to exaggerate the importance of the tasks to which we devote our time. One bank required that its branch managers record time spent under three headings: (a) time with customers, (b) time on administration, and (c) time with their own staff. The analysis demonstrated that too much time was expended on internal administration to the detriment of marketing and staff development.[19]

Identify and Plug Time Leaks. Many a landlord or homeowner has scurried around in recent years to identify and plug water or heat leaks. In years past, the money saved from stopping drips or drafts was rarely worth the effort. With the substantially increased cost of energy and water in recent years, plugging leaks has become more profitable. The cost of wasted time has also been inflated enough to justify your identifying and plugging time leaks. By putting more of normal working hours to good use, you can increase your output without increasing your number of hours worked.

A common time leak is the practice of *schmoozing*—informal nonjob-related discussions held during working hours, including social phone calls.

Other common leaks include 90-minute lunch breaks, excessive time spent in warming up to get started working, too much time spent winding down to stop working, and visiting other people in the office instead of phoning them to discuss a work problem.

GF Business Equipment has developed a guide to protecting your privacy from small-talkers in the office. They suggest that a direct statement is the most effective. Simply say, "I'm sorry, but I'm busy and can't be disturbed." They also suggest that if you are concerned that others will take this personally, or consider you to be antisocial, compensate by going out of your way to be friendly with these people at other times.[20]

Schedule Similar Tasks Together. An efficient method of accomplishing small tasks is to group them together and perform them in one block of time. To illustrate, you might make most of your telephone calls in relation to your job from 11 to 11:30 each workday morning. Or you might reserve the last hour of every workday for correspondence. When you go downtown, think of all the errands that you have that can best be done downtown. Over a period of time you save a number of wasted trips.

By using this method, you develop the necessary pace and mental set to knock off chores in short order. In contrast, when you flit from one type of task to another, your efficiency may suffer.

Concentrate on One Task at a Time. Effective executives have a well-developed capacity to concentrate on the problem or person facing them, however surrounded they are with other obligations. Intense concentration leads to crisper judgment and analysis, and also minimizes major errors. The thousands of fingers lost each year by the owners of home power tools attest to this observation! Another useful byproduct of concentration is that it helps reduce absent-mindedness. If you concentrate intensely on what you are doing, you decrease the chance of forgetting what you intended to do. Walter Olesky provides a dramatic statement of the link between concentration and personal productivity.

> Most of the really successful people, in whatever field, subordinate everything to the main purposes of their lives. When they are working, they display extraordinary powers of concentration. These men and women often bewilder their fellow workers, because they never seem to work hard, or for any period of time. Their secret lies in their power to concentrate, and thus obtain maximum results with a minimum of apparent effort.[21]

Deal with Distracting Problems. When you are preoccupied with a personal or work problem, it is difficult to concentrate in the manner just described. The solution is to do something constructive about whatever problem is sapping your ability to concentrate. Suppose a person is so far in debt that his or her monthly debt payments and fixed living expenses allow no room for unanticipated expenses that seem to arise every month. As dire as the solution seems, it might be to that person's advantage to obtain a debt-consolidation loan. The monthly payment might be low enough to allow "breathing room." Once the consolidation loan is paid off, that person might choose to never reenter debt, thus contributing to his or her peace of mind for the long term.

Sometimes a relatively minor problem such as being long overdue for a dental checkup can impair your work concentration. At other times, a major problem such as a child custody dispute between two divorcing parents interferes with work. In either situation, your concentration will suffer until you take appropriate action.

Delegate When Feasible. A boss who tries to do too many tasks alone eventually becomes overwhelmed and somewhat unproductive. A sounder approach is to delegate that portion of those assignments that can be properly handled by a subordinate. In order to delegate effectively, it is necessary to have competent and willing subordinates. Even under such conditions, it is important to exercise some control (follow up) on work that is delegated. If the subordinates do not produce results, *you* are still responsible for the lack of results.

For delegation to have a payoff, it is important to delegate interesting assignments of substantial size. One manager was criticized by a subordinate for the type of work he delegated. Said the subordinate, "Am I really helping you by following your instructions to simply 'look over' something? It's difficult to provide you any real input for those jobs." In other words, such delegation is neither effective nor efficient.

Harness your Natural Energy Cycles. The old saying, "I'm a morning person," has scientific substantiation. According to the advocates of biorhythms, people vary somewhat as to their hours of peak efficiency. A week of charting should help you determine the hours at which your mental and physical energy is apt to be highest or lowest.

After you have determined your strong and weak energy periods, you should be able to arrange your work schedule accordingly. Tackle your intellectually most demanding assignments during your energy peaks. Avoid creative work or making major decisions when fatigue has set in. It may be all right for a 25-year-old intern to patch a wound in his or her 23rd consecutive hour of work, but for most of us, crucial tasks demand a fresh outlook.

Schedule Yourself by Computer. Software is available that allows one to use a personal computer as an electronic calendar to help keep track of appointments and lists of chores.[22] The first step is implementing these programs would be to enter into the computer's memory your appointments, tasks, and errands. For instance, a person might use these items as input:

April 2	Meet with Brady to discuss budget.
April 17	Get strategic plan for department started.
May 3	Lunch with Rachel to discuss affirmative action plan.
May 18	Make request for new office furniture.

From this point forward, the computer's information-processing capabilities could be tapped. Suppose you couldn't remember the date of your lunch with Rachel. You would command the computer to "Find lunch date with Rachel." Or, if you were an extremely busy person, you might have reason to ask the computer to tell you when you had the next opening for lunch. Another use of this type of software is to command the computer to flag key appointments and tasks. An indicator such as **URGENT** might be used. Some managers who use electronic calendars (and word processing) believe that their personal computers take over many secretarial chores.

Break the Task Down into Manageable Units. A person may be faced with a large, complex job to accomplish that leads to feelings of being overwhelmed and immobilized. You will recall that this feeling of being overwhelmed can lead to procrastination. The problem is more acute when more than one of these "elephants" is facing you. A well-accepted principle in this situation is to "Eat the elephant one bite at a time." Break the project down into logical parts and begin with a few simple parts of the project. You might begin by assigning a clerk to help you, or ordering the necessary supplies to get the project done.

Make Use of Bits of Time. As a final suggestion, remember that a truly productive person makes good use of miscellaneous bits of time, both on and off the job. Time spent waiting in lines can be profitably invested in professional reading, reading work memos and reports, or composing a fresh list of chores. While waiting for an elevator you might be able to read a 100-word report. And if you have finished your day's work 10 minutes before quitting time, you can use that 10 minutes to clean out a drawer in your desk. By the end of the year, your productivity will have increased much more than if you had squandered these bits of time.[23]

Set Time Limit for Certain Tasks. As managers and professionals become more experienced with certain projects, they become able to make more accurate estimates of how long a project will take to complete. A department head might say, for example, "Getting this preliminary budget ready for my boss's approval should take seven hours." A good time management practice to develop is to estimate how long a job should take and then proceed with a strong determination to get that job completed within the estimated period of time.

A productive variation of this technique is to decide that some low- and medium-priority items are only worth so much of your time. Invest that much time in a project, but no more. Preparing a file on advertisements that cross your desk is one example.

Be Aware of Diminishing Returns. A time management principle closely related to setting time limits for tasks is to know when to get off a project to avoid low productivity. Stephanie Winston points out that "knowing when to stop a project is as important as knowing when to start one."[24] If you can only concentrate on doing a spreadsheet analysis on a computer for three hours, stop as soon as your time in front of the computer approaches three hours. If your neck muscles ache, and you are making too many errors, it is time to quit. If it is not the end of your normal workday, move on to some other less tedious task such as making telephone calls.

As you acquire more skill on a difficult task, you are likely to find that you are able to work productively on the same task for longer periods of time. Thus, the point of diminishing returns takes longer to reach. One reason is that as people become more skilled in performing a task, they become less tense and more relaxed. Working under moderate tension, in turn, leads to fewer errors than working under high tension.

The Case for Good Work Habits and Time Management

Common sense and experience suggest that there is much to be gained by improving your approach to work along the lines suggested in this chapter. Good work habits, including time management, may be as important as high intelligence and appropriate personality characteristics in bringing about career success. To use an extreme example, if you are in charge of issuing payroll checks, your employees will be more concerned about your timeliness than your personal warmth and enthusiasm.

Another important reason for improving your work habits is that they make a multifaceted contribution to your life. Good work habits can improve job performance, personal life, and mental health. A person who performs efficiently and effectively on the job has more time (and often money) for personal life. Simultaneously, he or she escapes the stress stemming from a constant feeling of being behind in work.

Good work habits are also important because, to a large extent, they underlie the basic management functions of planning and controlling. To illustrate, planning involves setting priorities and controlling includes following up on progress toward achieving goals.

The Case against Good Work Habits and Time Management

Almost no experienced manager or individual contributor would say that poor work habits and time management are the keys to success, yet the converse is not always true. Many successful, creative people do not appear particularly well organized. Successful executives often behave in an impulsive manner, responding to the demands of the moment. Their work is characterized by frequent interruptions.[11]

Another fundamental argument against placing too much emphasis on good work habits is that they are a reflection of underlying personality characteristics. As such, they are difficult to change. For instance, if you are a compulsive personality (tidy, highly concerned about details), your natural inclination will be to have good work habits and time management. If you are not compulsive, trying to behave compulsively may not be worth the effort. Also people who are basically patient have an easier time developing good work habits than do impatient people.

Despite these arguments that could conceivably be advanced against improving your work habits and time management, almost any manager or professional person would become more productive by practicing some of the suggestions made in this chapter.

GUIDELINES FOR ACTION AND SKILL DEVELOPMENT

As you embark upon a program of improved efficiency and effectiveness, guard against becoming an annoyance to everybody else. If you become too concerned about time squandering and inefficiency, it is possible that you will irritate more than motivate others. The true goal of the suggestions in this chapter is to improve your productivity but still retain some flexibility in your work and compassion for people.

To get started improving your work habits, select an aspect of work where you are hurting the most, then choose an appropriate remedial strategy. A good starting point for most people is to clean up their work area or develop a prioritized list.

Practice faithfully and patiently whichever work habits and time management approaches you select. Poor work habits and time management usually develop over the years and therefore require at least several months to turn around. Once you have mastered one new habit or habits, proceed to another strategy appropriate to your situation.

Questions and Activities

1. Benjamin Franklin said, "To love life is to love time, since time is the stuff that life is made of." What is your reaction to this statement?

2. What is your reaction to the statement, "A clear and orderly desk reflects a clear and orderly mind"?
3. When you meet a stranger, how can you tell if he or she is well organized?
4. Give an example for your own life in which striving for perfection was not worth the effort.
5. In what type of work will good work habits and time management most likely lead directly to increased money (earnings) for the individual?
6. What is the best use of your time right now?
7. Which three of the 27 suggestions offered in this chapter are particularly important for people at the early stages of their careers? Explain your reasoning.
8. Which three of the 27 suggestions offered in this chapter are particularly important for top executives? Explain your reasoning.
9. Interview a person you know to be highly productive. Try to discover which of the time management and work habits presented in this chapter he or she practices regularly.

Notes

[1] A scholarly analysis of the meaning of productivity is found in Harold J. Tragash, "A Model for Managing Productivity," *National Productivity Review* (Summer 1983) pp. 323–325.

[2] Strategies for improving your work habits and time management tend to be quite similar from source to source. Where credit to one particular source is deserved, it will be indicated by footnotes.

[3] Michael LeBoeuf as cited in Priscilla Petty, "Saying No to Unproductive Jobs Frees Time for High-Priority Goals," Rochester *Democrat and Chronicle* (June 21, 1983) p. 10D.

[4] Alan Lakein, *How to Gain Control of Your Time and Your Life* (New York: Peter H. Wyden, 1973) pp. 141–151.

[5] LeBoeuf, in "Saying No to Unproductive Jobs," p. 10D.

[6] Albert Ellis and William J. Knaus, *Overcoming Procrastination* (New York: New American Library, 1979) p.111.

[7] Ronald N. Ashkenas and Robert H. Schaffer, "Managers Can Avoid Wasting Time," *Harvard Business Review* (May-June 1982) p. 99.

[8] Peter A. Turla and Kathleen L. Hawkins, "The Flaws of Perfectionism," *Success* (December 1982) p. 23.

[9] Edwin C. Bliss, "Give Yourself the Luxury of Time," *Mainliner* (December 1976) p. 55.

[10] "Confessions of a Happy Workaholic," *Success* (June 1983) p. 8.

[11] Bliss, "Give Yourself the Luxury," p. 55.

[12] Lakein, *How to Gain Control*, p. 99.

[13] Dru Scott, *How to Put More Time in Your Life* (New York: New American Library, 1980) pp. 92–100.

[14] John Humble, "Time Management: Separating the Myths and the Realities," *Management Review* (October 1980) p. 27.

[15] Lakein, *How to Gain Control*, pp. 21–22.

[16] Among the many places in which this concept is espoused is Andrew Grove, *High Output Management* (New York: Random House, 1983).

[17]Humble, "Time Management," pp. 28, 49.
[18]LeBoeuf, cited in Petty, "Saying No to Unproductive Jobs," p. 10D.
[19]Humble, "Time Management," p. 27.
[20]"Protecting Your Privacy," *Success* (April 1982) p. 10.
[21]Walter Olesky, "Concentration," *Success* (October 1983) pp. 28, 30.
[22]William Brohaugh, "Computerizing Your Calendar," *Success* (November 1983) pp. 14–16.
[23]Warren Keith Schilit, "A Manager's Guide to Efficient Time Management," *Personnel Journal* (September 1f983) p. 740.
[24]Stephanie Winston, *Getting Organized* (New York: Warner Books, 1979) p. 40.

Some Additional References

Bartolome, Fernando. "The Work Alibi: When It's Harder to Go Home." *Harvard Business Review* (March-April 1983) pp. 66–74.

Douglass, Merrill E., and Donna N. Douglass. *Manage Your Time, Manage Your Work, Manage Yourself*. New York: AMACOM, 1980.

Machlowitz, Marilyn. *Workaholics: Living with Them, Working with Them*. Reading, Mass.: Addison-Wesley, 1980.

Turla, Peter A., and Kathleen L. Hawkins. *Time Management Made Easy*. New York: E. P. Dutton, 1984.

Webber, Ross A. *Time is Money: The Key to Managerial Success*. New York: Free Press, 1980.

Appendix to Chapter 1

Time Feelings Self-Quiz

		Yes	*No*
1.	Are you concerned about wasting time?	_____	_____
2.	Do you wish you had more time?	_____	_____
3.	Do you want to be on time?	_____	_____
4.	Do you make the most of your time?	_____	_____
5.	Can you find time for important things?	_____	_____
6.	Do you want to save time?	_____	_____
7.	Do you feel the pressure of time?	_____	_____
8.	Do you spend your time wisely?	_____	_____
9.	Do you wait until the last minute?	_____	_____
10.	Do you have plenty of time?	_____	_____
11.	Do you put things off until another time?	_____	_____
12.	Do you rush projects because of time pressure?	_____	_____
13.	Is your time well-organized?	_____	_____
14.	Do others rob your time?	_____	_____
15.	Do you have free time?	_____	_____
16.	Are you trying to do too much at one time?	_____	_____
17.	Are you realistic in setting time deadlines?	_____	_____
18.	Are you in control of your time?	_____	_____
19.	Do you have the time to think?	_____	_____
20.	Have you tried to change your time habits?	_____	_____

This self-quiz is designed to identify three basic patterns associated with time attitudes:

1. Pattern U: A sense of time urgency. If you've answered "Yes" to questions 3, 6, 7, and 12 and "No" to question 10, you are in the proper frame of mind to undertake a time-management system. Time is playing havoc with you. It's straining and stretching you, forcing you to rush through the day watching the clock.

Without a sense of time urgency, it's unlikely that you will have the incentive to change your work habits. Why should you want to manage your time if you aren't having any major problems?

2. Pattern C: Concern about time. If you answered "Yes" to questions 1, 2, 4, and 14 and "No" to question 19, you not only have a sense of time urgency, but you have a genuine concern about effective time management. This attitude is a prerequisite to initiating a time-improvement program.

On the other hand, if you answered "Yes" to questions 9, 11, and 15, you possess attitudes which interfere with time management.

3. Pattern S: Self-critical about time management. If you answered "Yes" to question 16 and "No" to questions 5, 8, 13, 17, 18, and 20, you already know that you have to change your work habits and you're ready to consider some of the ideas to follow.

If, however, you answered "No" to question 16 and "Yes" to questions 5, 8, 13, 17, 18, and 20, stop reading. Either you are already a very effective time manager or you resist recognizing any of your weakness in managing time.

Source: The Time feelings self-quiz and interpretation from Ed Roseman, "How to Gain Control of Your Time," *Product Management,* July 1975, p. 25.

Chapter 2

Improving Your Creativity

The manager of a department within a government agency sought a way to improve the creative response of her people to work problems. She chose a consultant to conduct brainstorming sessions with the key people in her department, including herself.

"Thanks for being so prompt for our brainstorming session," said Pam to her five supervisors. "As you know our executive director believes strongly that we must become a more creative government unit. I totally support his thinking. In fact, I'll be the sixth person in today's session. I'm going to sit down now and turn the meeting over to Gus Gaston, a creativity trainer with a fine reputation." Gus began:

> I appreciate the accolade. What Pam has told you is correct. My role here today is to help ignite the creativity within you. Just as all of you are not the same height, or equally good in seeing or hearing, the six of you have different amounts of creativity. It is scientifically unsound to classify people as creative on the one hand or uncreative on the other. Since virtually everybody has some creative potential, you can learn to make better use of that potential through training.
>
> Today we are going to conduct a brainstorming session. We have two purposes in mind. The first is to give you some practice in liberating your creative impulses. The second is to work on a real operational problem. Thus you will not only benefit personally from practicing creative thinking, you will also help the organization solve a real organizational problem.
>
> Our task will be to generate a number of suggestions for reducing costs and saving money. Pam tells me that the grim reaper from on high has struck again. Every department head must bring forth a budget slash of 10 percent. We will spend about two hours on this task today.

Before jumping right into our idea generating session, it is important that I suggest some rules for brainstorming. I do not want to constrain you, but I also want to improve the chances that the session will be worthwhile. I'll keep these rules posted on my flip chart. They are very straightforward and easy to follow.

Rule 1 is that we should have about five to seven people in the group. We've already taken care of that rule. That's how many people are here today. If too few people are used, you lose the feeling of ideas floating all over the place. If we have too many people, you might lose the feeling that your contribution is important. Too big a group seems intimidating to some people.

Rule 2 is that everybody is given the chance to spew forth alternatives to the problem without asking permission to speak. You spontaneously call out alternatives to the problem facing the group.

Rule 3 is that no criticism is allowed. All suggestions are welcome. It is particularly important not to use derisive laughter or make sarcastic comments about other people's ideas. Remember, people laughed when somebody first brought up the idea of television.

Rule 4 is that freewheeling is encouraged. The crazier the idea the better. It's easier to tone down an idea than to think one up.

Rule 5 is that quantity and variety are essential. The greater the number of ideas put forth, the higher the probability of a breakthrough idea.

Rule 6 is that combinations and improvements are encouraged. Building upon the ideas of others is very fruitful. I like to call this approach "piggybacking."

Rule 7 is that notes must be taken during the session, either electronically or manually. I'll be taping the sessions, but I also recommend that one of you act as recording secretary. It takes much less time to review a few pages of notes than to play a tape.

Rule 8 is not to take the preceding seven rules too literally. Brainstorming is a spontaneous process.

While you folks are carrying out the brainstorming, I'll be making observations of what you are doing. After the session, I'll share my comments with you.

After you have basically drained your minds, you'll conduct the editing phase. This is a fairly simple process. First, you eliminate the duplications from your list, then you salvage the 10 or so ideas that you will consider further or actually implement.

Pam, Ralph, Terry, Ruth, Lester, and Dan then gathered themselves around a circular conference table to commence brainstorming. The following is an abridged transcript of the session.

Ralph: I'll be first. I got it, let's decrease meal allowances by 10 percent. So what's the difference if we learn to order fried chicken instead of steak when traveling on business?

Ruth: While we're at it, why not simply cut travel 10 percent? That would result in a real cost saving.

Dan: Or we could all try to do 10 percent more work. That would make 1 out of 10 employees redundant. One tenth of the people who left the agency would not have to be replaced. Who knows maybe our department could get by with one less supervisor?

Terry: Let's get down to some short strokes. What about everybody hanging onto pencils until they're down to a little stub?

Pam: Or maybe we could encourage people to empty their pockets of ball pens and pencils before they left work in the afternoon. If this were done nationwide, the Bic people would be in trouble.

Lester: You could add yellow memo pads to that list. I have to admit some guilt there. My kids make paper airplanes out of lined, yellow paper paid for by the taxpayers.

Terry: Let's clean out the storerooms and put to work some of the supplies that have been collecting dust for years. Why not put a freeze on ordering anything new until an employee's supervisor is convinced we do not already have a good substitute in the storeroom?

Dan: A brainstorm just hit me! Why not place a moratorium on hiring creativity training consultants until the budget crunch has passed?

Ruth: What about cutting down on duplicate subscriptions to the same magazine or newspaper? I think we get two subscriptions to *The Wall Street Journal* for our department. One would seem to be enough.

Pam: Maybe we should have some interagency and interdepartmental suggestions. The governor might be able to get by without that big limousine. Maybe he should be driven around in a compact.

Lester: While you're slashing into transportation costs, let's buy only compact cars for the state from this point on. No more gas guzzlers at the taxpayer's expense.

Terry: Why not have employees use a carpool when on government business? Furthermore, why not travel by bus rather than airplane? The fares are lower and you can make up for the longer time by doing paperwork on the bus.

Dan: Let me get back to inside our own office. It looks to me like we waste an awful lot of electricity. We keep the venetian blinds open and the fluorescent lights on. Let's cut out lights when we don't need them.

Pam: And what about shutting off lights after the cleaning crew is finished at around 11 P.M.? My husband and I have driven by after midnight. Every light is left on in our building.

Ralph: The amount of heat we waste in our agency is a tragedy. Even the room right here is too hot. Let's start a "wear a sweater and hat in the office" campaign. Since 10 percent of your body heat escapes through the top of your head, we could cut the thermostat down to 60° if we wore hats indoors. If somebody brought a medical excuse saying they needed more heat, they could use a space heater near their desk.

Lester: Or what about taking off your shoes and socks during the summer months? That would cool you down enough whereby the thermostat could be turned up to 80°.

Terry: Watch out Lester, I think the brainstorming session is getting to you. Oops. I forgot about not criticizing!

Lester: That's OK, they laughed at Thomas Edison.

Pam: Here's an idea I heard about someplace else. Storage of paper is a big cost. Why not use the back of letters received for the photocopy of your reply to that letter? We'd also save a few bucks on copy paper.

Ralph: So long as we're being so efficient, why not use envelopes mailed to us as scrap paper? Many a good idea has been recorded on the back of an envelope.

Pam: I've got it. Instead of trying to have every state employee's mind and desk filled with hundreds of cost saving tips, let's get to the root of the problem. What we really need is to have our consciousness raised about the importance of cost savings. Group discussions about the importance of cost savings should be held in every department and agency at least once a month. And, in typical government style, people would bring their own coffee or tea.

Dan: This session is raising my consciousness. Why have hot and cold water in the restrooms and sink closets? Why not just use hot water heated to about 100° Fahrenheit? We have no real need for water any hotter than that. We don't run dishwashers or clothes washers around here.

Ralph: It looks like it's taking longer and longer between ideas. Let me review with you the suggestions I have written down. Tell me if I have the idea recorded correctly.

Gus: Let me give you some feedback on what I've observed. First of all, I think that you've made a terrific start. You've brought forth a number of fine suggestions that I suspect the agency will be able to implement. Another good thing I've noticed is that there has been a balanced contribution from people in the group. No one person is dominating. Also, you're not mechanically following a set pattern of whose turn it is to contribute. That allows for more spontaneity.

Something else I noticed is also very significant. You are beginning to overcome mental blocks in your thinking. For example, Pam decided that there was no real reason to restrict your thinking to your own department. Her idea about consciousness raising also reflected an expanded mental set. Overcoming mental sets or perceptual blocks is an important part of learning to become more creative.

I noticed one little incident of putting someone else's thinking down. But I don't think it hampered the flow of ideas.

I have a constructive suggestion to offer. I notice that at several times you seemed concerned because an idea was not forthcoming at the moment. You should not be particularly concerned. In most brainstorming sessions, there is an immediate, initial outpouring of ideas. Once these are used up, there is likely to be a lull. A mysterious inner consolidation then takes place and a new set of suggestions will emerge. The graph is shaped a bit like two adjacent normal curves or humps on a camel.

Let's dig into the problem again. I think you will be pleasantly surprised at the results.

IMPROVING YOUR CREATIVITY ON YOUR OWN

The standard approach to creativity improvement just described has considerable merit. But it does require a group setting and usually some kind of organizational support. In this section we will describe several other techniques to build creativity that you can use on your own. (As defined here, creativity is the degree to which one can think of different, more effective approaches to a problem. Similarly, creativity can be defined as the generation of a new or relatively infrequent idea.)

Conduct Private Brainstorming Sessions. Brainstorming originated as a group method of creativity improvement. It has also had widespread application as an individual method. Some writers even suggest that brainstorming is more effective conducted individually than in groups.[1] Similar to the group method, you spew forth a large number of possible solutions to the problem facing you. An important requirement of private brainstorming is that you set aside a regular time (and perhaps place) for generating ideas. Even five minutes per day is much more time than most people are accustomed to thinking creatively about job problems. Give yourself a quota with a time deadline.

A good deal of self-discipline is required to conduct private brainstorming sessions because you do not have the support of the group. The idea is to discipline yourself to develop a number of alternatives to the job problem you are trying to solve—or the opportunity you are trying to create. Faced with a situation calling for a creative response, you might sit quietly with a pencil and pad and begin to generate possible solutions. For example, "How can I shorten the time it takes our customers to pay their bills without creating ill will?" Most people accept the first one or two alternatives to such a problem. Through private brainstorming, you can learn to search for many alternatives.

Overcome Mental Locks. An important part of learning to behave creatively is to overcome familiar approaches to problems that lock us into one way of doing things. According to Roger von Oech, president of Creative Think in Menlo Park, California, people become prisoners of familiarity. The more often you manage a project, run a meeting, or design a marketing strategy the same way, the more difficult it becomes to think about doing it any other way. Von Oech refers to these perceptual blocks as "mental locks."[2] Originally, he concentrated on developing creativity-training programs to help high-technology companies arrive at more creative solutions to scientific and marketing problems. The application of his methods has spread to many different organizations and individuals. Von Oech suggests a few ways he believes will help most people get in a creative frame of mind:

Allow the Foolish Side of You to Come Out. Humor has long been observed to be a helpful way of getting into a creative mental set. "For example, one of my clients manufactures satellites. They had a design meeting not too long ago and everyone started making fun of the satellites. They made weird jokes about it, bad puns, and were just really silly with it. In the course of this, they came up with two major innovative design breakthroughs."[3]

Be a Hunter. Says von Oech, "I've worked with creative people in many industries, disciplines, and professions, and the really good ones are hunters. These people look outside their areas for ideas, and when they find an idea, they bring it back to their own area and apply it."

Use Stepping Stones. Crazy-sounding, impractical, infrequent ideas, even though you are unable to execute them, can sometimes serve as a stepping stone to a practical, creative new idea. A paint company representative said a few years ago, "Let's put gunpowder in our housepaint. Then when the paint cracks and it's a real pain to get off, we could just blow it right off the side of the house."

Von Oech notes the silliness of the idea. However, that idea was used as a stepping stone to ask another question: "What other ways could we put additives in our paint at the front end so they would remain inert, but combined with another solution a few years later, would react and make the paint easy to get off?" This paint is now available commercially.

Be a Revolutionary. Most new ideas and advances in technology, science, and business come about when someone either breaks or bends the rules. Microprocessors and recombinant DNA break the rules. Ask yourself, "What if we tried it another way?" "What if we didn't do this?" One company president says his most difficult task is getting his subordinates to challenge the rules.

Don't Be Afraid to Try and Fail. If you try a large number of projects, ideas, or things, a large number of them are likely to fail. Yet your number of "hits" will be much higher than if you tried only a few projects, ideas, or things and all of them were successful. It is the absolute number of successes that counts the most—not the percentage of successes. von Oech maintains, "You learn by trial and error, not trial and rightness."[4]

Develop a Synergy between Both Sides of the Brain. Developments in the understanding of the human brain in recent years shed some light on creativity improvement. Researchers have been able to demonstrate that the left side of the brain is the source of most analytical, logical, and rational thought. It performs the tasks necessary for well-reasoned arguments and working with standard applications of a computer. The right side of the brain grasps the work in a more intuitive, overall manner. It is the source of impressionistic, creative thought. People with dominant right brains thrive on disorder and ambiguity—both characteristics of creative people.[5]

A seemingly logical conclusion would be that if you develop the right side of your brain by such means as brainstorming, and de-emphasize the left, you will become more creative. This is only partially true. To be creative you usually need to have a fund of facts readily available to your mind. (Creativity is sometimes defined as the combining of ideas into a new and meaningful pattern.) And the left side of the brain is best suited for fact gathering. Therefore the highly creative individual achieves *synergy* (the combination is more than the sum of the parts) between the two sides of the brain. Both brain hemispheres are used as needed. Robert Gundlack, a physical scientist who had been awarded 128 patents in his first 30 years of work, explains this approach to creativity improvement in these terms:

> Being creative means developing a synergy between the left half of the brain—the analytical half—and the right half of the brain—the creative half. I learned that at home during my childhood. My mother was an artist, a painter of landscapes. My father was a chemist and inventor of Wildroot hair oil. Both my parents influenced me equally well.[6]

Identify Your Creative Time Period. As you begin to make creativity a habit, it is helpful to identify those times of the day (or week) when your capacity for creative thought is the highest and lowest. For most people, creative capacity is best following ample rest. (So many people in our culture are addicted to caffeine, that they require coffee before they can capitalize upon a rested brain.) It is, therefore, helpful to tackle creative problems at the start of a workday.

Some executives and researchers tackle their biggest thought problems while on vacation or while jogging. The solution to the problem is conceptualized in broadest outline, and the details are worked out back on the job. Among such "vacation problems" might be "What new service might our agency offer?" or "What hypothesis is worthy of researching?"

Other individuals report that their best time for creative thought is immediately before falling asleep. We have all heard of the energetic people who keep a pen and notebook adjacent to their bed in order to jot down such nocturnal flashes of inspiration. One manager reports that he gets his best ideas during meetings conducted for other purposes. The point is to chart your individual creative time period.

Be Curious. Curiosity frequently underlies creative ideas. The person who routinely questions why things work or don't work is on the way toward developing a creative suggestion to improve on what already exists. Many new ideas for products and services stem from the curious attitude of their developer. An office supervisor in a plumbing supply company encouraged his firm to develop a new mechanism that would help stop leaking water closets. His suggestion stemmed from his curiosity as to why so many places he visited had troubles with continuously running toilets. The resultant product is built upon a new principle. It uses water pressure to replace the troublesome floating bulb arrangement found in most water closets.

Borrow Creative Ideas. Duplication—copying the success of others—is a type of creativity. Knowing when and which ideas to borrow from other people can help you behave as if you were an imaginative person yourself. Many useful ideas brought to an organization are simply lifted directly from others or a simple combination of them. Trade magazines, books, and newspapers are fertile sources for innovative ideas. Another source might be other people engaged in similar work. Many career-minded individuals use luncheon engagements as an opportunity to hunt for new ideas. We are, of course, referring to borrowing ideas that are public information, not trade secrets. Finally, many entrepreneurs borrow ideas that have worked for others in order to start their own businesses.

Maintain (and Use) an Idea Notebook. It is difficult to capitalize upon creative ideas unless you keep a careful record of them. A creative idea trusted to memory may become forgotten in the press of everyday business. An important suggestion kept on your daily log of errands to run or duties to perform may become obscured. Because it is creative ideas that carry considerable weight in propelling your career forward, they deserve the dignity of a separate notebook. The cautious or forgetful person is advised to keep two copies of the idea book: one at home and one in the office.

The Demand for Creativity in Managerial Work

Managerial work requires more creativity than most people realize. Above all, the manager or professional is frequently faced with a complex problem to solve for which programmed alternatives are not available. By searching for a new alternative, the manager engages in creative behavior. Robert E. Kaplan, a behavioral scientist and project manager at the Center for Creative Leadership, contends that good managers are creative all the time: "They have to be to meet the confusing, fast-changing procession of demands on their intelligence, adaptability, and people-handling skill."[7]

Some of the need for creativity in management stems from the hectic nature of a manager's job. A manager's day includes such diverse activities as scheduled meetings, reading, writing, making presentations, greeting visitors, and going on tours. Managers jump from one task to another. According to Kaplan, to fashion order out of this potential chaos is a creative act.[8]

Entrepreneurial managers are continuously faced with the need to be creative. The entrepreneur needs to be creative in such matters as identifying a new product or service that customers will accept, getting by with a small staff, and arranging for financing—particularly when business is bad or the firm is facing bankruptcy.

Another way of developing one's managerial skills is thus to improve one's creativity. The suggestions described in this chapter and the Guidelines section are directly relevant. In addition, the essential skill to develop in becoming more creative is to search for several good alternatives to the problem at hand before reaching a decision. The less creative manager or professional will tend to grab at the first alternative rather than stretching his or her mind one step further.

The Strengths of Creativity Improvement

Few people would argue that improving your creativity is not of some benefit to the individual and the organization. A statement in a management journal cogently argues the case for creativity:

> Creative decision making and problem solving are two of the most important talents that employees can possess, talents that are necessary for the financial health and prosperity of any firm. Unless a firm can respond with unique products/services, innovative marketing strategies and creative responses to complex problems, it may find itself losing sales, shares of the market and profits.[9]

Assuming the suggestions for creativity improvement described here (or in the additional references) worked for you, it could propel you forward in your career. Many high ranking executives gained early momentum in their careers because they spearheaded a breakthrough idea. Edwin Land with instant photography and Lee Iacocca with the Mustang are but two legendary examples.

A key strength of these methods of creativity improvement is that they are highly cost effective. For a modest investment of time, and virtually no money, they can yield a major return. Brainstorming, both in groups and individually, has helped bring forth thousands of creative suggestions in its close to 50 years of history.

The Weaknesses of Creativity Improvement

Improving your creativity is not without some subtle disadvantages. For one, many organizations are not looking for more creative ideas. They already have too many good ideas floating around that they are unable to implement, or even process, because of limited resources. Being creative is usually far removed from creating change. Noted management authority Ross A. Webber points out that creativity exists in large supply because it is merely the generation of ideas. But *innovation* (his term for creating change) is rarer, because it includes the application of the creative idea to the solution of a problem.[10]

However, if you carry creativity improvement too far, you will be perceived as more of a dreamer than a realist. Most organizations are looking for an occasional good idea, not a spate of them.

A related argument against creativity improvement is that some organizations do not want creativity because the key people are unclear as to the true meaning of creative behavior. They may perceive creativity as being synonymous with far-fetched thinking, rather than as primarily looking for new alternatives to solving problems. Thus, the creative individual may be shunned as a person with unworkable ideas.

An argument against the creativity-improvement exercises described in this chapter is that they are not validated with substantial empirical evidence. Therefore, a person could be investing time in exercises that will not really achieve their purpose.

GUIDELINES FOR ACTION AND SKILL DEVELOPMENT

Select several or a combination of creativity-improvement techniques that seem best suited to your personal preferences. To illustrate, you might find it comfortable to conduct private brainstorming sessions but too much of a long-term commitment to try to develop synergy between both sides of your brain. Unless you have an extraordinary gift for remembering things, using an idea notebook will be beneficial to you.

Improving your creativity requires a great deal of self-discipline and concentrated effort. The techniques and strategies described here and in the references are intended to supplement, not substitute for diligent application of your mental efforts toward finding creative alternatives to problems.

Avoid overemphasizing creativity to the point that you develop a distaste for the repetitive aspects of your job. Every position from the data-entry clerk to the chief executive officer includes some noncreative tasks.

An idea cannot be considered truly creative until other people

---

pass judgment on its utility. The reason is that your idea must be converted to action before it is classified as creative. It is, therefore, helpful to give your ideas a "pilot run" by asking others for their reaction to your innovative suggestions. To keep the process alive, it is important that you establish a reciprocal relationship with those people by providing them feedback about their ideas.

Questions and Activities

1. Which method of creativity improvement discussed in this chapter do you think is best suited to you? Why?
2. It has been often said that innovation in business and industry has shown a decline in the last decade (in North America). Assuming this statement is true, what factors do you think have contributed to this decline?
3. What stage, or aspect, of decision making requires the most creativity? Explain.
4. A federal government official once told this author, "Don't forget to tell your readers how creative and flexible a bureaucracy can be." What is your evaluation of the creativity of managers in large bureaucracies?
5. How can a person who borrows creative ideas from others avoid being accused of stealing or plagiarizing?
6. To what extent is the type of creativity displayed by inventors and artists the same type as that displayed by businesspeople?
7. Try one or two of the creativity-improvement suggestions in this chapter for 10 days. See if you actually become more proficient at searching for creative alternatives to problems. Report your observations back to your classmates.

Notes

[1]Thomas J. Bouchard, "Whatever Happened to Brainstorming?" *Industry Week* (August 2, 1971) p.29.

[2]Roger von Oech, *A Whack on the Side of the Head* (New York: Warner Books, 1984). Some of the information in this section is based on two interviews with von Oech: Priscilla Petty, "Break Out! Routine Thinking Can Be Hazardous to On-the-Job Creativity," *Rochester Democrat and Chronicle* (November 22, 1983) p. 1D; Robert S. Wieder, "How to Get Great Ideas," *Success* (November 1983) pp. 29–31, 59, 60. All the quotes in this section are from the Petty Article.

[3]Petty, "Break Out," p. 1D.

[4]Ibid.

[5]Information on this topic is synthesized in Thomas V. Bonoma and Gerald Zaltman, *Psychology for Management* (Boston: Kent Publishing, 1981) pp. 111–113.

[6]John J. Byczkowski, "Invention's a Necessity at Xerox," *Rochester Democrat and Chronicle* (January 9, 1983) p. 1F.

[7]Robert E. Kaplan, "Creativity in the Everyday Business of Managing," *Issues & Observations* (May 1983) p. 1.

[8]Ibid.

[9]David R. Wheeler, "Creative Decision Making and the Organization," *Personnel Journal* (June 1979) p. 374.

[10]Ross A. Webber, *Management: Basic Elements of Managing Organizations*, rev. ed. (Homewood, Ill.: Richard D. Irwin, 1979) p. 475.

Some Additional References

Asimov, Issac. "Creativity Will Dominate Our Time after the Concepts of Work and Fun Have Been Blurred by Technology," *Personnel Administrator* (December 1983) pp. 42–46.

Gryskiewicz, S. S., and J. T. Shields. "Targeted Innovation," *Issues & Observations* (November 1983) pp. 1–4. Center for Creative Leadership, Greensboro, North Carolina.

Tushman, Michael L., and William L. Moore. *Readings in the Management of Creativity.* Marshfield, Mass.: Pitman Publishing, 1982.

Gardner, Howard. *Art, Mind, and Brain: A Cognitive Approach to Creativity.* New York: Basic Books, 1982.

Appendix to Chapter 2

How Creative Are You?*

By Eugene Raudsepp
President Princeton Creative Research, Inc., Princeton, New Jersey

In recent years, several task-oriented tests have been developed to measure creative abilities and behavior. While certainly useful, they do not adequately tap the complex network of behaviors, the particular personality traits, attitudes, motivations, values, interests and other variables that predispose a person to think creatively.

To arrive at assessment measures that would cover a broader range of creative attributes, our organization developed an inventory type of test. A partial version of this instrument is featured below.

After each statement, indicate with a letter the degree or extent with which you agree or disagree with it: **A** = strongly agree, **B** = agree, **C** = in between or don't know, **D** = disagree, **E** = strongly disagree. Mark your answers as accurately and frankly as possible. Try not to "second guess" how a creative person might respond to each statement.

1. I always work with a great deal of certainty that I'm following the correct procedures for solving a particular problem. _____
2. It would be a waste of time for me to ask questions if I had no hope of obtaining answers. _____
3. I feel that a logical step-by-step method is best for solving problems. _____
4. I occasionally voice opinions in groups that seem to turn some people off. _____
5. I spend a great deal of time thinking about what others think of me. _____
6. I feel that I may have a special contribution to give to the world. _____

7. It is more important for me to do what I believe to be right than to try to win the approval of others. _____

8. People who seem unsure and uncertain about things lose my respect. _____

9. I am able to stick with difficult problems over extended periods of time. _____

10. On occasion I get overly enthusiastic about things. _____

11. I often get my best ideas when doing nothing in particular. _____

12. I rely on intuitive hunches and the feeling of "rightness" or "wrongness" when moving toward the solution of a problem. _____

13. When problem solving, I work faster analyzing the problem and slower when synthesizing the information I've gathered. _____

14. I like hobbies which involve collecting things. _____

15. Daydreaming has provided the impetus for many of my more important projects. _____

16. If I had to choose from two occupations other than the one I now have, I would rather be a physician than an explorer. _____

17. I can get along more easily with people if they belong to about the same social and business class as myself. _____

18. I have a high degree of aesthetic sensitivity. _____

19. Intuitive hunches are unreliable guides in problem solving. _____

20. I am much more interested in coming up with new ideas than I am in trying to sell them to others. _____

21. I tend to avoid situations in which I might feel inferior. _____

22. In evaluating information, the source of it is more important to me than the content. _____

23. I like people who follow the rule "business before pleasure." _____

24. One's own self-respect is much more important than the respect of others. _____

25. I feel that people who strive for perfection are unwise. _____

26. I like work in which I must influence others. _____

27. It is important for me to have a place for everything and everything in its place. _____

28. People who are willing to entertain "crackpot" ideas are impractical. _____

29. I rather enjoy fooling around with new ideas, even if there is no practical payoff. _____

30. When a certain approach to a problem doesn't work, I can quickly reorient my thinking. _____

31. I don't like to ask questions that show ignorance. _____

32. I am able to more easily change my interests to pursue a job or career than I can change a job to pursue my interests. _____

33. Inability to solve a problem is frequently due to asking the wrong questions. _____

34. I can frequently anticipate the solution to my problems. _____

35. It is a waste of time to analyze one's failures. _____

36. Only fuzzy thinkers resort to metaphors and analogies. _____

37. At times I have so enjoyed the ingenuity of a crook that I hoped he or she would go scotfree. _____

38. I frequently begin work on a problem which I can only dimly sense and not yet express. _____

39. I frequently tend to forget things such as names of people, streets, highways, small towns, etc. _____

40. I feel that hard work is the basic factor in success. _____

41. To be regarded as a good team member is important to me. _____

42. I know how to keep my inner impulses in check. _____

43. I am a thoroughly dependable and responsible person. _____

44. I resent things being uncertain and unpredictable. _____

45. I prefer to work with others in a team effort rather than solo. _____

46. The trouble with many people is that they take things too seriously. _____

47. I am frequently haunted by my problems and cannot let go of them. _____

48. I can easily give up immediate gain or comfort to reach the goals I have set. _____

49. If I were a college professor, I would rather teach factual courses than those involving theory. _____

50. I'm attracted to the mystery of life. _____

Scoring Instructions. To compute your percentage score, circle and add up the values assigned to each item.

	Strongly Agree	Agree	In-Between or Don't Know	Disagree	Strongly Disagree
	A	B	C	D	E
1.	−2	−1	0	+1	+2
2.	−2	−1	0	+1	+2
3.	−2	−1	0	+1	+2

4.	+2	+1	0	−1	−2
5.	−2	−1	0	+1	+2
6.	+2	+1	0	−1	−2
7.	+2	+1	0	−1	−2
8.	−2	−1	0	+1	+2
9.	+2	+1	0	−1	−2
10.	+2	+1	0	−1	−2
11.	+2	+1	0	−1	−2
12.	+2	+1	0	−1	−2
13.	−2	−1	0	+1	+2
14.	−2	−1	0	+1	+2
15.	+2	+1	0	−1	−1
16.	−2	−1	0	+1	+2
17.	−2	−1	0	+1	+2
18.	+2	+1	0	−1	−2
19.	−2	−1	0	+1	+2
20.	+2	+1	0	−1	−2
21.	−2	−1	0	+1	+2
22.	−2	−1	0	+1	+2
23.	−2	−1	0	+1	+2
24.	+2	+1	0	−1	−2
25.	−2	−1	0	+1	+1
26.	−2	−1	0	+1	+2
27.	−2	−1	0	+1	+2
28.	−2	−1	0	+1	+2
29.	+2	+1	0	−1	−2
30.	+2	+1	0	−1	−2
31.	−2	−1	0	+1	+2
32.	−2	−1	0	+1	+2
33.	+2	+1	0	−1	−2
34.	+2	+1	0	−1	−2
35.	−2	−1	0	+1	+2
36.	−2	−1	0	+1	+2
37.	+2	+1	0	−1	−2
38.	+2	+1	0	−1	−2
39.	+2	+1	0	−1	−2
40.	+2	+1	0	−1	−2
41.	−2	−1	0	+1	+2
42.	−2	−1	0	+1	+2
43.	−2	−1	0	+1	+2
44.	−2	−1	0	+1	+2
45.	−2	−1	0	+1	+2
46.	+2	+1	0	−1	−2
47.	+2	+1	0	−1	−2
48.	+2	+1	0	−1	−2
49.	−2	−1	0	+1	+2
50.	+2	+1	0	−1	−2

80 to 100	Very creative	20 to 39	Below average
60 to 79	Above average	−100 to 19	Noncreative
40 to 59	Average		

Further information about the test, "How Creative Are You?" is available from Princeton Creative Research, Inc., 10 Nassau St., P.O. Box 122, Princeton, NJ 08540.

Chapter 3

Assertiveness Training

The company described below was concerned that minorities and women were not doing enough to propel themselves into management. Furthermore, when members of these groups were placed in management positions, many of them were more hesitant than necessary in making their work demands known. The company therefore looked toward assertiveness training (AT) as a method of helping minorities and women realize their potential as managers.

Bette Falco, manager of Equal Employment Opportunity, welcomed participants to the career development program:

> During our two days together, you'll be participating in an assertiveness training workshop. Assertiveness training, or AT as we often call it, has three important goals: We want you to know how you feel; to say what you want; and get what you want.[1]
>
> I suspect some of you are wondering why you have been extended the invitation to participate in an AT workshop. In other words, what organizational and individual problems are we attempting to solve? Quite frankly, much of it has to do with equal employment opportunity. AT was first applied in business and government when some people began to realize that women and minorities were themselves partially to blame for their modest progress in organizations. If women and minorities would be more assertive, in a sensible way, more of them would be chosen for higher-level assignments.
>
> You realize this program is designed primarily for women and minorities of our corporation. However, nobody has been excluded because of his or her race or sex. I'm glad to see that we also have several male majority members signed up for the program. AT can help anybody who experiences problems in the area of

self-assertion. AT can also help people who are obnoxious and abrasive when they try to get what they want.

Quite specifically, the reason top management has been eager to sponsor our AT workshop is that they believe many women and minorities employed by us are too timid in getting their point across and making their demands known. Top management also believes that many employees are too easily bullied by several of our more aggressive department heads. Before we begin with our first exercise, what questions might you have about AT or our workshop?

After 20 minutes of questions and answers, Bette Falco proceeded with the first role-playing exercise designed to teach assertion skills:

To begin we must make the vital distinction among the three types of behavior—assertive, passive, and aggressive. *Assertive behavior* is when an individual makes a clear statement of what he or she wants, or how he or she feels in a given situation. All this is accomplished without being abusive, abrasive, or obnoxious. *Passive* or *nonassertive* people let things happen to them without letting their feelings be known. They are hesitant to take the initiative to express their point of view. *Aggressive* people are obnoxious and overbearing. They push for what they want with almost no regard for the feelings of others.

Another way of looking at it is that the nonassertive person is stepped on and the aggressive person steps on others. The assertive person deals with a problem in a mature and explicit manner.[2]

In our first role-playing situation, Jed, one of our workshop trainers, will play the role of the boss. A couple of you will play the role of the subordinate. After you have acted out the role for a few minutes, I'll present my critique of the interaction that I have observed. Here is the scenario: You are a market research analyst for a major brewery that has just appointed a new president. The president has sent a suggestion to marketing that the brewery should use a purple can for its new light beer. A study conducted by your department suggests that the majority of beer drinkers would have an aversion toward purple beer cans.

Your boss, to be played by Jed, says to you: "I know your analysis reveals that consumers don't want beer in purple cans. But you must realize that our new president believes strongly that purple cans will work. Couldn't you manipulate your data just a bit, so our department does not appear to be contradicting the president's first big suggestion? As you know, market research is not infallible."

Our first volunteer will respond to this statement from Jed. Go ahead Audrey McIntosh.

Audrey: You mean to say, Jed, that you will not accept my findings as they are. That I'm going to have to adjust my conclusions to fit the president's opinions?

Jed: You're getting the point, Audrey. It would be kind of naive to kick sand in the face of our president's first big contribution to marketing. He has built his reputation on having a good feel for the market.

Audrey: I've worked long and hard on this survey. I would hate to junk it. But I do see some data here suggesting that about 25 percent of consumers do like the idea of a purple beer can. Maybe the idea would catch on, once the purple cans were out on the shelves and shown on color TV advertisements.

Bette: Okay, you two can stop now. Audrey I like your acting ability, but I'm somewhat concerned about your assertiveness. You did get your feelings across a little bit. Yet, you were completely bulldozed by your boss. It could be an authority problem. Both Jed and, of course, the president, have much more power than you do. However, we must learn to assert ourselves with authority figures. Let's get another person to play the role of the market research analyst. Thanks so much, Audrey, for being our first volunteer of the workshop. Okay, how about Jenny Tindall?

Jenny: I hear you saying, Jed, that I should reinterpret my data to fit the president's preconception. I understand how you feel, but I am unwilling to change my conclusions about the acceptance rate for purple beer cans.

Jed: How nice to hear from goodie two shoes, but even market research must sometimes face up to harsh political realities. How can you be so sure you're right?

Jenny: As my boss, you are, of course, entitled to your opinion about the accuracy of my work. No market researcher can offer 100 percent confidence in her work. If you do not think my report is accurate, do not use it. However, I would not be able to change my interpretations of the data.

Bette: Good enough for now. Let's stop at this point for a brief analysis. Jenny must have done her homework. She is being assertive without being totally inflexible. She has offered a proposition to her boss that could be interpreted as a workable compromise. She continues to assert her right to her professional opinions. Yet, she is suggesting to her boss the option of not using the report. Jed is probably not compelled to present all market research reports to top management. Nevertheless, Jenny goes on record as having stood by her professional position. She was appropriately assertive.

To finish up with this role play, could we please have a volunteer to act in an agressive mode? Thank you Rich Hodgetts.

Rich: Hold on, Jed, I resent your telling me to lie just to please the new president. He's making a foolish mistake and you're willing to sacrifice ethics to avoid confronting him.

Jed: I think you're taking a harsh position.

Rich: If we manufacture beer in purple cans, we'll be the laughing stock of the industry. Whatever the company decides to do is okay with me. But I'll resign from my job before I fake data.

Jed: If you want to resign, that's your decision.

Bette: Thank you, Rich, for a clever role play. You have seen how Rich placed himself in an untenable position by being aggressive and abusive. A disagreement over market research ethics has escalated almost to the point of resignation from the company. Rich Hodgetts does not seem headed toward a constructive resolution of the problem.

THIRTEEN STEPS TO ASSERTIVENESS

The sample role playing interchanges just presented have given you preliminary insight into the mechanics of an AT workshop. Assertiveness training usually also involves a series of steps that, if properly followed, lead you toward becoming an assertive individual. These steps are provided in some detail here to provide further insight into the process involved in changing your behavior from passive to assertive (or from aggressive to assertive).[3]

Step 1: Observe Your Own Behavior. Above all, are you asserting yourself adequately? Or are you being too pushy, obnoxious, or abrasive? Do you believe you get what you want when you want it, without stepping on the rights of others? A frequent work situation, that of being appointed to a committee, can be used to help sensitize you to the differences among passive (nonassertive), aggressive, and assertive behavior.

Opening her morning mail, supervisor Phyllis notices a memo from the human resource director, which says in part, "Congratulations, you have been appointed chairperson to organize the holiday party for needy children. You will find it both an honor and a privilege to serve your community in this manner."

Unfortunately, Phyllis is already heavily committed to community activities, including serving as a special representative to change zoning laws to encourage more industrialization of her town. She also thinks that perhaps her being female contributed to the decision to appoint her to organize the children's party. Phyllis can respond in three different ways:

1. *Passive behavior:* Phyllis does nothing and awaits further instructions. She is simmering with anger but grits her teeth and hopes that the assignment will not be as time consuming as she now estimates.

2. *Aggressive behavior:* Phyllis grabs the phone, calls the human resources director, and says: "Who do you think you are, assigning me to head up this committee? When I want to run a children's holiday party, I'll volunteer. Try asking a man next time. Maybe a man should be organizing childrens' activities for a change."

3. *Assertive behavior:* Phyllis calls the human resources director and says, "I appreciate your thinking of me as the head of the committee to

organize the holiday party. However, I choose not to serve. It sounds like an interesting assignment and I doubt that you will have trouble finding another chairperson. If this is an assignment that is rotated between males and females, please keep me on your list of potential committee heads."

The appendix to this chapter will provide you some clues to your present level of assertiveness.

Step 2: Keep a Record of Your Assertiveness. Devote an entire week to this project, keeping a careful log or diary of situations in which assertive behavior might have been called for. Record each day when you behaved assertively, when you were too passive, or when you were too aggressive. Also, look carefully at situations which you avoided altogether in order to avoid confrontation. Such a diary entry might be, "The head of the duplicating department told me I would have to wait two weeks to have my report duplicated. I needed it within 10 days. I guess I should have pursued the matter further rather than just grumbling to myself." It is crucial that you be candid and systematic in keeping this diary.

Step 3: Concentrate on a Specific Situation. As instructed by two pioneers in AT, "Spend a few moments with your eyes closed, imagining how you handle a specific incident (being shortchanged at the supermarket, having a friend 'talk your ear off' on the telephone when you had too much to do, letting the boss make you 'feel like 2 cents' over a small mistake). Imagine vividly the actual details, including your specific feelings at the time and afterward."[4]

The market researcher in the situation described earlier in this chapter might express feelings of this nature:

> Here I was facing my boss in a heavy ethical situation. Jed actually wanted me to fake data in order to agree with some mammoth blunder about to be initiated by the new president. It seemed like I was caught between a rock and a hard place. If I agreed with my boss, I couldn't live with myself as a professional person. On the other hand, if I stood up to the boss, it would be like criticizing him and the president. It won't be easy to assert my rights in this situation.

Step 4: Review Your Responses. Write down your behavior in Step 3 in terms of the key components of assertiveness (eye contact, body posture, gestures, facial expression, voice, and message content). Ask yourself questions such as these: Did my body language communicate how I really felt about the situation? Did I look disappointed about being asked to reinterpret my research data? Did I express my disagreement in a forceful, well-modulated conversational statement? Or did I murmur or fly off the handle? Was I able to look Jed straight in the eye? Did I state clearly that it would be upsetting to me to interpret my data in a manner contrary to what I really believed?

As you review your responses, it is helpful to note the things you did right. Also be aware of those statements which represented passive or aggressive behavior. An example of passive behavior is Audrey's statement, "But I do see some data here suggesting that about 25 percent of the consumers do like the idea of a purple beer can." An example of aggressive response was Rich's statement, "I'll resign from my job before I fake data."

Step 5: Observe an Effective Model. People who attend AT workshops are encouraged to observe another person in action who appears to be assertive. It is as important to observe that person's style, as well as what that person says. Observing an assertive person in a staff meeting is one method of finding an appropriate model. Interviews shown on public television are useful in providing a variety of effective models. Some public figures are adept at behaving assertively when interviewed by a television reporter.

Style refers to body language rather than content. The timing of messages is also part of a person's style. A good person to model is one who times his or her assertions well. For instance, it is poor practice to behave assertively with your boss when the both of you are around others in the office. The boss may be forced to behave defensively in such a situation.

Step 6: Consider Alternative Responses. Think of a situation you recently handled. How else could it have been handled? Larry was using a public photocopying machine at a library. Those waiting in line in back of him could readily see that he had a large stack of papers to be photocopied. Four different people said something to the effect, "Do you mind if I jump in for a second and use the machine? I only have two pages to copy." Larry did mind, but each time his response was "Well, okay, if you only have one or two pages."

An assertive response Larry might have tried would be, "It may not be what you would prefer but you will have to wait 10 minutes until I've completed my copying. My time is very valuable today."

Step 7: Imagine Yourself Handling the Situation. Close your eyes and visualize yourself behaving assertively in the situation reported in Step 6. You might act similarly to the model you have used for Step 5. It is important to be assertive but not to behave in a manner out of character with yourself. This step is much like a rehearsal or role play, except that it all takes place by yourself. You might also practice saying the assertive statement: "I appreciate your asking me first, but I cannot let other people in to use this machine until I have finished. My time is very valuable today."

Some readers will think to themselves at this point, "AT is much like the old standby 'I should of said' when you have recently argued with somebody." The difference is that in AT, you relive the past and rehearse the future.

Step 8: Try It Out. At this point you have examined your own behavior, explored alternatives, and observed a model of an assertive individual. You are now prepared to begin trying out assertive behavior in a specific problem situation or two. It may be helpful to repeat Steps 5, 6, and 7 until you are ready to proceed. Prior to trying out your new assertive behavior, it may be beneficial to role play the situation with a friend.

One engineer used role playing to prepare herself to assertively handle an annoying situation at work. Although she was equal in organizational rank to other engineers in her department, her boss typically introduced her to strangers by her first name only: "This is Pam, one of our mechanical engineers." Males were introduced to visitors in a manner such as "This is Pete Nowacki, one of our mechanical engineers." Pam's assertive response to her boss was:

> Gerry, something has been troubling me. I notice that when I'm introduced to visitors, you only use my first name. When you introduce male engineers to visitors, you use their first and last names. I would like to be given the same courtesy as males.

Pam's boss apologized and never repeated this personal slight.

Step 9: Get Feedback. Here you try to obtain feedback on how well you did in trying out the assertive behavior. Step 4 called for the same type of self-examination. In this step you emphasize what you did right. Pam might provide herself this type of feedback, "You handled things well. You leveled with Gerry in a way that did not make him defensive or retaliatory. You now feel much more comfortable when Gerry introduces me to new people. Although I thought I would appear nervous in making my assertion, I came across pretty cool."

Step 10: Behavior Shaping. Steps 7, 8, and 9 should be repeated as often as necessary to shape your behavior in the desirable direction. Step by step you build up toward the final desired result. You build yourself up to a point where you feel comfortable dealing in a self-enhancing manner with a situation that was bothersome in the past. Suppose you work for a superior who characteristically tells you, "Don't you see that my way is better?" Your final goal might be to say, "I must disagree. Your way has some merit, but my careful analysis of the situation reveals . . ." Since you are somewhat fearful of disagreeing with somebody in a position of authority, you may have to begin with a very mild assertion such as, "You could be right. But could you explain your position to me more fully?"

Step 11: No Further Delays in Trying Out the Assertive Behavior. The illustrations presented earlier indicate that many people will have put their AT to actual use from Step 8 forward. However, some particularly nonassertive people may have still restricted their assertive behavior to practice sessions. Rehearsals and role plays are a relatively secure environment. It is now time to do what Pam did—behave assertively in a natural setting. As a final preliminary, some people will try out AT in low stake situations such as demanding a larger portion of french fries at a restaurant, or asking a clerk in a dry cleaning store to replace a button broken during the dry cleaning process. People who still cannot behave assertively through Step 11 may need professional assistance in defending their rights and expressing what they think and feel.

Step 12: Further Training. The developers of this program of AT state, "You are encouraged to repeat such procedures as may be appropriate in the development of the behavior pattern you desire."[5] Some people will repeat steps 1 through 11 for one or two other situations in life that call for assertiveness. A person with a work-related problem of assertiveness might want to repeat the same process for a vexing marital problem.

Step 13: Social Reinforcement. No program of self-development will work unless the new behavior receives frequent reinforcement. As you practice assertive behavior, observe the beneficial consequences. (For example, "Yes, it felt great to explain patiently to my boss that I want to be considered for promotion to another division even if I have a husband and three children.") Positive comments from other people about your assertions will prove of more value than self-reinforcement. A shy systems analyst went through a program of assertiveness training. He practiced the new skills back on the job with apparent success. His self-confidence elevated a notch when he overheard the comment, "Whatever happened to Tim? He's a new man these days. He lets people know exactly what he thinks of their work procedures."

The Argument For and Against AT

A compelling argument for the use of assertiveness training in personal development programs is that a substantial number of career-minded people are either too shy or too outspoken. AT is designed to help with both extremes of behavior. AT is also quite useful in reducing and preventing stress. Many people develop psychosomatic disorders because they overcontrol their feelings instead of expressing them directly to people with whom they are in contact. Assertiveness training is also valuable because it can contribute to leadership effectiveness. Competent leaders are usually assertive individuals—they lay out their demands clearly to subordinates, and they express their feelings and attitudes constructively. Finally, AT is at worst harmless, and can be conducted for a relatively modest cost.

A major argument against AT is that only anecdotal evidence exists that it does work. It has been observed that people who undergo assertiveness training often become assertive over minor issues such as not losing their place in a movie theatre line. Changes in more significant aspects of behavior are not forthcoming. Another disadvantage of AT is that despite its claims, it has an adverse impact on people who are already too assertive. Instead of making them more tactful, they become overly abrasive. As one insurance company executive told a personnel manager, "Please stop sending women to assertiveness training indiscriminately. Some of the women you sent were already assertive. They are now much too outspoken in making their demands known to management."

Another potential concern about AT is that if too many people in the workforce became assertive, management would spend an inordinate amount of time responding to their demands. Even if they are tactful, and many of their demands are legitimate, assertive people require a lot of individual attention. For instance, one man who returned from assertiveness training began to make demands such as wanting new office furniture, more secretarial help, and a larger salary increase. Because of these large number of demands, his manager began to dread meeting with him.

GUIDELINES FOR ACTION AND SKILL DEVELOPMENT

As explained by psychologist Anthony F. Grasha, there are three things to remember when becoming more assertive. First, avoid behaving in ways that will probably make others overly defensive or angry or lead them to shun you. Such behavior will guarantee that you will not get what you want. Second, remember that others have the same rights as you. "You should not try to get what you want by ignoring the legitimate needs and rights of other people." Third, behaving assertively does not mean that you will get what you want everytime. Sometimes a compromise is necessary; at other times you will simply fail to get what you want.[6]

Watch out for immediate swings from one extreme of behavior to another shortly after participating in assertiveness training. Psychiatrist Helen A. De Rosis cautions: "Swooping from an extreme nonassertive position to an extreme position of hard, critical abrasiveness can be very offensive and often abrasive. There are some women who have moved from one of these extremes to the other and have found it to be counterproductive."[7]

Use flexibility in applying the program of assertiveness training featured in this chapter (13 steps to assertiveness). One important factor subject to individual differences is the amount of rehearsal you will need before carrying out an assertion. A few people can modify their behavior from passivity to assertiveness, or from aggressiveness to assertiveness after just being made aware of the differences. Some people require considerable rehearsal in order to overcome the anxiety associated with behaving assertively.

As with any program of self-development, there is no appropriate substitute for the active practice of assertive behavior both on and off the job. Behave assertively when you choose to, not as an arbitrary exercise. The basic steps in becoming more assertive are deceptively simple. "The execution of these steps, however, requires knowledge, skill, and a great deal of practice."[8]

Questions and Activities

1. How does being assertive contribute to one's managerial effectiveness?
2. If you were the market researcher who discovered that most beer drinkers would dislike purple beer cans, how would you deal with the situation?
3. Describe how AT might be a useful technique for helping sales representatives become more comfortable in making cold calls.
4. Would you recommend AT for a supervisor who has a severe stutter? Why or why not?
5. Describe how AT might help you get a generous salary increase.
6. From top management's standpoint, what are some of the potential problems with using AT at lower levels in the organization?
7. Take an informal poll of about six experienced businesspeople and get their opinions on the following question: In what organizational functions (divisions) is assertiveness the most important? Bring your findings back to class and discuss them with your classmates.

Notes

[1]Lynn Z. Bloom, Karen Coburn, and Joan Pearlman, *The New Assertive Woman* (New York: Dell Publishing, 1975) p. 1.

[2]The original source of the assertive, nonassertive, and aggressive behavior categories is Robert E. Alberti and Michael L. Emmons, *Your Perfect Right: A Guide to Assertive Behavior* (San Luis Obispo, Calif.: Impact Publishers, 1970) Chapter 2.

[3]This presentation follows closely Alberti and Emmons, *Your Perfect Right*, 2nd ed. (1974) pp. 35–38. The examples and illustrations within the 13 steps, however, are original.

[4]Ibid., p. 35.

[5]Ibid., p. 37.

[6]Anthony F. Grasha, *Practical Applications of Psychology*, 2nd ed. (Boston: Little Brown, 1983).

[7]Helen A. De Rosis, *How to Be Assertive Without Putting Someone Down* (New York: Bonomo Culture Institute, 1977) p. 55.

[8]Malcolm E. Shaw, "Making Your Way Assertively," *Supervisory Management* (March 1982) p. 3.

Some Additional References

Burley-Allen, Madelyn. *Managing Assertively: How to Improve Your People Skills*. New York: John Wiley, 1983.

Kahn, Sharon E. "Adding Affect to Assertion Training." *Personnel and Guidance Journal* (April 1979) pp. 424–426.

Paul, Nancy. "Assertiveness Without Teams: A Training Programme for Executive Equality." *Personnel Management* (April 1979) pp. 37–40.

Powell, Barbara. *Overcoming Shyness: Practical Scripts for Everyday Encounters*. New York: McGraw-Hill, 1981.

Shyne, Keven. "Shyness: Breaking Through this Invisible Barrier to Achievement." *Success* (July 1982) pp. 14, 16, 36, 37, 51.

Weisinger, Hendrie and Norman M. Lobsenz. *Nobody's Perfect (How to Give Criticism and Get Results)*. New York: Warner Books, 1981.

Appendix to Chapter 3

Are You Passive, Assertive, or Aggressive?

The following questionnaire is designed to give you tentative insight into your current tendencies toward nonassertiveness (passivity), assertiveness, or aggressiveness. As with other questionnaires presented in this book, The Assertiveness Scale is primarily a self-examination and discussion device. Answer each question Mostly true or Mostly false, as it applies to you.

	Mostly True	Mostly False
1. It is extremely difficult for me to turn down a sales representative when that individual is a nice person.	_____	_____
2. I express criticism freely.	_____	_____
3. If another person were being very unfair, I would bring it to that person's attention.	_____	_____
4. Work is no place to let your feelings show.	_____	_____
5. No use asking for favors, people get what they deserve on the job.	_____	_____
6. Business is not the place for tact; say what you think.	_____	_____
7. If a person looked like he or she were in a hurry, I would let that person in front of me in a supermarket line.	_____	_____
8. A weakness of mine is that I'm too nice a person.	_____	_____
9. If my restaurant bill is even 25 cents more than it should be, I demand that the mistake be corrected.	_____	_____
10. I have laughed out loud in public more than once.	_____	_____
11. I've been described as too outspoken by several people.	_____	_____
12. I am quite willing to have the store take back a piece of furniture that has a scratch.	_____	_____

13. I dread having to express anger toward a co-worker. _____ _____
14. People often say that I'm too reserved and emotionally controlled. _____ _____
15. Nice guys and gals finish last in business. _____ _____
16. I fight for my rights down to the last detail. _____ _____
17. I have no misgivings about returning an overcoat to the store if it doesn't fit me properly. _____ _____
18. If I have had an argument with a person, I try to avoid him or her. _____ _____
19. I insist on my spouse (roommate, or partner) doing his or her fair share of undesirable chores. _____ _____
20. It is difficult for me to look directly at another person when the two of us are in disagreement. _____ _____
21. I have cried among friends more than once. _____ _____
22. If someone near me at a movie kept up a conversation with another person, I would ask him or her to stop. _____ _____
23. I am able to turn down social engagements with people I do not particularly care for. _____ _____
24. It is poor taste to express what you really feel about another individual. _____ _____
25. I sometimes show my anger by swearing at or belittling another person. _____ _____
26. I am reluctant to speak up in a meeting. _____ _____
27. I find it relatively easy to ask friends for small favors such as giving me a lift to work when my car is being serviced or repaired. _____ _____
28. If another person was smoking in a restaurant and it bothered me, I would inform that person. _____ _____
29. I often finish other people's sentences for them. _____ _____
30. It is relatively easy for me to express love and affection toward another person. _____ _____

Scoring and Interpretation

Score yourself plus 1 for each of your answers that agrees with the scoring key. If your score is 10 or less, it is probable that you are currently a nonassertive individual. A score of 11 through 24 suggests that you are an assertive individual. A score of 25 or higher suggests that you are an aggressive individual. Retake this score about 30 days from now to give yourself some indication of the stability of your answers. You might also discuss your answers with a close friend to determine if that person has a similar perception of your assertiveness. Here is the scoring key.

1.	Mostly false	16.	Mostly true
2.	Mostly true	17.	Mostly true
3.	Mostly true	18.	Mostly false
4.	Mostly false	19.	Mostly true
5.	Mostly false	20.	Mostly false
6.	Mostly true	21.	Mostly true
7.	Mostly false	22.	Mostly true
8.	Mostly false	23.	Mostly true
9.	Mostly true	24.	Mostly false
10.	Mostly true	25.	Mostly true
11.	Mostly true	26.	Mostly false
12.	Mostly true	27.	Mostly true
13.	Mostly false	28.	Mostly true
14.	Mostly false	29.	Mostly true
15.	Mostly true	30.	Mostly true

Chapter 4

Preventing and Overcoming Job Burnout

Troy Bannerstone, sales manager at a large branch of a financial services firm, by his own admission was becoming emotionally exhausted and cynical. He and his manager both agreed that Troy should attend a burnout workshop—to learn techniques designed to both remedy and prevent burnout. In this chapter, we describe portions of the workshop Bannerstone attended.

Drew Jordan, the workshop leader, began the session by making a few introductory comments about the nature of burnout to the 21 participants: "At one time we believed that burnout was a special type of stress disorder that affected workers in the human services field almost exclusively. It was thought to be a form of battle fatigue from trying to be a conscientious people helper. When the rewards weren't there, conscientious human services workers would eventually lose their spark. Individuals would suffer a host of mild stress symptoms such as backaches, muscle aches, and headaches.

"Later burnout was observed among people not directly involved in the mental health or human services field. Police workers, fire fighters, and high school teachers were found to be frequent victims of burnout. Then, specialists in the field began to notice that conscientious workers in any type of work, and at any job level, could suffer from job burnout. So long as the rewards were not there, or you were working under oppressive organizational conditions, you could become emotionally exhausted, depleted, cynical, irritable, and impatient.

"You people may be particularly interested in knowing that managers are now known to be frequent victims of burnout. It's partly because managers are often conscientious, well-motivated people, and so much is expected of them. Often managers are supposed to reward other people, but they may not be receiving much stroking themselves." (More than half the attendees nod their head in approval at the last statement.)

"Later on this morning we'll get into some of the techniques and strategies for treating and preventing job burnout," said Dr. Jordan. "But for now, I think we should start learning from each other. I would like each person here to explain to the rest of the group, why you are here. Tell us about the specific concerns you have that have brought you to this workshop. Between now and the coffee break, let's hear from you six people seated to my right."

Person A: I came here, quite frankly, because I'm frightened. I'm not nearly the hard-driving, hard-charging sales rep I used to be. After 20 years in the territory, I really don't care too much whether or not customers buy from us. Our line of office furniture is pretty good, but our competition also has good equipment. I'm also tired of jumping up and down telling people that what we sell is service, when our service really isn't that hot.

Dr. Jordan, if you can recharge my battery, I'll consider this day time and money well spent. (A spontaneous burst of laughter takes place within the group.)

Person B: My reason for being here is to try and help some of my supervisors. As plant superintendent, I see burnout every day. You didn't mention it in your little speech, but burnout has driven some of my best supervisors into overdoing it with drugs and alcohol. My team is suffering from trying to motivate employees who are suffering from a weak work ethic. Also, the heavy turnover among our production workers leads to burnout for the supervisor. Training new employees all the time gets very discouraging.

Person C: I'm a high school teacher in a city school. I'm getting very discouraged about trying to help young black Americans. So many of them in my district have such poor home conditions that they have a negative image of themselves. As hard as I try, I just can't get almost any of them to develop an upbeat attitude and identify with successful black people. I'm proud of my black heritage, and I want them to be proud too. It's too bad, but I'm becoming very discouraged myself. I just don't know how I can ever reach enough of my students to do any good.

Person D: I'm a manager of a technical publications group in a large company. I've been in the same spot for about 10 years. There's not much hope of a promotion, and I'm not seeing many problems that I haven't seen before. But that's not the real reason I feel burned out. It's the lack of appreciation and recognition that's getting to me and my whole group. Management treats us like a necessary evil. There's not much glamor in "tech pubs."

Person E: My problem is probably a little bit different than the problem most of you people are facing. I've been put on a shelf and it bothers me. I'm about seven years away from retirement, but I feel that the company is treating me as if I were already retired. I'm a senior engineer who is supposed to have a lot of wisdom and knowledge. My problem is that nobody comes to me for advice anymore. My boss gives all the interesting problems to the younger engineers. I try to keep up with my field a little bit. However, I just don't have the educational background to cope with electronic engineering as the field is today. My energy supply is so low I sometimes go to bed right after dinner. And I still have trouble waking up in the morning.

Person F: I'm Troy Bannister, sales manager of a large suburban branch of one of the big financial services firms. I supervise about 20 people all together. If the group doesn't mind, I'd like to take an extra minute or so to describe my situation. I think that most of us here today are experiencing some of the same problems that I am facing.

First of all, both my boss and I agreed that I need help. I'm definitely a classic case of burnout. I'm exhausted; I'm cynical; I've lost my zip; and most of the time, I'm not much fun to be around. It all started a couple of years ago. I began to notice that I was no longer so concerned about our branch making quota. I used to think that making or exceeding quota was one of the biggest items in my life. I would call my wife immediately once I learned that we made or surpassed quota.

I began to question the value of my work when I read a report concluding that most of our customers would have been better off financially if they had not taken our advice. They would have fared just as well by putting their money in no-load mutual funds, money market funds, and bank certificates of deposit. Soon thereafter I began to experience tension and anxiety when I tried to get our representatives excited about getting our clients to invest more money with us.

I also began to see that the whole financial services industry was involved in some very nonproductive work, particularly mergers and acquisitions. I'm especially referring to the situation where one company tries to buy out another, against the will of the first company. The only people who benefit in these games are lawyers, financial analysts, and some stockholders who are wealthy enough to own large numbers of shares. But no new jobs are created.

My level of discouragement with our business also increased when our clientele became increasingly unsophisticated. In years past, most of our customers were knowledgeable about investments. For many it was a hobby. Today our sophisticated investors are more sophisticated than they ever were because there is so much valid information available for them to read. However, we are also serving customers today who know absolutely nothing about investments. These are the people who literally used to stuff their money under their mattresses in the past. One man came to our office last month with $10,000 in $100 and $50 bills. He said, "Will you please put this in a safe place for me? I've heard that you guys are doing the same kinds of things banks used to do."

After awhile my disenchantment with my work began to spill over into my home life. Sometimes I would feel so down that I couldn't get involved with my wife and two children. Soon they started to do things without me. I heard my six-year-old say one day, "Why has Dad turned into such a sour-puss?"

I know it's break time, so I'll make just one more statement. It really helps explain the magnitude of my burnout problem. My boredom with my job sometimes interferes with my sex life. When I'm depressed about having to face another week in the office, I lose my interest in sex. And that's really bad because it hurts the feelings of somebody I love very much—my wife.

After the break, the remaining 15 workshop participants presented a brief description of their problem. The workshop leader then described a number of techniques and strategies all people might use to combat burnout. Jordan then asked each participant to spend 30 minutes writing down some tentative approaches to dealing with his or her problem. Participants would then be asked to share their plans with the other members of the group. In addition, Jordan would react to their plans. Other participants were also encouraged to comment.

When it was Troy Bannister's turn to present his action plan, he offered these comments to the other workshop participants:

"First of all, as Dr. Jordan has suggested, I should take care of the stress aspects of my burnout. Combined with my occasional down-in-the dumps feelings, I am very tense and wound up. I have kind of slipped away from regular, robust physical exercise. I think I'll get back into chopping wood and jumping rope. That should make me feel better. A bigger issue is that I take my job too seriously. I like the strategy of not putting all my emotional eggs in one basket. If I could convince myself that kicks from personal life are as legitimate as kicks from work life, I think my burnout problem would benefit.

"I also like your suggestion of getting a new toy or gadget to play with on the job. Most of the customer representatives use the computer, but I rarely do. If I learned to use it well, it could conceivably give me a new kick on the job that would serve me well.

"I think I'll stick with these three suggestions as a starting point. Implementing them will keep me pretty busy for awhile."

Dr. Jordan had these reactions to Bannister's action plans:

"I think your approach is sound. Yet I have the feeling that you are overlooking one of the most important factors that is behind your particular burnout situation. Earlier today you mentioned your growing concern about whether or not your firm was really helping people. I think you should give careful thought to the number of people you really are helping. Your branch is probably making a positive impact on more lives than you realize. I suspect that without the services of your firm—or a comparable one—many of your customers would not have been able to send their children to college or purchase a home.

"One of the core reasons many conscientious people like Troy suffer burnout is that you want to help everybody. Learn to relish in the victories of the lives that you have touched."

STRATEGIES FOR MANAGING BURNOUT

Burnout is an evolving concept centering around the idea of a job-related condition of discouragement and apathy, stemming from receiving fewer rewards than anticipated. A current conception of burnout defines it as a syndrome (a pattern of symptoms) of emotional exhaustion and cynicism toward's one's work in response to stressful circumstances.[1] As implied from the statements made by the workshop participants, each case of burnout is based on a slightly different set of factors. An appropriate strategy for managing burnout must therefore be based on individual circumstances.

In this section of the chapter we will describe a variety of measures that can be taken to both treat and prevent burnout. Described first are actions the individual can take, followed by actions that the organization might take to help manage burnout. Each burnout victim should select several techniques and strategies that make the most sense in his or her unique circumstances—as illustrated by the comments of Troy Bannister and the response from Drew Jordan.

Individual Strategies

Take the Problem Seriously. Unfortunately many career people are reluctant to admit that they are experiencing burnout. They deceive themselves into believing that the situation will mysteriously pass away, similar to many bodily aches and ailments. It is strategically sounder to admit that the problem exists and formulate remedial action quickly. Toward this end, hundreds of workshops have been conducted for teacher victims of burnout. Only recently has it been recognized that managerial workers might also need such help.

Reading the vignette about the burnout workshop may have helped sensitize you to the phenomenon of burnout. The appendix to this chapter might prove useful in providing preliminary insight into whether or not you are experiencing a similar problem.

Deal with the Stress Aspects of Burnout. Job burnout and stress are inextricably related. The usual conception is that burnout stems from being exposed to uncomfortable stressors. The threat of physical violence and violence itself, for example, are documented stressors contributing to teacher burnout. Another conception is that burnout itself becomes a stressor—it is stressful to feel discouraged, apathetic, and cynical. Whether burnout is a reaction to job stress or a stressor itself, the burnout victim is therefore well advised to practice relaxation techniques. Among the more successful everyday methods of relaxation are physical exercise, rest, maintaining a nutritious diet, and learning to relax your muscles. Information about stress management techniques is widely available today.[2]

Develop Realistic Expectations. Management development specialist Ivan was the quickest victim of burnout known to this author. After two months in his position, he began to exhibit the classic symptoms of burnout—apathy, irritability, and disappointment. The sudden onset of his condition seemed closely tied in with his unrealistic expectations of what he could accomplish. As Ivan describes it:

> Was I deceived. My first assignment as management development specialist was to conduct a leadership training program for middle managers. I thought I would hit them with some of the latest developments in leadership theory and practice. My boss and higher management liked the basic idea of my program and gave me the green light. Once the programs actually began, I knew something was wrong. Some of the managers yawned during the sessions. They laughed; they joked; they bragged about having stayed up half the night. A few of them patronized me. One woman in her 50s told me that after I had some practical knowledge under my belt, I would become a first-rate trainer.
>
> I don't think that more than 1 in 10 was really interested in the program. I thought since everybody assigned to the training program was a manager they would automatically be interested in leadership theory. I thought they would be eager to sop up any information I could give them. I was crushed by their lack of response.

Realign Goals. Closely related to developing realistic expectations is the process of realigning your goals once it appears that they might be too difficult to achieve. For instance, in the future Ivan might strive to capture the interest of one third of his trainees, not all of them. Hundreds of case workers have burnt out because they expected poor people to take their admonitions about food habits and financial management seriously. You can only save a small proportion of people in any occupation. (Troy Bannister received similar advice.)

Here is an illustration of how developing realistic goals might help prevent burnout for an occupational safety and health specialist. Jim, one such worker in a large firm, has decided that despite its importance, "Not everybody is sold on safety and health." He claims that he intends to fight one battle at a time and will be happy if he has a positive impact on safety and health in his area. He puts it this way, "I can bang my head against the wall until the year 2000, but my company will never make safety and health its number 1 priority. However, at least they are beginning to listen to me."

Rotate Assignments. Job rotation often brings about a new perspective and new rewards, and it prevents the staleness which often contributes to burnout. According to one authority on burnout, "Varying assignments and routines so that a worker can spend at least part of the time on work with a definite end, or "closure," is helpful because long periods of working without visible results makes a fertile environment for burnout."[3]

Alter Working Conditions. Sometimes a constructive way of alleviating burnout is to modify job conditions so that the primary contributor to the problem is softened in impact. Often this modification can be made for a group of workers. One hospice for dying patients was faced with an unacceptably high turnover among nurses. Management intervened by giving the nurses places to eat lunch and take breaks by themselves. Previously, they had to share lunches and cafeterias with the dying patients. In that hopeless environment, the nurses had limited opportunity to offer each other peer support or advice and encouragement. After this modified work condition, the turnover rate fell to a more acceptable level.[4]

Try New Activities. "Remember, the more well rounded your life is, the more protected you are against burnout, " contends a psychoanalyst who specializes in treating the problem.[5] New activities could include hobbies, sports, community activities, attending different restaurants, eating different foods, or enriching your social life. This advice is similar to the old idea of taking a vacation when things are not going well for you. Trying out new activities is helpful but is only supplemental to strategies designed to change your work activity or modify your perception of them.

Find a Second Career or New Job. For many burnout victims the only real solution is a drastic one—placing yourself into a new occupational role. Finding a second career requires long-range planning. The economy can only absorb so many small retail store owners or freelance operators. Sometimes a long-term avocation can be converted into an occupation, provided a high level of skill has been developed. One manager had been hand-crafting furniture since age 20. By age 43 he was tired of spending so much time working directly with people. He converted his savings plus a bank loan into an initial investment in his own custom furniture business. He worked longer hours in his new occupation at slightly lower net income, but his psychic income increased dramatically. He enjoyed shifting the balance of his activities from so much concern with people to more concern with things (furniture).

Finding a new job can also be an antidote to burnout providing the new job does not contain the same contributors to the problem as did the old one. A guidance counselor may experience temporary relief from the condition if he or she becomes a personnel specialist. But after a while, the ex-guidance counselor may feel unappreciated and unrewarded as a personnel worker. One manager dealt with his burnout problem by joining a firm that placed more emphasis on the development of subordinates. He felt that in his previous firm the efforts he invested in developing subordinates were largely unappreciated by management. The new firm rewarded such activity. Consequently he felt rejuvenated in his new position.

Closeness to Yourself and Others. Therapist Herbert J. Freudenberger suggests that closeness is the enemy of burnout and distance its ally. The remedy to burnout is, therefore, to get close to yourself or others. [6] Closeness is a difficult-to-pin-down concept that means much the same as getting in touch with your feelings or tuning in to others. Supposedly you can achieve closeness to yourself by such means as going for a walk in the country alone. You might get close to another individual by listening carefully to that person express his or her feelings, desires, concerns, and so forth. Our society tends to emphasize preoccupation with busyness (including television watching) to such an extent that closeness is usually avoided. It is, therefore, possible to spend time with people without really getting close to them.

Stroking Yourself. Burnout is a form of mental depression. As with mild depression, a sometimes workable antidote is to pamper yourself with small rewards, or in modern terms "stroke yourself." Give yourself rewards for a job well done, such as a luxurious meal (I personally opt for a submarine sandwich accompanied by Canadian ale). Suppose you perform well on a people-related task such as conducting a performance evaluation. The world may not pay you a compliment, but you can tell yourself that you did a good job and deserve to be complimented. Or when you do something well, buy yourself a new piece of athletic equipment, suit, jacket, or dress. In short, take care of yourself rather than waiting for others to reward or "stroke" you.

Rewarding yourself becomes particularly important when placed in a work environment in which few contingent rewards are given to employees. Although this strategy sounds simplistic, experience suggests that it is effective in combating burnout. Stroking yourself, as with realigning your goals, has a built-in problem: It often suffers from a lack of authenticity. Realigning your goals is sometimes perceived by the individual as lowering personal standards or copping out. Self-rewards, to many people, don't seem nearly as potent as those conferred by other individuals.

Get a New Gadget. A broad generalization about managing burnout is that something must be done to initiate a process of constructive change. Sometimes the change may appear to be small, like a manager using a personal computer in his or her daily work. We mention personal computers because there is something both partially addictive and tension reducing (sometimes) about working with a computer. For some managers and staff specialists, the high point of their day arrives when they can "play" with their computers. Another gadget that might help combat burnout is a video-cassette recorder. It could be used for such purposes as practicing sales presentations, and presentations to top management.

Try Humor and Laughter. A minor tactic for coping with burnout is to find ways to inject humor and laughter into the stressful aspects of one's job. A good example of gallows humor took place at International Harvester, when the company was experiencing financial losses. The chief executive, Don Lennox, took a vacation to play in an American Airlines, Inc., golf tournament in Hawaii. Some old friends noticed that Bethlehem Steel Corporation had just amassed a loss larger than Harvester. They sent Lennox this telegram: "Forget American tourney. Harvester needs you. Bethlehem now in first place."[7]

Humor and laughter can actually produce physiological changes in the body, and these can help combat some forms of disease. Similarly, laughter can be effective in displacing stress that can push a person toward burnout.[8]

Maintain a Growing Edge. An almost philosophical strategy for preventing burnout is to maintain a lifelong positive attitude toward self-development and self-improvement. By so doing, the individual continues to receive a new trickle—and sometimes a flood—of rewards. The logic behind this strategy is that if you avoid going stale, you decrease the probability of burning out. Here is how the situation might work for a manager whose work primarily involves supervising word processing technicians:

Over a period of time, the manager begins to hear the same complaints from her subordinates; she watches person after person leaving the word processing center for transfer, promotion, or personal reasons; she hears the same old rush requests week after week. Under these circumstances many managers would experience burnout. Using the growing edge strategy, the word processing manager would continue to develop as a manager and as an individual. One month she might learn a new technique of disciplining subordinates. She tries it, and the method works. The manager thus receives the reward of self-satisfaction for having used a personnel technique which proved effective. Each new increment of personal development yields a new reward. Fed by a long series of rewards, the word processing manager avoids burnout.

Maintaining a growing edge could prove to be the most important technique for improving your professional effectiveness and personal vitality.

Organizational Strategies

Several valid reasons exist why organizations should take constructive action in the treatment and prevention of burnout. Many instances of burnout are triggered by adverse organizational conditions, thus creating an obligation on the part of management to solve problems it creates. Burnout also adversely affects performance. Remedying the problem would thus elevate performance and productivity. Further, managing burnout is part of a humanitarian obligation to provide employees a good quality of work life. Described next are some potentially effective organizational strategies for managing burnout.

Confront the Burnout Victim. A starting point in effectively managing burnout is to confront burnout victims with the consequences of their problem. The confrontation should be done in a helpful and sympathetic manner, focusing on the work behavior that is suffering (review the Guidelines for Action in Chapter 3). Although a given individual may talk about being burned out, he or she may not realize the full implications of the problem. In addition, burnout is often said to be contagious.

Establish a Contract with the Burnout Victim. After the burned out person is confronted, and shows some awareness of the problem, a verbal contract between the organization and the individual should be established. It should specify what is expected of the individual in terms of performance improvement and what types of help the employer is willing to offer.[9] A clause in one such contract specified, "We are willing to find you a special assignment for a month or two. In return we expect you to stop telling your subordinates how oppressive it is to work here." One form of help is a stress management program.

Conduct a Stress Management Program. Previously we described the necessity of individuals managing their own stress levels. The process is facilitated when organizations offer a company-sponsored stress-management program. Oliver L. Niehouse has worked with the United States federal government in helping several of its agencies develop such programs. Aside from helping individuals deal with stress disorders in general, these programs are useful in combating the stress associated with burnout. A popular program of this nature is the READ program of relaxation, exercise, attitude and awareness, and diet. Niehouse argues that the READ program is cost effective. Its cost of several hundred dollars per participant can be contrasted to the much larger (yet unknown) cost of a decline in a burn-out staff member's productivity.[10]

Employee assistance programs can also be used to help individuals cope with burnout. At a minimum, employees can receive help in dealing with stress. Today, most assistance programs have a counselor on the staff who is familiar with the problem of job burnout.[11]

Alter Stressful Working Conditions. A macro solution to the burnout problem is for the organization to make the total environment less stressful, both physically and mentally. The less chronic stress experienced by employees, the less the likelihood of burnout. Physical working conditions can be improved by such relatively small factors as improved ventilation, heating, and lighting.[12] Recent research evidence suggests that managers play a more important role than family members in helping subordinates cope with stress. It has been found that managers can reduce stress levels by offering encouragement and other forms of emotional support . Stress researcher, Kenneth Pelletier, reports these findings about another aspect of the boss's role in controlling stress:

> The boss is crucial in how much stress his or her workers feel , and whether their health will suffer. One key is whether the boss lets subordinates feel in control of their jobs.[13]

Give Ample Rewards, Including Recognition. Many burnout sufferers believe that their apathy and indifference stems from not receiving the recognition (and other rewards) they think they deserve. The self-stroking strategy described earlier is designed to help with this problem. Of greater potential impact, the organization should implement a carefully designed system of rewards that includes recognition from superiors for a job well done. Susan E. Jackson and Randall S. Schuler recommend that supervisors be trained to offer more rewards based on performance to employees, thus reducing the frequency of the comment, "If you don't hear anything, you must be doing okay."[14]

Give Increased Feedback on Performance. A general case of the point just mentioned is to provide substantial feedback on performance to employees at all levels. It has been noted that in human service organizations, for example, there is a dominant tendency for employees not to receive feedback for a job well done.[15] Presumably, this is one factor contributing to a high burnout rate among human service professionals.

Increase the Use of Participative Decision Making. A major contributor to job stress is the feeling that the job controls you rather than your controlling the job. Previously it was mentioned that the manager can reduce stress by helping subordinates gain more control. When opportunities for control are missing, and employees feel trapped in an uncontrollable and unpredictable environment, both their physical and mental health are likely to suffer.[16] A standard technique for turning over more control to subordinates is participative decision making (PDM). Besides increasing employees' feelings of control, participation may help prevent burnout by clarifying what is expected of employees and giving employees a chance to reduce some of the role conflict they experience. In the process of PDM, for instance, the employee might contribute the input that he or she cannot satisfy the competing demands of two bosses.

Strengths and Weaknesses of Burnout Strategies

Although we do not yet have much research-based information about the prevention and treatment of burnout, many of the strategies described earlier have proven clinically effective. In other words, counselors and therapists have recommended them to people experiencing burnout and they seem to work. Also of significance, the strategies suggested for managing burnout are based upon well-established principles of human behavior (such as the value of establishing realistic goals).

Except for suggesting that you switch your job or career, these strategies are relatively conservative. They are unlikely to do any harm even if they fail to help you cope with burnout. Should you misdiagnose your situation (you are not really experiencing burnout), these strategies would still prove valuable for your personal development. The radical strategies of job or career switching are things a person might do for any type of chronic job dissatisfaction.

Also on the positive side, the organizational strategies for managing burnout suggested above are likely to help the organization in other ways even if they do not cure or prevent burnout. A case in point is the establishment of an effective reward system. Almost any organization would benefit from such a strategy.

On the negative side, many instances of burnout could be explained away as situations of extreme job dissatisfaction. And we know that a small percentage of the workforce is going to be dissatisfied no matter what action management takes. It could therefore be a waste of resources to try and eliminate some cases of burnout. Another weakness is that most of the strategies suggested here are superficial if your basic problem is that you hate your work. To illustrate, no matter how close you get to others you are unlikely to become happy about supervising a group of ungrateful and resentful subordinates.

GUIDELINES FOR ACTION AND SKILL DEVELOPMENT

Burnout is a serious problem that concerns your basic means of earning a living. Problems of burnout are, therefore, worth discussing with a mental health professional, career counselor, or professional human resource specialist. Reading about the problem should be an important supplement, not a substitute for, seeking outside assistance.

Move cautiously in choosing a radical solution to burnout such as changing jobs or careers. First try to modify that portion of your work which seems to produce the most frustration. Observe the results and see if burnout sensations still abound.

Recognize that every form of job dissatisfaction is not burnout. After reading this chapter and the additional references, do not talk yourself into a case of burnout.

If you are a manager, a potentially valuable human skill to develop is to be able to detect burnout among your subordinates. This skill begins with an awareness of burnout symptoms (such as apathy, indifference, cynicism, and emotional exhaustion). When these symptoms are manifested repeatedly by a person in your group, it would be time for you to intervene. You could ask the subordinate if he or she wanted to talk about the dissatisfaction and loss of enthusiasm you have observed. You might also discuss the possibilities of sponsoring the person at a burnout workshop, or make a referral to an employee assistance program (see Chapter 18).

Questions and Activities

1. To what extent do you think a burned-out manager creates burnout among subordinates? Explain your reasoning.
2. In what way might a burned-out manager contribute to the demotivation of subordinates?
3. Many managers and professionals talk openly about being burned out, almost to the point of bragging. What reasons do you think underlie this behavior?
4. Why do you think burnout has become so prevalent among professionals who work primarily with economically poor individuals?
5. Identify several techniques described in other chapters of this book that you think might be helpful in dealing with burnout.
6. Why do you think it is true that perfectionistic people are more likely to suffer from burnout than their less perfectionistic counterparts?

7. Find somebody who claims to be a burnout victim. Interview that person and try to establish the factors contributing to his or her burnout.

Notes

[1]Jeannie Gaines and John J. Jermier, "Emotional Exhaustion in a High Stress Organization," *Academy of Mangement Journal* (December 1983) p. 568.

[2]Two such sources are: Walter H. Gmelch, *Beyond Stress to Effective Management* (New York: John Wiley, 1982); Michael T. Matteson and John M. Ivancevich, *Managing Job Stress and Health* (New York: The Free Press, 1982).

[3]Jerry E. Bishop, "The Personal and Business Costs of 'Job Burnout'," *Wall Street Journal* (November 11, 1980) p. 39.

[4]Ibid.

[5]Herbert J. Freudenberger, with Geraldine Richelson, *Burn Out: The High Cost of High Achievement* (Garden City, N.Y.: Anchor/Doubleday, 1980) p. 175.

[6]Ibid., pp. 123–142.

[7]"Can Don Lennox Save Harvester?" *Business Week* (August 15, 1983) p. 83.

[8]Oliver L. Niehouse, *The Road Away from Burnout: A Traveler's Guide for Public Management*, AMA Management Briefing (New York: AMA Membership Publications Division, 1982) p. 55.

[9]Ibid., p. 64.

[10]Ibid.

[11]Morley D. Glicken, "A Counseling Approach to Employee Burnout," *Personnel Journal* (March 1983) pp. 222–228.

[12]Niehouse, *The Road Away*, p. 55.

[13]Quoted in Daniel Coleman, "Controlling Stress Starts with the Boss," *New York Times* story reprinted in Rochester *Democrat and Chronicle* (January 31, 1984) p. 3A.

[14]Susan E. Jackson and Randall S. Schuler, "Preventing Employee Burnout," *Personnel* (March-April 1983) p.63.

[15]Ibid., p. 67.

[16]Ibid., p. 65.

Some Additional References

Farber, Barry A. *Stress and Burnout in the Human Services Profession.* Elmsford, N.Y.: Pergamon Press, 1983.

Maslach, Christina. *Burnout—The High Cost of Caring.* Englewood Cliffs, N.J.: Prentice-Hall, 1982.

Paine, Whiton Stewart. *Job Stress and Burnout: Research, Theory, and Intervention Perspectives.* Beverly Hills, Calif.: Sage Publications, 1982.

Veninga, Robert L., and James P. Spradley. *The Work Stress Connection: How to Cope with Job Burnout.* Boston: Little, Brown, 1981.

Welch, I. David; Donald Mederios; and George A. Tate. *Beyond Burnout: How to Prevent and Reverse the Effects of Stress on the Job.* Englewood Cliffs, N.J.: Prentice-Hall, 1982.

Appendix to Chapter 4

The Burnout Checklist*

Directions. Answer the following statements as mostly true or mostly false as they apply to you.

	Mostly true	Mostly false
1. I feel tired more frequently than I used to.	___	___
2. I snap at people too often.	___	___
3. Trying to help other people often seems hopeless.	___	___
4. I seem to be working harder but accomplishing less.	___	___
5. I get down on myself too often.	___	___
6. My job is beginning to depress me.	___	___
7. I often feel I'm headed nowhere.	___	___
8. I've reached (or am fast approaching) a dead end in my job.	___	___
9. I've lost a lot of my zip lately.	___	___
10. It's hard for me to laugh at a joke about myself.	___	___
11. I'm not really physically ill, but I have a lot of aches and pains.	___	___
12. Lately I've kind of withdrawn from friends and family.	___	___
13. My enthusiasm for life is on the wane.	___	___
14. I'm running out of things to say to people.	___	___
15. My temper is much shorter than it used to be.	___	___
16. My job makes me feel sad.	___	___
17. Most days I feel emotionally exhausted.	___	___
18. I look forward to vacations much more than I do to work.	___	___
19. I know I have a problem but I just don't have enough energy to do anything about it.	___	___
20. I don't get nearly enough appreciation from my employer.	___	___

*Based in part on the questionnaire printed on the dust-jacket of Freudenberger's *Burn Out*.

Interpretation. The more of these questions you can honestly answer mostly true, the more likely it is that you are experiencing burnout. If you answered 15 or more of these statements mostly true, it is likely you are experiencing burnout or another form of mental depression. Discuss these feelings with a physical or mental health professional.

■ Part 2

Improving Interpersonal Relationships

■

The next four chapters concentrate on methods and techniques of strengthening one-on-one relationships in organizations. However, these one-on-one, or face-to-face, relationships can also take place within the context of a group.

Chapter 5, Effective Negotiating, described strategies for improving your ability to negotiate for what you want. Since the first edition of this book, behavioral science strategies for negotiating have received considerably more attention in the organizational behavior and management literature. The topic has also received substantial attention in general-interest books (including the bestseller, *You Can Negotiate Anything*) and magazine articles. The negotiating strategies presented are rooted in behavioral approaches to conflict resolution and the social psychology of bargaining. Several of the strategies stem from research conducted in the Harvard Negotiation Project.

Chater 6, Nonverbal Messages in Organizations, deals with the most speculative topic in this book. Although nonverbal communication has been widely researched, its readiness for direct application is subject to debate. Despite this, the practicing manager should know something about the transmission of nonverbal messages in the workplace. Improving nonverbal communication skills can enhance job effectiveness.

Chapter 7, Resolving Conflict between Subordinates, describes several hands-on tactics for managing conflict between two people reporting to a manager. This material is thus an important supplement to more general information on the nature of conflict and its resolution. Skill development in resolving conflict between subordinates is sometimes incorporated into organization development (OD) programs.

Chapter 8, The Prevention and Control of Sexual Harassment, presents information about a sensitive topic that has received widespread attention both in the formal literature and popular press in recent years. The purpose of this chapter is not to present another exposition indicating that sexual harassment is prevalent in the workplace, but to describe experience-based suggestions for its control. This information is of particular interest to human resource professionals who have formal responsibility for controlling sexual harassment in the organization.

Chapter 5

Effective Negotiating

The chief administrator at a health maintenance organization (HMO) was one of the key figures involved in negotiating the terms for her HMO's acquisition of a smaller HMO. To prevent the takeover from falling through, she relied heavily on the general negotiating strategy of looking for win-win solutions to the points at issue.

Maxwell Health Center is a health maintenance organization that functions much like a large self-contained health clinic, or a "medical supermarket." It currently has a membership of 45,000 subscribers. To belong, members pay a fee of $125 per family, per month. All medical and nursing care received at the center is covered by this monthly fee in addition of a $4 per visit charge. Medicine and medical supplies (such as crutches and back braces) are paid for directly by the patient.

The Maxwell Health Center is divided into eight medical departments including opthalmology, obstetrics and gynecology, pediatrics, and radiology. Each department is administered by a medical director and an office supervisor. The patient intake and billing departments are managed by nonmedical personnel. Each medical department is staffed by physicians, nurses, nurse practitioners, licensed practical nurses, medical assistants, and other appropriate health service professionals. Top management of Maxwell consists of the chief medical director, Frank Whitcomb, M.D., Lisa Tonnelli, M.S. H.A. (M.S. Health Adminstration), a chief financial officer, Al Canton, C.P.A., and several administrative assistants.

About six months ago, Canton submitted a report on the health center's financial status to Whitcomb, Tonnelli, and the board of directors. The report pointed out that although the membership of the Center was growing steadily, and the membership fee structure was appropriate for local circumstances, operating expenses were cutting heavily into profits. Canton's recommended action plan to increase profitability was to acquire Northside Group Health, a competitive HMO. Both top management and the board thought highly enough of Canton's plan to empower him to speak to Northside top management about the proposed acquisition.

Northside Group Health is located about 12 miles north of Maxwell, in another section of the city. Northside has an organization structure quite similar to Maxwell's; however the total operation is about two-thirds the size both in membership and employees. The top management team is headed by medical director Barry Phillips, M.D., chief administrator Clint Griffin, M.B.A., and chief financial officer Karen Lacey, M.B.A.

At the time of Canton's original inquiries, Northside was operating at a loss and therefore was willing to discuss terms of a possible acquisition by Maxwell. Karen Lacey thought the acquisition would bring consolidated advertising costs, centralized billing, less need to have expensive specialized medical equipment at both HMOs, and reduction in payroll costs, among other benefits. One day a month for as long as needed was set aside for the negotiating teams to work out the details of an acquisition agreement. Both boards agreed the acquisition would be approved providing the negotiating teams could arrive at some mutually satisfactory agreements.

The negotiating teams for each side consisted of the three members of top management, each headed by the chief administrative officer of the HMO: Lisa Tonnelli for Maxwell, and Clint Griffin for Northside. Portions of the final negotiating session are presented below.

Tonnelli: Welcome back, gang, to what we all hope could be the final session needed to reach agreement on big issues causing us some concern. For openers, we haven't yet agreed on a suitable name for the surviving HMO. Since we are the acquiring organization, I thought it would be appropriate for both places to carry the name Maxwell Health Center. What problems does this create for you people?

Phillips: I'm much older than anybody else in this room, so perhaps that's why I'm more sentimental. I just can't see us dumping entirely the good Northside Group Health name. It means too much to too many people. [*Griffin and Lacey nod in agreement.*]

Tonnelli: Now I understand. You feel there is good will attached to the Northside Group Health name. You have a good point. We think the Maxwell name is valuable for similar reasons. Also, we are the acquiring organization. Let me suggest a name for the new HMO that might serve both our purposes: Maxwell Group Health. In that way the Maxwell fans could refer to it as "Maxwell," and the Northside fans could refer to it as "Group Health."

Griffin: I've just conferred with my two colleagues. We buy your idea. The new name should work just fine.

Canton: We still have some key items to resolve in terms of reducing overhead in the new organization. We have already reached agreement about the clerical and data processing staffs. After normal attrition, one early retirement, and the laying off of two problem employees, those support groups will be down to the right size. At the top of the major issues is the problem of two medical directors. Dr. Phillips, what are your current feelings about your position?

Phillips: I'm 63 and I intend to remain professionally active until retirement.

Tonnelli: We think a person of your stature should remain active. Here's what we have in mind. We would like you to become a member of the board of directors and also to serve as a consultant to Maxwell Group Health, effective the first day of acquisition.

Phillips: That's not exactly what I meant by remaining professionally active, but I'll give your offer warm consideration.

Griffin: I'm happy to know that Dr. Phillips is taken care of. We now have to deal with my situation. You tell us, Lisa, that Al Canton will have to stay as chief financial officer, and I could stay on as office manager of the combined office operations, providing we find other jobs for our two present office managers. Well, that's not satisfactory to me. If that's my only alternative, I won't be in favor of the acquisition. One of the major tentative agreements we reached is that all personnel would be handled equitably.

Tonnelli: What do you see as the biggest problem with your proposed new job as officer manager?

Griffin: It's the pits. I don't want a decrease in status at this point in my career.

Tonnelli: What career alternative do you see that would give you the status you need, aside from your present job?

Griffin: To be candid, I want to establish my own consulting firm to provide data processing and financial services to small medical and dental offices.

Tonnelli: Our negotiating team has the authority to give a key executive up to six-month's salary and benefits as severance pay if that person's job is collapsed as a result of the acquisition.

Griffin: Although I would prefer one year's salary as severance pay, I think I could live just fine with that deal. It could fund me while I'm getting my new business started.

Tonnelli: Another major issue we face is the salary differentials for physicians at our two HMOs. Al Canton has shown me the figures. Apparently physicians at Northside Group Health receive salaries that are about 20 percent higher than paid by other HMOs in this area. For example, your two opthalmologists are paid $175,000 per year. That's out of line; $150,000 per year is much more in line with our salaries.

Phillips: But if you tell a doctor today that he or she is going to receive a pay cut, you can say goodbye to that doctor.

Tonnelli: You think, then, that the underlying problem is that physicians on your staff would want to maintain their same total income?

Phillips: I don't think so, I *know* so.

Tonnelli: In that case, hear my proposal. I think it will satisfy everybody. We'll explain to the overpaid doctors that their salaries are out of line with our pay scales, but that we do not want to cut their incomes. As a compromise, we'll ask them to forgo cost-of-living increases for the next three years. However, we will do what we can to help them maintain their current income levels. We will authorize them to spend an additional five hours per week on private practice patients if they so desire. This should enable them to maintain their same high incomes during the time the Maxwell pay scales are catching up with those of Northside.

Phillips: Your idea just won't work. If you think you can cut the pay of our physicians, you're wrong. They'll quit for sure, under the terms you propose.

Tonnelli: But, as I explained, their total income won't be reduced. We will be giving them time for private practice.

Lacey: You're being too naive, Lisa. Our doctors are already seeing some private practice patients. No matter how you try to work the deal, you're asking our doctors to take a pay cut. And they won't buy it. I'm beginning to think you're not bargaining in good faith.

Tonnelli: You're the one who is intractable, not me. It looks like we're getting nowhere today. Think through carefully our offer about the pay for our doctors before we meet again.

By the end of this negotiating session, one major issue remained to be resolved. However, the issue of the disparity between physicians' pay at the two HMOs was such a major one, that it threw negotiations into a serious deadlock. Unless the parties can effectively negotiate a solution to this problem, the merger acquisition will not be consummated.

NEGOTIATING STRATEGIES

Although behavioral and social scientists have studied negotiation extensively, relatively little of this work has been reported in the literature of management, organizational behavior, or human resource management. It appears, however, to be a field of emerging interest. The topic warrants our attention because negotiating strategies are required for effectiveness in such diverse work activities as finding a job, agreeing upon goals, agreeing upon provisions of a contract, buying and selling, determining the size of a departmental budget, obtaining human resources for your project or task force, or drawing up technical specifications for a machine part. And, as illustrated in the HMO case, negotiation is a vital part of working out the provisions of a merger or acquisition.

A helpful starting point in sorting out the many negotiating strategies available is to classify them as either *collaborative* or *competitive*.[1] Collaborative strategies and tactics are based on a win-win philosophy. The user of these approaches is genuinely concerned about arriving at a settlement that meets the needs of both parties, or at least does not badly damage the welfare of the other side. Competitive approaches are based more on a win-lose philosophy. Each side is trying to maximize gain with little regard for the needs and welfare of the other side. We also classify as competitive, those techniques that are more devious or "tricky," than open and honest.

Fifteen of the strategies described below are classified as collaborative, and 11 as competitive. Two limitations to this dichotomy should be kept in mind. First, a good deal of subjective judgment is used in classifying the strategies: you may not agree with the categorization for every strategy. Second, the intent of the person using a given strategy counts heavily as to whether it is honest or devious. For example, one person may use the strategy "make small concessions gradually," as a way of out-foxing the other side. Another person may rely on this strategy in a genuine attempt to arrive at a fair negotiated agreement.

Collaborative Approaches to Negotiation

Use the Harvard Negotiation Project Strategy. The best field-tested and researched overall program for effective negotiation has been developed by the Harvard Negotiation Project, as described in the book *Getting to Yes*.[2] Their program for resolving conflict through negotiation encompasses many of the other strategies described in this chapter. As you read through the four-step Harvard program, you will observe that the HMO negotiating teams negotiated in the same spirit. The underlying philosophy is that one bargains over underlying issues, not positions. The strategy is referred to as *principled negotiation*, meaning about the same thing as collaborative negotiation.

The basic point is to decide issues on their merits rather than through a haggling process focused on the position held by each side. It implies that you look for mutual gains wherever possible. In situations where your interests conflict, the parties insist that the result be based on some fair standards independent of the will of the other side. (For instance, it was determined that the physicians' salaries should be brought in line with wage rates at other HMOs in the area.) Principled negotiation is based on the merits of the situation, and uses no tricks or posturing.

Principled negotiation, or negotiation by merit, centers around four basic points (described next). These points define an open and honest form of negotiation that its developers believe can be used in almost any negotiating situation.

I. People. Separate the people from the problem. According to this point, human beings, unlike computers, are not entirely rational problem solvers. People have strong emotions, and often have radically different perceptions of the same event. When negotiating, their emotions become entangled with the objective merits of the problem. It is therefore important to disentangle the people problem before working on the substantive problem. Fisher and Ury recommend "The participants should come to see themselves as working side by side, attacking the problem, not each other."[3]

Lisa Tonnelli showed good sensitivity to human behavior when she suggested a solution to the problem of having one surplus medical director. She appealed to Dr. Phillip's need for status by offering him a position as a board member and a consultant. (Whether or not displaced executives in a merger ever do much consulting, their egos are usually satisfied by having the title, consultant.) Fisher and Ury point to another of the infinite possible applications of this general principle. Should you be negotiating with a company to repair your broken machinery, focus on the problem but do not attack the company representative. Here is an example:

> Our rotary generator that you service has broken down again. That is three times in the last month. The first time it was out of order for an entire week. This factory needs a functioning generator. I want your advice on how we can minimize our risk of generator breakdown. Should we change service companies, sue the manufacturer, or what?"[4]

II. Interest. Focus on interests, not positions. The intent here is to overcome the drawback of focusing on peoples' stated positions when the true object of a negotiation is to satisfy the underlying interests on both sides. A negotiating position often obscures the nature of what a person is really trying to achieve. The standard remedy of compromising positions infrequently produces an agreement that effectively takes care of the human needs that led people to adopt these positions.

A detail not provided in the HMO acquisition case is that both sides initially took the position that they wanted to retain the original organizational name. During the session, the underlying interest was revealed: both sides were looking for a way of preserving the identity of their HMO. The proposed solution of combining the key elements of both names—Maxwell Group Health—was therefore a workable compromise that satisfied both sides. An unworkable compromise might have been for the acquiring firm to give the acquired firm a cash bonus for scrapping its name.

III. Options. Invent options for mutual gain. An effective negotiating strategy is to generate several workable options before you enter into the heat of the actual negotiating session. Trying to select a good option in the presence of your adversary may create emotional interference with your thinking. When the stakes are high, the stress created by the negotiating session may be at such a high level that creativity is dampened. Thus, you may not arrive at creative alternatives to the points at issue.

Under ideal circumstances, the two parties can join together in a brainstorming session to arrive at options that will satisfy the needs of both. Or, both parties may engage in brainstorming separately and then bring these new options to the negotiating session or bargaining table. However, a major hurdle must be overcome before a systematic search for options is possible. Both sides must realize that the outcome of negotiation is not inevitably one position winning out over the other.

A germane example of the search for creative options has taken place at several business colleges seeking accreditation by the American Association of Collegiate Schools of Business (AACSB). Schools with an evening program separate from the day program cannot qualify for full accreditation unless they gain administrative and curriculum control over the evening program. The evening program administrators, of course, resist turning over control to the day program. The creative option chosen was for the day school to take over control only of the third and fourth year of the evening programs. AACSB approves of this option, and it has met with the approval of the college administrators involved in a number of settings.

IV. Criteria. Insist on using objective criteria. To overcome stubbornness and rigidity on one or both sides, it is helpful to insist that the agreement reached must reflect some fair (objective) standard such as market value, expert opinion, customary settlements, or law. For instance, if you are negotiating with a new car dealer about repairing your "lemon," you can insist that the amount paid for by the dealer is in line with customary handling of this problem. Similarly, the dealer should not be forced to make a settlement with you exceeding this standard.

Base Your Demands on a Solid Rationale. Related to the above point, it is useful to base your demand on a solid rationale. A typical setting for applying this strategy is when asking for a raise. A weak rationale is to demand an above average raise because you need more money. It is more tactically sound to provide a valid reason why you deserve a big raise. Gerard I. Nierenberg, founder of the Negotiation Institute, offers this example of how to get results:

> I want a raise so I can work harder for both of us. I want a raise so I can be more productive and give you more of my time. I want a raise because if you can't give me one, I'll have to take another job that is offered to me at a higher salary.[5]

The present author has some concern that the last sentence might be so abrasive as to trigger counterhostility from the boss.

Plan in Advance. A negotiation session is a meeting. As such, it will proceed more smoothly if both sides prepare an agenda and make other necessary preparations (including looking for creative options, as described above). You should plan in advance what major and minor points you plan to negotiate. Your opponent should do the same. Ideally, the two sides should agree beforehand on what items will be dealt with during the formal negotiating session. The agenda places control on what will be said and not said. It has also been suggested that one should plan for the negotiating session by role-playing the opponent's most likely responses to your suggestions.[6] Assuming you were going to ask for a large salary increase, it would be helpful to role play the scenario in which your boss says, "It's too bad you feel that way. But there are loads of good people out there who will perform your job at less pay than you demand."

Give Yourself Time to Think. A hasty decision made in a negotiating session is often a poor one. Although it may seem that you are pressed to make a fast decision, there are many legitimate and ethical stalling tactics that will enable you to reflect upon the proposition coming from the other side. You might call for a lunch break; request time to obtain some backup information from your files; demand that you first consult an expert advisor before committing yourself; or suggest that both sides resume negotiations in the morning.

Create a Positive Negotiating Climate. Negotiation proceeds much more swiftly if a positive tone surrounds the session. It is therefore helpful to take the initiative to take a positive outlook about the negotiation meeting. Nonverbal behavior such as smiling and making friendly gestures both help create a positive climate. Nierenberg maintains that by staying positive, you'll stop a negative person cold. "It will be like a child who throws a tantrum until the child sees that it's not working, that nobody's giving in. Then he or she will move on to something else."[7]

Avoid Macho-Chicken. Many tough-minded negotiators play a standoff game in which they become bull-headed, entrenched, and committed to a win-lose conception of the outcome (defined in this chapter as the essence of competitive bargaining). Howard Raiffa cautions that if the negotiation gets down to Macho-Chicken it has escalated out of your control.[8] The antidote is to focus on the many collaborative bargaining tactics described throughout this section of the chapter.

Allow Room for Negotiation. The most basic negotiating strategy is to begin with a demand that allows you room for compromise and concession.

Anybody who has ever negotiated the price of an automobile, house, or used furniture recognizes this vital principle. If you are the buyer, begin with a low bid. If you are the seller, begin with a high demand. If you are negotiating next year's budget for your department, begin by asking for a liberal budget—one higher than the absolute minimum required for your functioning. Labor unions typically allow themselves negotiating room by bringing many more items into negotiating than they believe will be granted (such as complete dental coverage or treating a person's birthday as holiday). As negotiations proceed, the union will drop several of these lesser demands.

Allowing room for negotiation does not preclude the importance of beginning negotiations with a plausible demand.[9] To begin with an unreasonable and potentially destructive demand will often be interpreted by the other side as bargaining in poor faith. Thus, serious negotiations will be delayed or even cancelled. One 40-year old manager was approached by an executive search firm to be considered for a vice-president's position, paying around $95,000 per year. The prospective employer was warmly interested in the candidate. He was immediately dismissed from consideration, however, when he asked for an annual salary of $145,000.

Make the Opposing Negotiator Feel Good. A useful, positive negotiating tactic is to make the adversary feel good, to facilitate that person thinking in a win-win mode. One "feel-good" tactic is to reward the opposing negotiator's concession. A series of laboratory simulations of union-management negotiations over wages showed that granting counter-concessions (or reciprocating) serves as a reward. It results in large concessions by a quick agreement with the opponent.[10] Of considerable value, these large concessions continue after the rewards cease—as would be predicted from reinforcement theory. An example of a reward might be, "Since you were gracious enough to decrease the number of forms we have to process per week, we'll set higher quality standards in the department."

Gary Whitney offers another way of making the opponents feel good: simply let them know you understand their position. One way to accomplish this is to paraphrase their position accurately. This lets them know that you understand their objective even if you do not necessarily agree with it.[11] You may recall that when Barry Phillips said that he could not see dumping the Northside Group Health name, Lisa Tonnelli, replied, "Now, I understand. You feel there is good will attached to the Northside Group Health name."

Be Truthful. In many instances, laying all the cards out on the table is an effective negotiating tactic. It communicates the fact that you are not game playing and that you respect the intelligence of the opponent. It may also encourage the other side to make more honest demands since their distorted demands will be contrasted to a set of more honest ones. Howard Raiffa has concluded from his experiements that subjects who did the best in negotiating games were the ones who simply announced the truth.[12] One reason is that most people expect negotiation to be filled with duplicity. Consequently, they are overwhelmed by the truth.

Use Negotiation Jujitsu. Another suggested strategy stemming from the Harvard Negotiation Project deals with parrying the aggressive thrusts from your opponent. Called negotiation jujitsu, it centers around the idea that you do not push back or counterattack when they attack your idea. Instead you "sidestep their attack and deflect it against the problem."[13] One such approach is to look at the consequences of their proposal or position. Here is an example:

Union representative: Our last and final offer is a wage rate of $21.75 for machinists in this labor grade.

Company representative: That certainly is a handsome rate of hourly pay. But what do you think that would do to the cost our our gear-cutting equipment?

Union representative: The cost would go up, I guess.

Company representative: You guessed right. It would raise the price so high that foreign competition would take over our market. Then we would probably have to close our Michigan plant.

Union representative: Let me get back to my people and study this issue some more.

Know Your Best Alternative to a Negotiated Agreement (BATNA). The reason people neogitate is to produce something better than the results obtainable without negotiating. When you are aware of your best alternative to a negotiated agreement it sets a floor to the agreement you need to accept. Your BATNA thus becomes the standard which can protect you both from accepting terms that are too unfavorable and from walking away from terms that would be beneficial for you to accept.[14]

In the situation above, the company representative may know ahead of time that if machinists are to be paid more than $18.50 per hour, it would be more cost effective for the company to subcontract out a good portion of its manufacturing. Thus, he or she can negotiate calmly and accept only an option that the company can afford. The union representative may not have have a BATNA in this situation. One conceivable option is to ask the union members to vote on a strike. However, this could lead quickly to the subcontracting option on the part of the company.

Allow Room for Face Saving. People prefer to avoid looking weak, foolish, or incapable during negotiation or when the process is completed. If you do not give your opponent an opportunity to save face, you will have most probably created a long-term enemy. The president of a small company was committed to the idea of relocating the office in a setting overlooking a body of water within the same city. Steve, the office manager, was given the tough assignment of locating a suitable property. One such piece of property was found, which overlooked a scenic canal. After weeks of negotiation, Alice, the person negotiating the deal for the seller, would only agree to a price 30 percent above what the president wanted to pay originally. The president then reluctantly agreed to the deal. During the formal closing on the property, Alice made this face-saving statement in the presence of Steve and the president: "Steve must have been psychic in agreeing to the minimum price at which we could afford to let this property go. Only this morning another party made a tentative offer at $38,000 over what you are paying."

Some experimentation exists supporting the importance of face-saving maneuvers. In one study, subjects who made concessions in accordance with a mediator's suggestion were apparently able to dispel their feelings of personal weakness for having made the concessions. They simply passed much of their responsibility for having made the concession on to the mediator.[15]

Competitve Approaches to Negotiation. The emphasis in the approaches described in this section is win-lose, or one of trying to maximize gain for your side even if it involves some trickery and deceit. We strongly recommend a collaborative approach wherever possible, but a discussion of negotiation tactics and strategies would be incomplete without a description of competitive approaches. Besides, some of these competitive approaches are not particularly devious.

Maintain Emotional Control. Table thumping during a negotiating session is often said to bring results. But the table thumper is usually in control of his or her emotions. If you lose emotional control during a negotiating session, you run the risk of making a poor decision. An outside negotiator sometimes makes a contribution because that negotiator can remain more detached about the issues. As one lawyer said to his client, "In your desperation to get divorced, you have agreed to indentured servitude to your former wife for perhaps the rest of your life. While fighting with your wife is no time to reach a divorce settlement."

Ask "What Do I Have to Gain?" Negotiation can be seen as a way of resolving conflict. Recent laboratory experiments suggest that your mental set about conflict can influence the level of your success in negotiating a favorable outcome. Apparently when negotiators use a positive frame of conflict ("What do I have to gain?"), they tend to be more successful then when they use a negative frame ("What do I have to lose?").

Margaret A. Neale demonstrated this by giving two different negotiating teams opposite mental sets (conflict frames). The subjects with a negatively framed condition were told:

> Any concession beyond those granted will represent serious financial losses to the company. Please remember that your primary objective is to minimize such losses to the company. I cannot emphasize the severity of this situation enough. It is mandatory that you secure the necessary concessions from the union to reduce our losses to a tolerable level.

In the positively framed condition, subjects received these instructions:

Any union concession from their current position will result in gains for the company. Please remember that your primary objective is to maximize such gains for the company. I cannot emphasize the importance of these gains to the company enough. It is mandatory, that you, as the company representative, secure such concessions from the union to increase these gains to a meaningful level.

The results of the experiment showed that the frame of conflict significantly affected the negotiation process. Negotiators who viewed the interaction from the standpoint of what they stood to lose behaved in such a way as to reduce concessions. In contrast, the negotiators who had a positive frame ("What do I have to gain?") granted more concessions and won more issues for their side. Success was measured by such factors as the number of issues resolved and the dollar amount of the concessions received.[16]

The implication of this experiment is that all things being equal, you are likely to be more successful in negotiating when you attempt to achieve gains rather than prevent losses. This strategy is akin to raising your level of expectation, or having a positive mental attitude when you enter into negotiation.

Raise Your Level of Expectation. People who set higher targets for themselves in negotiation and stick firmly to them will do better than those people willing to settle for less. In an experiment testing this proposition, a barricade was built betwen bargainers so that neither could communicate with the other. Demands, offers, and counteroffers were passed under the table. Instructions to both sides were identical except for one fact: One side was told that he or she was to achieve a $7.50 settlement; the other a $2.50 settlement. From an arithmetical standpoint, both sides had an equal chance to get $5. In test after test, subjects who expected $7.50 received around $7.50 while those told to expect $2.50 got close to $2.50.[17]

Make Small Concessions Gradually. Social scientists describe this approach as a soft approach to bargaining. Experimentation suggests that making steady concessions leads to more mutually satisfactory agreements in most situations. The hard approach to bargaining is to make your total concession early in the negotiation and to grant no further concession. ("Okay, you can have three of my people for your project. That's my final concession to you.") Another extreme approach (which is really neither hard nor soft) is to make no concession until the very last moment, and then surrender all your concession amount. ("Okay, I've decided to lend you three of my people for your project.")

Negotiating consultant Karrass recommends that if you are a buyer (leading from strength), start low and give in very slowly over a long period of time. If you are a seller (leading from weakness), just turn it around. Start higher and give in slowly over a long period of time. Buyer or seller, the principle remains the same—grant small concessions over the length of the negotiating session.[18]

Use Deadlines. Many deadlines imposed on us are fictitious. You can still obtain the same deal after the deadline is passed. One example came in my mail. It stated, "A free $500 camera is waiting for you just for using our film processing service. But you must act within five days." I called 20 days after the deadline and was informed that the free $500 camera was still waiting for me. (The only hooker was that I had to purchase 200 rolls of film and processing in advance!) Despite these fictitious deadlines, many deadlines do force people into action. Among them are file your income tax by April 15 or begin work by 8:30 in the morning. Here are several examples of deadlines that will usually move the negotiation in your favor:

> Will I be receiving that promotion to senior engineer by December 31? If not, I will feel impelled to act on this job offer from another firm. It has become a matter of pride.
>
> If we don't have your order in by February 1, you will not receive your supplies for 45 days after ordering.
>
> My boss has to approve this deal and she'll be leaving for the west coast tomorrow.

Use Silence. A patient negotiator is often a successful negotiator. If negotiations proceed at a deliberate pace, both sides learn more about the real issues involved. Another value of patience is that it enables the negotiator to probe more carefully before taking a stand. Howard Raiffa reports on a negotiation experiment in which Israeli subjects played against Americans. It was found that the Israelis fared better because they were less impatient to arrive at negotiated settlements. Many Americans become anxious with long pauses in the give-and-take of negotiations. Instead, they prefer to say something or do something to move negotiations forward.[19]

Check with Home Office. According to John L. Graham and Roy A. Herberger, Jr., overseas executives use the concept of limited authority quite effectively when negotiating with North Americans. In reality the foreign executive is saying, "To get me to compromise you not only have to convince me; you've got to convince my boss, who is 5,000 miles away." This may force the other side to come up with very persuasive arguments (and very good deals). Graham and Herberger believe that Americans are generally uncomfortable about checking with the home office in the midst of negotiations.[20]

Use Impasse Breakers. When negotiations are at an impasse, something needs to be done to get things moving. Sometimes a minor change in the nature of the deal can break an impasse. Suppose, as a manager, you are given additional responsibility but not enough new help to accomplish the job properly. An impasse breaker might be to request that you be temporarily relieved of some minor responsibility that your department is now performing. Among the many other possible impasse breakers are changing a negotiating team leader, calling in a mediator, making changes in specifications or terms, or setting up a joint study committee.[21]

Avoid Final Negotiations When Exhausted. A fashionable stunt is for union-management negotiating teams to work around the clock as negotiations move toward their final stages. Nevertheless, people think more clearly and are more in control of their emotions when properly rested.

One school district arrived at a final contract for school teachers and related personnel that proved to be quite unpopular with both the teachers union and the school board. The lawyer for the school district and the chief negotiator for the union pointed out that the all-night negotiating sessions made it difficult to avoid making a few errors. What the negotiators failed to point out was that there was no valid reason for negotiating through the night. They frittered away three summer months of potential negotiating time. When formal sessions began, too much negotiating was crammed into little time. Negotiators from both sides were physically and mentally exhausted.

Play Hard to Get. Another common sense negotiating strategy is for you to make it appear that you will not readily grant concessions to the other side or buy their proposition. The job applicant who is overly anxious to land employment may meet with less success than the applicant who remains mildly aloof. "I might be interested under the right circumstances," is a more effective tactic than, "Please let me have the job. I'll begin as soon as you want."

Make a Last and Final Offer. In many circumstances offering the other side your final offer, or "doorknob price," will break a deadlock. Over 10 years ago I was trying to sell a house I owned for what I considered to be the very fair price of $53,000 (the market value was around $56,000). I received an offer in writing for $43,500 from a woman who was genuinely interested in the property. She contended that money was a problem for her. To help break the deadlock, I told her over the phone, "My house is for sale at an absolute minimum price of $50,000. Please get back in touch with me should you be willing to pay $50,000 for my house." Two weeks later she found the means to meet my last and final offer (which was an excellent deal for her and a minimum satisfactory deal for me.)

Watch out for Game Playing. One of the reasons many negotiating sessions fail is that the opposing parties play games—they go through the motions of acting in good failth, but they have a concealed, somewhat dishonest motive. In some way, both sides want to put each other down. Game playing while negotiating is usually not productive. Recognizing that such games exist may help you confront the game player with his or her game.

Two of many possible negotiating games are presented next in capsule form:[22]

Snow job. Facts and figures are the main tool of this game, as one side or both attempts to establish credibility. Snow job is played by A and B trying to overwhelm or dazzle the other side.

A: It is clear by your proposal the 30 percent increase affects the lower 72 percent of the employees with gains of less than 9 percent increase, and top 10 percent wage earners with $1.22 per hour. Our membership can hardly tolerate this proportion, particularly when our two biggest competitors are doing 30 percent better for their workers.

B: I don't think that's necessary. It's obvious from the facts presented that we must have a 57 percent increase in the sake of fairness.

So what? This game is played by the parties immediately after a concession has been won at the bargaining table. The postconcession posture is that the concession was not really significant. The aim is to deemphasize the concession so that the party granted the conceded item can maintain leverage for gaining other concessions. In other words, "What you gave us was trivial, now let's get on to significant items." The transaction often takes this form:

A: We both agree then that one company-paid holiday per year will be added to the contract.

B: Agreed. Now, let's move on to some of the demands central to negotiations.

A: What could be more major than this one holiday? We've spent hours negotiating an item which will have a major cost and scheduling impact on our operations. This item would eliminate from consideration some of the remaining negotiable items.

B: I see your point. But don't forget this is something we should not have had to bargain over in the first place.

Use Final Offer Arbitration. Arbitration is an increasingly common strategy for resolving labor-management disputes within both the private and public sectors. A relatively new form of arbitration, called *final offer arbitration*, has been shown to increase the effectiveness of negotiators.[23] In a sense, final offer arbitration helps convert competitive negotiation in to a collaborative mode.

Under conventional arbitration, a third party is asked to resolve the issues in dispute so that the final outcome balances the organizational and political needs of each party. Three problems with this conventional approach have been identified. First, the possibility that the arbitrator will "split the difference" compels the negotiators to make extreme demands (maintain polar positions) to offset the arbitrator's expected compromise. Second, since the arbitrator makes the final decision, negotiators feel less responsibility for resolving the dispute and consequently have less incentive to bargain. (This is referred to as the "narcotic effect.") Third, negotiators may feel uncommitted to the outcome since the final outcome was not their decision.

Under final offer arbitration, if negotiators do not reach an agreement among themselves, each must submit a final offer to the arbitrator. Instead of compromising, the arbitrator must choose a final offer from one of the parties. Resolutions tend to occur more frequently under final offer arbitration, partly because each side fears that the other side's final offer would be the one accepted by the arbitrator.

Final offer arbitration can also be used outside of labor-management negotiations. So long as the two parties agree to have a third party accept one of their final offers, the process can be used. Suppose two department heads are negotiating over who will get how much office space in an upcoming move to a new location. Under normal human gluttony, both sides will make exaggerated claims about their needs for new space. If final offer arbitration is agreed to, or imposed, both sides may behave differently. Rather than risk a reasonable demand of the other side being selected as the best final offer by an arbitrator, both sides may bargain in a more collaborative mode.

Improving Your Negotiating Skills

A starting point in developing your negotiating skills is to recognize when a situation calls for negotiation. According to the research of Richard E. Walton, bargaining to reach a decision occurs when the joint pool of resources available to the parties is fixed, yet so far their relative shares have not been determined.[24] The situation described previously of two department heads each trying to capture a larger share of the new office space fits this category. Whatever one side gains is at the expense of the other—the classis case of the zero-sum game. On the other hand, if the potential gain to both parties is variable, joint problem solving can take place. If the two department heads could help each other decide on how much space each really needed, without having to worry about dividing up a fixed amount of resources, they could engage in joint problem solving.

After learning to identify which situations call for negotiation, the next step in skill development would be to practice negotiating in nonthreatening and relatively inconsequential situations. For instance, one might try out one or two negotiating tactics when buying a piece of furniture or home appliance. Once confidence is developed in these lesser situations, one might try negotiating for bigger stakes—such as buying an automobile or arriving at a starting salary on a new job. Again, it is important to incorporate several of the strategies described into one's negotiating.

Another recommended method for improving one's negotiating skills is to use role playing. Two people can first study the description of one of the many strategies descrilbed here. Next, they can develop a scenario approximating a bargaining situation they have faced on the job. The tactic "Use Negotiation Jujitsu," described earlier in this chapter lends itself well to role playing.

Additional suggestions for improving one's negotiating skills are presented in the section, Guidelines for Effectiveness and Skill Development.

Negotiating Tactics: Pro and Con

Pro. Negotiating is an important aspect of life, both on and off the job. Despite its importance, negotiating is often carried out ineffectively. Two researchers note that many negotiating practices today "lead to long and tedious dickering which brings severe hardship to many who should not be involved and many who cannot bear such a hardship."[25] If more people followed the experienced-based guidelines presented in this chapter, more agreements between people would be settled in an equitable fashion.

Con. Many of the tactics described are manipulative in nature. Some of the tactics that appear valid need to be researched more carefully. In many instances, they are based on small support from simulated negotiating sessions with college students. A person may not need to pay heed to these strategies if he or she has good common sense and a well-developed sense of ethics. Finally, if people strived for openness and honesty with each other there would be very little need for negotiating tactics.

GUIDELINES FOR ACTION AND SKILL DEVELOPMENT

Follow those negotiating tactics described in this chapter that best fit your particular circumstances. Be alert to possible negotiating errors you have made in the past. For instance, perhaps your pattern has been to not allow room for negotiating. Next time you are bargaining about something, begin with a demand that allows you some flexibility in negotiating for your final price or position.

Chester Karrass provides some research-based tips about the ideal concession pattern. Making use of these findings will go a long way toward improving your effectiveness as a negotiator:

1. Buyers who start with low offers do better.
2. Buyers who gave a large amount in a single concession raised the expectation of sellers.
3. Sellers who were willing to take less received less in the end.
4. Buyers and sellers who gave just a little at a time did best.
5. Losers tended to make the first concessions on major issues.
6. Deadlines were useful in forcing decisions and agreements.

> 7. Quick negotiations proved ineffective for either side.
> 8. People who made the largest single concession in a negotia-
>   tion did poorly.[26]
>
> All things being equal, use the homecourt advantage in conduct-
> ing negotiations. Included here is your office, a conference room
> housed in your office building, plant, laboratory, or mill. A neutral
> location, such as a hotel or motel, is preferable to negotiating with
> the other party on his or her home court.
>
> If the setting for your negotiations is a large organization, and
> time is an important factor, send high-ranking people to the negoti-
> ating session. Research evidence indicates that when representa-
> tives from both sides held high power in their own subunits, negotia-
> tions were completed in less time than were negotiations between
> one high and one low or between two low power representatives.[27]

Questions and Activities

1. Identify three situations in personal (social) life in which negotiating skills are important.
2. How effective a negotiator is the current president of the United States or prime minister of Canada? Explain.
3. Based on your own observations, what are two frequent errors made by people when negotiating for themselves?
4. It is common practice these days for movie stars, big name singers, and professional athletes to hire agents to negotiate contracts for them. What do you see as the advantages and disadvantages of this practice?
5. To what extent can you negotiate the sale price of home appliances at large department stores?
6. To what extent can you negotiate with the Internal Revenue Service about the amount of taxes they think you owe them?
7. Identify a professional negotiator, such as a labor relations specialist, or an attorney involved in frequent negotiations, in your community. Interview that person to discover the several negotiating tactics he or she thinks are the most effective. Report your results back to the class.

Notes

[1]Robert W. Johnson, "Negotiation Strategies: Different Strokes for Different Folks," *Personnel*, May 1981, pp. 36–44.
[2]Roger Fisher and William Ury, *Getting to Yes* (New York: Penguin Books, 1981).
[3]*Ibid.*, p. 11.
[4]*Ibid.*, p. 26.

[5]"Negotiating: A Master Shows How to Head Off Argument at the Impasse, " *Success,* October 1982, p. 53.

[6]Gary G. Whitney, "Before You Negotiate: Get Your Act Together," *Personnel,* July-August 1982, p. 14.

[7]"Negotiating," p. 53.

[8]Howard Raiffa, *The Art and Science of Negotiation* (Cambridge, Mass.: Harvard University Press, 1983).

[9]Whitney, "Before You Negotiate," p. 23.

[10]James A. Wall, Jr., "Operantly Conditioning a Negotiator's Concession Making," *Journal of Experimental Social Psychology,* 1977, pp. 431–440.

[11]Whitney, "Before You Negotiate," p. 25.

[12]Raffa, *The Art and Science,* p. 306.

[13]Fisher and Ury, *Getting to Yes,* p. 114.

[14]*Ibid.,* p. 104.

[15]Bert F. Brown, "Face-Saving and Face-Restoration in Negotiation," in Daniel Druckman, ed. *Negotiations: Social Psychological Perspectives* (Beverly Hills, Calif.: Sage Publications, 1977), pp. 431–440.

[16]Margaret A. Neale, "Systematic Deviations from Rationality in Negotiator Behavior," *Academy of Management Proceedings '83,* p. 146.

[17]Chester L. Karass, *Give & Take: The Complete Guide to Negotiating Strategies and Tactics* (New York: Thomas Y. Crowell, 1974), p. 2. Most of the competitive strategies listed in this chapter are reported on directly or indirectly in Karass.

[18]*Ibid.,* p. 45. The supporting research is from W. Clay Hamner and Gary A. Yukl, "The Effectiveness of Different Offer Strategies in Bargaining," in Druckman, *Negotiations,* p. 157.

[19]Raiffa, *The Art and Science of Negotiation,* p. 306. See also John L. Graham and Roy A. Herberger, Jr., "Negotiators Abroad—Don't Shoot from the Hip," *Harvard Business Review,* July-August 1983, pp. 160–168.

[20]Graham and Herberger, "Negotiators Abroad," p. 163.

[21]Karass, *Give & Take,* p. 25.

[22]Frank L. Acuff and Maurice Villere, "Games Negotiators Play," *Business Horizons,* February 1976, pp.72–73.

[23]Max H. Bazerman and Margaret A. Neale, "Improving Negotiation Effectivess Under Final Offer Arbitration: The Role of Selection and Training," *Journal of Applied Psychology,* October1982, pp. 543–548.

[24]Research reported in Bernard M. Bass, *Organizational Decision Making* (Homewood, Ill.: Richard D. Irwin, 1983), p. 109.

[25]Acuff and Villere, "Games Negotiators Play," p. 70.

[26]Karass, *Give & Take,* pp. 40–41.

[27]Conrad N. Jackson and Donald C. King, "The Effects of Representatives' Power Within Their Own Organizations on the Outcome of Negotiation," *Academy of Management Journal,* March 1983, p. 153.

Some Additional References

Bachrach, Samuel B., and Edward J. Lawler. *Bargaining: Power, Tactics, and Outcomes.* San Francisco: Jossey-Bass Publishers, 1981.

Bazerman, Max H., and Roy J. Lewicki (eds.). *Negotiating in Organizations.* Beverly Hills, Calif.: Sage Publications, 1983.

Ewing, David W. "How to Negotiate with Employee Objectors." *Harvard Business Review,* January-February 1983, pp. 103–110.

James, Lawrence R., and Jeanne M. Brett, "Mediators, Moderators, and Tests for Mediation." *Journal of Applied Psychology,* May 1984, pp. 307–321.

Warschaw, Tessa Albert. *Winning by Negotiation.* New York: McGraw-Hill, 1980.

Appendix to Chapter 5

Test Your Negotiating Potential

The following questionnaire is designed to give you tentative insight into your current tendencies toward being an effective negotiator. As with other instruments presented in this book, The Negotiator Scale, is primarily a self-examination and discussion mostly true or mostly false, as it relates to you.

	Mostly true	Mostly false
1. Settling differences of opinion with people is a lot of fun.		
2. I try to avoid conflict and confrontation with others as much as possible.		
3. It is very important to me to be liked.		
4. I am generally unwilling to compromise.		
5. How the other side feels about the results of our negotiation is of little consequence to me.		
6. I think very well under pressure.		
7. People think I'm tactful and diplomatic.		
8. I'm known for my ability to express my viewpoint clearly.		
9. Very few things in life are not negotiable.		
10. I always accept whatever salary increase is offered to me.		
11. A person's facial expression often reveals as much as what that person actually says.		
12. I wouldn't mind taking a few short-range losses to win a long-range battle.		
13. I'm willing to work long and hard to win a small advantage.		
14. I'm usually too busy talking to do much listening.		

15. It's fun to haggle over prices at a garage sale. ———— ————
16. I prepare in advance for my negotiating sessions. ———— ————
17. When there's something I need from another person, I usually get it. ———— ————
18. It would make me feel very cheap if I offered somebody only one half of their asking price. ———— ————
19. People are usually paid what they are worth, so no use haggling over starting salaries. ———— ————
20. I rarely take what people say at face value. ———— ————
21. It's easy for me to smile when I'm in a serious discussion. ———— ————

Scoring and Interpretation. Score yourself plus one for each of your answers that agrees with the scoring key. The higher your score, the more likely it is that you currently have good negotiating skills, *providing your self-assessment is accurate.* It might prove useful to also have a boss, spouse, or close friend answer The Negotiator Scale for you. Scores of below 5 and above 16 are probably the most indicative of weak or strong negotiating potential. Here is the scoring key:

1. Mostly true   11. Mostly true
2. Mostly false   12. Mostly true
3. Mostly false   13. Mostly true
4. Mostly false   14. Mostly false
5. Mostly false   15. Mostly true
6. Mostly true   16. Mostly true
7. Mostly true   17. Mostly true
8. Mostly true   18. Mostly false
9. Mostly true   19. Mostly false
10. Mostly false   20. Mostly true
21. Mostly true

Chapter 6

Nonverbal Messages In Organizations

The executive-in-action described in the following case has such an important message to deliver that she does not rely exclusively on written and spoken modes of communication. Instead, she makes a conscious effort to buttress the spoken and written word with a variety of nonverbal messages, also referred to as nonverbal communication, silent messages, and body language.

Jan Winters, executive director of the Thomas Street Center, has called a meeting with the center's board of directors to discuss a major issue. An approximate transcript of a portion of her meeting will be presented here. In addition, we will also include an analysis of some of the nonverbal messages sent simultaneously by Jan as she delivered her verbal messages. Videotape would be a preferable medium for studying nonverbal messages. Nevertheless, with special effort paid toward visualization on your part, our written messages will sensitize you to the role played by unwritten messages.

Jan: It's wonderful that all six of you could make it here this afternoon. I know you are busy people and that your time is very valuable. As my memo stated, I have requested a meeting with the board to discuss our needs for expanding the Thomas Street Center. We need more space; we need more staff.

Jan has already sent several unspoken messages in her opening comments. She quickly established eye contact with all the directors—Garth, Moses, Franklin, Carol, Tracy, and Rex. By leaning forward on her chair and positioning her body out toward the table, she communicated a sense of urgency. Jan's voice tone increased several decibels on the key words, *more space, more staff* which served to indicate the gravity of her request.

Moses: I certainly want to hear your entire story, Jan, but it sounds like your request is running against the census tide. The Thomas Street Center is serving a declining population. According to the latest census, population in our city has declined 8 percent in the last decade. How do we justify expansion when the population is running the other way?

Jan: Moses, you're a better statistician than that. The general inner city population may be declining, but the remainders have a great need for our services. As job opportunities decline, more of our public gets into trouble. We have more broken homes, more drug abuse, more teenage pregnancy, and more old people without a place to live. Besides, the demands for our day-care center alone have shot up 30 percent in the last year. As an increasing number of women work outside the home, families need our services. The families that are still together also place more demand on our services.

Owing to inflation it usually takes two paychecks to meet family expenses.

Jan made forceful use of body language in delivering this message. At the outset, she tapped Moses's shoulder several times as she said ". . . you're a better statistician than that." Touching in this manner, combined with her voice tone, communicates a tone of condescension and criticism. Jan also wrinkled her face in mild disappointment toward Moses.

Tracy: How much staff, and how much space are you talking about? Jan, why not just lay your facts right out on the table?

Jan: As you board members well know, Thomas Street is no mental health retreat for the wealthy. Our cabinets and files are stuffed. Our counselors and clerical help work almost on top of each other. Each one of my counselors carries a double workload. Our clerks are a month behind in their typing and bookkeeping. We need three more full-time counselors, two more clerk-typists, and another 1,000 square feet of space. We could expand the back of our building to do us nicely.

As Jan delivered the verbal message "Thomas Street is no mental health retreat for the wealthy," she also delivered a few nonverbal messages. She used the illustrator message of pointing to her surroundings. The environment she pointed to supported her claims of austerity. The conference table is old and battered with a chipped formica top. Folding metal chairs are scattered around the table. Instant coffee is served in styrofoam cups and with plastic spoons. Powdered milk is used for cream. Grime covers the walls, and there are many patches of gray where the wallboard has been chipped. Consciously or unconsciously, Jan has also worn clothing to the meeting to suggest that she is not bathed in affluence. She is wearing a polyester pants suit and a few small items of costume jewelry.

Carol: I'd like to see exactly what you mean by expanding the back of the building. Could you give us a tour?

Jan: Fine idea. Come on gang, let's get out of the room and into the bullpen. Follow me. It might do us some good to see what the center looks like on a busy afternoon. The kids are back home from school by now and have poured into the neighborhood. That means we're jumping.

Jan's gestures and the tone of her voice communicate substantial enthusiasm. She gestures toward the door; she displays a wide-mouth grin; her emphasis on the word *gang* conveys a feeling of group cohesiveness.

Rex: *[As the group is walking through the bullpen area of the center]* I guess it's been too long since I saw what it was like at the client level of a community agency. You become kind of insulated from the public as a bank officer. I haven't seen so many people doing so many things in such little space in a while.

Jan: Rex, old buddy, I'm glad you could make this board meeting today. I figured you might be too busy lending $10 million to a shopping center developer to talk about our small problems.

Jan sent two different silent messages during this brief interchange. For one, as she toured the facility with the board, she sent an emblem signal to her assistant director who was seated across the room. Jan made a circle with her thumb and index finger, while extending her other three fingers upward and slightly separated—the symbol for "things are going okay." Second, her comment about Rex being too busy for the center's small problems, was delivered with a warm smile, and her hands extended outward. Delivered with different body language, Jan's message could have been interpreted by Rex as a sign of sarcasm, even ridicule.

Franklin: I'm glad Carol suggested we take that little tour. Thanks too, Jan, for your willingness to have the board pay an unannounced visit on your professional and clerical staff. Those folks are certainly working hard to help a needy public. My tentative thoughts as a member of the Community Chest are that your plea for expansion funds has merit. Of course, you would have to draw up an elaborate set of objectives plus an operating plan. It's never easy to obtain funds. We only have so many funds available to help a large list of needy causes.

I suspect your other sources of funding such as the local, state, and federal governments might also be receptive to your ideas. Of course, it would take even more work to get money from them than from the Community Chest.

Garth: I would agree with Franklin. From the little that you have told us about your needs for expansion, your request has merit. But funding is not an easy matter these days. Every worthy cause in our society has its rightful priority.

Jan: Thanks so much everybody. I think we have accomplished quite a bit today. I agreed that we would break by 5:45 and it's 5:50 right now. I'm pleased with your receptiveness to my ideas. Shortly, you'll be receiving a formal proposal for expansion in staff and space. Of course, we are so shorthanded with clerical help around here. Thanks again for coming. See you all at a future board meeting.

Jan could not help but convey mixed messages about her enthusiasm for the outcome of the meeting. She pursed her lips slightly as she thanked the group, almost in the manner of forcing a smile of gratitude. Jan would have much preferred a reaction from the board suggesting that nothing would stop them from helping her find expansion funds.

Jan's second comment about time has significance. By acknowledging that she would keep her promise to set a specific limit to the duration of the meeting, Jan was deferring to the status of the board members. The more you value a person's time the more importance you attach to that person. Jan solidified this notion by apologizing for running the meeting five minutes late. Finally, being a sensible executive, Jan did not emit nonverbal messages that would alienate the board. She did not pout or grimace at the outcome of the meeting. Yet, she did not disguise her feelings entirely. In the final moments of the meeting she communicated guarded enthusiasm for the board's reception to her ideas. Her comment about the clerical shortage was another stab at saying, "See what a bind I'm in. It's difficult for us to find the clerical support to help out on a task as vital as obtaining funds for expansion."

MODES OF TRANSMITTING NONVERBAL MESSAGES

As revealed by the Thomas Street Center board meeting, nonverbal messages are communicated in many ways. Here we will summarize the major nonverbal modes of communication used in job settings. In addition, we will present some of the research evidence that supports their validity. Research evidence is especially important when discussing nonverbal communication because of the many outlandish claims made for the meaning of minor, often random, body movements and gestures.

Head, Face, and Eye Behavior. When used in combination, the head, face, and eyes provide the clearest indications of attitudes toward other people.[1] Lowering you head and peering over your glasses, for instance, is the nonverbal equivalent of the idiom, "You're putting me on." As is well known, maintaining eye contact with another person improves communication with that person. In order to maintain eye contact, it is usually necessary to correspondingly move your head and face. Moving your head, face, and eyes away from another person is often interpreted as defensiveness or a lack of self-confidence. Would you buy a used car from somebody who didn't look at you directly?

The face is often used as a primary source of information about how we feel. We look for facial cues when we want to read another person's expression. You can often judge an employee's morale just by looking at his or her face. The popular phrase *sourpuss* attests to this observation. Happiness, apprehension, anger, resentment, sadness, contempt, enthusiasm, and embarassment are but a few of the emotions that can be expressed through the face. Two communications experts offer this sage advice about facial messages in a work setting:

> The ability to read these emotional cues . . . is extremely important, because it is through these cues that you can get . . . the feedback you are seeking from others. A subordinate, for example, might not be able to put in words exactly what it was that he or she did not understand in your instructions, but perhaps an expression of bewilderment might give you a clue that there was some misunderstanding. Being able to read this nonverbal message would then allow you to adapt your verbal message, that is, to rephrase the instructions so that they are understandable.[2]

Some research evidence has shown that eye contact is an important supplement to verbal messages. A pair of researchers found that messages accompanied by eye contact are more favorably interpreted by observers than are messages sent without eye contact.[3] An implication drawn from this study is that if a manager maintains eye contact with subordinates, communication with them will often be significantly improved. At a minimum do not deliver an important message if you do not have people's visual attention.

Posture. "Walk into your prospect's office straight and tall. Show him that you represent the finest line of ball bearings in the world," shouted the sales manager of the past. Observations made today by specialists in nonverbal communication support the sales manager's exhortation. Posture does communicate a message. Leaning toward another individual suggests that you are favorably disposed toward his or her messages; leaning backwards communicates the opposite. Openness of the arms or legs serves as an indicator of liking or caring. In general, people establish closed postures (arms folded and legs crossed) when speaking to people they dislike. Standing up straight (assuming a person is physically capable of such behavior) generally reflects high self-confidence. Stooping and slouching could mean a poor self-image.

A study conducted a number of years ago indicated that posture was a more reliable indicator of the attitudes of women than men. When facing someone they strongly dislike, women particularly tend to be very indirect in their facial direction, looking away from the disliked person as much as possible. If women like the person in front of them, they vary their direction of face, sometimes looking squarely at that person and sometimes looking away. Similar, although less consistent results, were found among men.[4]

Interpersonal Distance. The placement of one's body relative to someone else's body is another meaningful way of sending a message. One study showed that people located in relatively close proximity are seen as warmer, friendlier, and more understanding than people located farther away.[5] The implication is that if you want to convey positive attitudes to another person, get physically close to that person. As common sense suggests, putting your arm around somebody else in a job setting is interpreted as a friendly act. Cultural differences must be kept in mind in interpreting nonverbal cues. For example, a French male is likely to stand closer to you than a British male even if they have equally positive attitudes toward you.

Practical guidelines for judging how close to stand to another person (in the North American or similar culture!) are as follows:

Intimate distance is from actual physical contact to about 18 inches. Physical intimacy is usually not called for in business but there are exceptions. For one, confidential information might be whispered within the intimate distance zone.

Personal distance is the distance from about one and one-half to four feet. The interaction that takes place in this zone includes friendly discussions and conversation. An exception is a heated argument between two people, such as a baseball coach getting up close to an umpire and shouting in his face.

Social-consultative distance is about four to eight feet and is usually reserved for businesslike, impersonal interaction. We usually maintain this amount of distance between ourselves and strangers, such as retail store clerks and cab drivers.

Public distance is from 12 feet to the outer limit of being heard. This zone is typically used in speaking to an audience at a large meeting or in a classroom. An important exception is the insensitive individual who sends ordinary messages by shouting across a room. The unstated message communicated in such an interaction is that the receiver of the message is not worth the effort of walking across the room.[6]

Gestures. Whether or not you are a student of body language, you are most likely familiar with the use of hands to communicate meaning. Gestures made with the hand are universally recognized as conveying specific information to others. Positive attitudes are shown by frequent gesticulation (hand movements). At the other extreme, dislike or disinterest usually produces few gestures. An important exception here is that some people wave their hands furiously while in an argument. Some of their hand movements reflect anger. The type of gesture displayed also communicates a particular message. To quote one observer of body language:

> Random fidgeting, such as drumming the fingers or twiddling the thumbs, is a set of gestural activities which convey extremely negative attitudes. Similarly, aggressive gestures with clenched fists and menacing postures convey hostile feelings, while frequent use of relaxed, open-palm gestures toward the other person typically conveys positive attitudes.[7]

An attempt has been made to classify the many functions served by hand gestures. Some of these are familiar to anybody who has ever cut off another driver on a highway, or watched an irate coach communicate displeasure to an umpire or referee. From time to time, obscene gestures present themselves in the workplace. For instance, a foreman asked his boss one day, "Can I fire an employee who 'gives me the finger'?" Gestures can be used as illustrators, regulators, affect displays, and emblems.[8]

Illustrators are gestures that are used to add emphasis or drama or to clarify a message. Examples of illustrators include pointing toward the floor while saying "Our profits are nosediving," and punching your fist into an open palm while saying "I know we can do better than this." A less dramatic example of an illustrator is to point toward a door or explain the nature of a spiral staircase by twirling your finger.

Regulators are gestures we use to regulate both conversation and human interaction. Raising your hand or finger when you want to talk at a meeting or in class is a regulator. Raising one hand with the fingers pointed upward and the palm outward is used to tell another person to stop talking (usually interpreted as a rude nonverbal message). Parts of the body other than the hand can also be used as regulators. You might raise your eyebrows or nod your head to send the message that it is your turn to speak.

Affect displays are gestures used to communicate emotion that we are experiencing. Such displays are generally used in conjunction with other modes of nonverbal behavior, especially facial expressions. Clenched fists to communicate tension illustrates an affect display. Intensified nail biting and cuticle nibbling are obvious examples of affect displays in response to tension or worry. Belly scratching in a relaxed manner is often a tipoff that an individual is feeling contented (or itchy). Scratching the back of one's head usually suggests that a person is perplexed. Hand-over-mouth gestures usually indicate shock, surprise, or remorse.

Emblems are basically hand signals, not too different from the manual communication that is used by many deaf people. They are nonverbal signals or cues that have a specific verbal equivalent. A popular emblem is the okay signal made by Jan in the case presented earlier. The okay emblem, however, communicates more enthusiasm than a simple okay; it seems to mean very okay. An emblem in contemporary use is the hearty approval shown by an upward pointed thumb, combined with a clenching of the four other fingers—both done with the vigor and motion used in hammering a nail. It is similar to the spoken message, "Right on!" Conversely, a thumbs-down signal at a business conference indicates strong disapproval.

Traffic hand signals, manual signals used on the playing field (such as the time-out signal of placing the index fingers at right angles to each other), and certain obscene gestures are other examples of emblems.

Gestures are also useful in revealing dominant and submissive behavior according to the research of anthropologist David Givens and psychiatrist Albert Scheflen. Their findings pointed out that the gestures of the dominant person are usually directed outward, toward the other person. Examples include touching of partner, fingers splayed and pointed toward partner, palm-down gestures, and a steady, unwavering gaze. Submissive gestures are usually protective like shrugging one's shoulder, gazing downward, and touching oneself.[9] (A minor criticism of this research is that "gaze" seems to be misclassified as a gesture.)

Tone of Voice. We often attach more significance to the way something is said than to what is said. Voice tone is critical, but other aspects of the voice, such as volume, quality, and rate, are also part of the nonverbal message. As with all nonverbal cues, there is an ever-present danger of overinterpreting a single voice quality. A subordinate of yours might speak to you about the status of a project in a high-pitched voice, not out of fear but because of laryngitis. Anger, boredom, joy—three emotions which are frequently experienced on the job—can often be interpreted from voice quality. Two communication specialists summarize these nonverbal cues in this manner:

> Anger is best perceived when the source speaks loudly, at a fast rate, in a high pitch, with irregular inflection and clipped enunciation. Boredom is indicated by moderate volume, pitch and rate, and a monotone inflection; joy by loud volume, high pitch, fast rate, upward inflection, and regular rhythm.[10]

Voice tone is also used to emphasize various elements of the verbal message. Through the use of voice tone, you are able to question, make exclamations, to give extra emphasis to one part of the message at the expense of another part. A clever example is presented in *Communication for Supervisors and Managers* of how emphasizing a particular word in a message through voice tone can lead to different interpretations of the same statement:

The *boss* is giving Sheila a promotion.
The BOSS is the one giving a promotion, not the president of the company, not the boss's supervisor, but the boss.
The boss is *giving Sheila* a promotion.

The boss is GIVING the promotion, implying that perhaps Sheila is not qualified.

The boss is giving *Sheila* a promotion.

The person getting the promotion is SHEILA, not Art, not Betty, not Ken, but Sheila.

The boss is giving Sheila a *promotion*.

Sheila is receiving a PROMOTION, not a raise, not a demotion, not "the sack."[11]

The general quality of a person's voice is often used to make inferences about a telephone caller. How a person sounds over the phone provides us with clues about that person's age, education, intelligence, masculinity-feminity, and self-confidence. One employment recruiter insists he can size up a person's physical attractiveness based on his or her telephone voice quality. In reality, the recruiter may be reacting to the degree of self-confidence communicated by the quality of the caller's voice. People who perceive themselves to be attractive often communicate in more decisive terms.

Environmental Cues. The environment in which you send a message can influence the receiving of that message. Assume that your boss invites you out to lunch to discuss a problem. You will think it is a more important topic under these circumstances than if he or she met you for lunch in the company cafeteria. Other important environmental cues include room color, temperature, lighting, and furniture arrangement.

An experiment was conducted to explore the relationship between the environmental quality and a person's psychological mood. Some people were assigned to work in a pleasant room and others in an unpleasant room. Distinct differences were found between the two groups. People who worked in the pleasant room experienced feelings of comfort, pleasure, enjoyment, importance, and a desire to continue with the task to which they were assigned. People who worked in the unpleasant room experienced feelings of monotony, fatigue, hostility, and irritability.[12]

Office furniture, in combination with its neatness and orderliness, can project information about the office occupant. A person who sits behind an uncluttered large desk, for example, appears more powerful than a person who sits behind a small, cluttered desk. This power illusion may hold even if the two people express the same message such as "What you say has merit." Our case history illustrates how some people use environmental cues to communicate information about themselves.

Derek, a 45-year old sales manager for a tire manufacturer, has a thirst for power that expresses itself in many subtle and some not-so-subtle ways. A visitor to his office can immediately sense Derek's almost immature desire to appear powerful and important. In a company where most managers conduct their work in short sleeves and no jacket, Derek wears a vest and jacket even during the summer. His shirts are French-cuffed; his boots have three-inch heels. Derek's office is uniformly furnished in leather, chrome, and glass. Instead of the ashtray fashioned of a miniature tire found on the coffee tables of his coworkers, he utilizes oversized decorator trays.

Derek's desk consists of a six-foot-long piece of heavy glass placed on top of two chrome sawhorses. Guests have no choice but to sit in chairs set at a level six inches lower than the two chairs Derek uses. Several photos and plaques adorn Derek's wall: One photo shows him—wearing a captain's cap—seated at the helm of a large speedboat; another, shaking hands with the mayor of Cleveland; a third depicts him standing while his wife and three children are seated. One plaque attests to the extraordinary number of miles he has traveled on one commercial airline. Another plaque gives Derek the accolade, "Outstanding Alumnus Award," based upon both his community activities and his contribution to the alumni fund of his college.

Clothing, Dress, and Appearance. Few people would disagree that your external appearance plays a role in communicating messages to others. Job-seekers implicitly recognize this aspect of nonverbal communication when they carefully groom themselves for a job interview. People pay more respect and grant more privileges to people they perceive as being well dressed and attractive. Should you like to gather empirical evidence for this proposition, conduct this simple experiment. Try paying for merchandise by check at several stores under two different sets of conditions. In one condition, dress as businesslike and affluent as possible. In the other condition, dress in clothing that you use for such chores as yard work, car washing, or helping a friend move. Compare your degree of success under the two experimental conditions.

Dress and appearance is often said to influence how powerful you appear to others, as suggested in the case of sales executive, Derek. *Winning at Work: A Book for Women* presents an analysis of how a career woman might look powerful or powerless, depending upon her clothing and dress (see Figure 6-1). A similar set of ground rules would apply to males. For example, a three-piece grey pin-striped suit sends out more power signals than does a loud plaid sports jacket and slacks. We are assuming, of course, that other factors, such as body weight, size, and hair style, are held constant.

Use of Time. A subtle mode of nonverbal communication in organizations is the use of time. If we are late for meetings, it might be interpreted that

Figure 6–1
A comparison of power and powerless looks for career women

	Powerful	Powerless
Clothes	Tailored suit with blazer jacket	Dress with frills
Overcoat	Wrap-around camel coat	Flaired coat
Raincoat	Trench coat, umbrella	Poncho, plastic rain hat, shawl
Purse	Attache case or small clutch bag	Large, floppy bag
Jewelry	Round gold hoop necklace; large watch and ring; simple post or ball earrings	Anything dangling
Hair	Slightly short to medium length	Very long or very short
Make-up	Moderately dark lashes; precisely and moderately shaped eyebrows; slight cheek color; moderate color lipstick	Large false eyelashes; very thin eyebrows; heavy, red rouge; no lipstick

Source: Figure reprinted from Florence Seaman and Anne Lorimer, *Winning at Work: A Book for Women* (Philadelphia: Running Press, 1979), p. 132.

we are careless, uninvolved, or unambitious. However, a high-ranking official might be late for a meeting and that same amount of lateness might be perceived as a symbol of importance or being busy. Looking at your watch is usually interpreted as a sign of boredom or restlessness.

An experiment was conducted demonstrating the importance of time use as a nonverbal cue. The critical variable was the punctuality of job applicants: some of the applicants arrived on time, some 15 minutes early, and some 15 minutes late. Punctual applicants were perceived by the interviewers as the most sociable and composed. Applicants who were 15 minutes early were perceived as the least sociable. Those applicants who were 15 minutes late were perceived as the least composed, and the least competent.[13]

Mirroring to Establish Rapport. A form of nonverbal communication used to achieve rapport with another is *mirroring*. To mirror someone is to subtly imitate that individual. It is one small aspect of a new discipline called *neurolinguistic programming*, a method of communication that combines features of hypnosis, linguistics, and nonverbal behavior. "Neuro" refers to the way the human nervous system processes communication. "Linguistic" refers to the way that words, tone, timing, gestures, and inflection can be used in communication. "Programming" refers to using a systematic technique of communication with others.[14]

The most successful mirroring technique for establishing rapport is to imitate another's breathing pattern. If you adjust your own breathing rate to match someone else's, you will soon establish rapport with that individual. Mirroring is of relevance here because it is a method of establishing rapport through a nonverbal message. Eric H. Marcus describes one example of how mirroring can be used to solve a management problem:

> A manager is confronted by an angry shop steward concerning disciplinary action taken against a member. In the normal course of events, the breathing rate of both people will fluctuate in keeping with the progress of the discussion. In this case, rapid, shallow breathing, a subconscious signal of anger, will only elicit anger in response. But if the manager instead deliberately paces his own breathing rate to that of his antagonist, and gradually decreases his breathing rate, tension will be dispelled and rapport established.[15]

Marcus notes that it is also possible to engage in *cross-over mirroring*, or using a different part of your body to mirror another person. For instance, you could mirror a breathing rate by moving your hand at the same rate. Effective communicators, according to Marcus, engage in this kind of nonverbal behavior intuitively, and sometimes unconsciously.

The Case For and Against Making Systematic Use of Nonverbal Messages in Organizations

On the positive side, the fact that we send nonverbal messages along with verbal messages cannot be denied. As much as 60 percent of communication is nonverbal. If you learn to recognize the more reliable nonverbal messages (such as eye contact), you will become adept at sending and receiving messages. Support for this conclusion comes from studies conducted by John T. Molloy.

Based on research with 100 men and 62 women, he demonstrated that one can learn to read the nonverbal messages of people he or she deals with on a daily basis. Ninety percent of the study participants believed that the people around them gave off reliable nonverbal signals indicating mood. In some cases, the signals predicted specific actions. All participants agreed that the information they gained from studying nonverbal signals was useful in solving everyday problems. Molloy reports, for example, that "Two men and six women told us they asked for raises when they knew their boss was in a good mood, and all, except one woman, received them."[16]

A telling point about the validity of nonverbal communication is that if it were not meaningful, anybody could be an effective actor. You could act by simply reciting lines in a monotone; nonverbal behavior would not be required to communicate feelings and moods. Similarly, all managers would be equally effective at communicating enthusiasm to subordinates. They would merely have to recite words of enthusiasm such as "You're doing a fine job." How the message was sent would not be of significance.

On the negative side, much of what we label nonverbal communication is basically frivolous and an overinterpretation of minor cues. What is true about nonverbal messages is so obvious, that it does not merit formal study. Admittedly a sweaty palm, a yawning mouth, or chain smoking communicate messages, but you do not have to study nonverbal communication to interpret these signals. The nonverbal cues that are not so obvious, such as placing your hands at your side or lowering an eyebrow, are not consistent enough in their meaning to serve as guidelines for action.

Another problem with nonverbal messages is that, as a result of the attention nonverbal behavior has received in the popular press, too many people are willing to overinterpret trivial nonverbal cues, such as random fidgeting or facial movements. One manager, for example, accused one of his subordinates of being disinterested in his proposal, based on the subordinate's "body language." When confronted about the matter, the subordinate replied that he was interested in the topic but a toothache was causing the pained expression.

GUIDELINES FOR ACTION AND SKILL DEVELOPMENT

Your ability to send nonverbal messages effectively can be improved, although programs of this nature are relatively unknown. Here are six suggestions to tentatively consider.[17]

Obtain feedback on your body language by asking others to comment upon the gestures and facial expressions that you use in conversations. Have a videotape prepared of you conferring with another individual. After studying your body language, attempt to eliminate those mannerisms and gestures that you think detract from your effectiveness (such as moving your leg from side to side when being interviewed).

Learn to relax when communicating with others. Take a deep breath and consciously allow your body muscles to loosen. A relaxed person makes it easier for other people to relax. Thus, you are likely to elicit more useful information from other people when you are relaxed.

Use facial, hand, and body gestures to supplement your speech, but do not overdo it. A good starting point is to use hand gestures to express enthusiasm. You can increase the potency of enthusiastic comments by shaking the other person's hand, nodding approval, smiling, or patting that person on the shoulder.

Avoid using the same nonverbal gesture indiscriminately. To illustrate, if you want to use nodding to convey approval, do not nod with approval even when you dislike what another employee or subordinate is saying. Also, do not pat everybody on the back. Nonverbal gestures used indiscriminately lose their communication effectiveness.

Try to maintain the proper physical distance from people when conversing with them. The better you know someone, the safer you are in standing close to him or her. Most people consider it an invasion of their *territorial space* if you move within six inches of them while speaking.

Use role-playing to practice various forms of nonverbal communication. A good starting point would be to practice selling your ideas about an important project or concept to another person. During your interchange, supplement your spoken messages with appropriate nonverbal cues, such as posture, voice intonation, gestures, and so forth. Later, obtain the other person's perception of the effectiveness of your nonverbal behavior.

Questions and Activities

1. What methods of nonverbal communication do you use to communicate enthusiasm to other people in a job setting?
2. What methods of nonverbal communication tend to be used more socially than occupationally?
3. Give a couple of specific examples of nonverbal signals that are more appropriate for the executive suite than the shop floor (or similar setting).
4. Give a couple of specific examples of nonverbal signals that are more appropriate for the shop floor (or similar setting) than for the executive suite.
5. What is your opinion of the validity of the powerful versus powerless analysis presented in Figure 6-1? Explain your reasoning.
6. What nonverbal cues might a manager use to appear confident in front of his or her subordinates?
7. This week engage two different people in conversation, and mirror their breathing rate. Observe what happens, and report your observations back to class. (It would be even more illuminating to try mirroring with someone who is angry with you.)

Notes

[1]John E. Baird, Jr., and Gretchen K. Wieting, "Nonverbal Communication Can Be a Motivational Tool," *Personnel Journal*, September 1979, p. 609. A substantial portion of our chapter is based on the literature review included in this article.

[2]Lyle Sussman and Paul D. Krivonos, *Communication for Supervisors and Managers* (Sherman Oaks, Calif.: Alfred Publishing, 1979), p. 75.

[3]Robert V. Exline and Carl Eldridge, "Effects of Two Patterns of Speaker's Visual Behavior Upon the Perception of Authenticity of His Verbal Message"(Paper presented to the Eastern

Psychological Association, Boston, 1967), cited in Baird and Wieting, "Nonverbal Communication," p. 610.

[4]Albert Mehrabian, "Influence of Attitude from the Posture, Orientation, and Distance of a Communicator," *Journal of Consulting and Clinical Psychology,* 1968, 296–308; cited in Baird and Wieting, "Nonverbal Communication," p. 610.

[5]Miles L. Patterson, "Spatial Factors in Social Interaction," *Human Factors,* 3, 1968, 351–361.

[6]Sussman and Krivonos, *Communication* pp. 80–81. Based on Nancy Russo, "Connotation of Seating Arrangement," *Cornell Journal of Social Relations,* 2, 1967, 37–44.

[7]Baird and Wieting, "Nonverbal Communication," p. 609.

[8]Paul Ekman and Wallace V. Friesen, "Hand Movements," *Journal of Communication,* 1972, pp. 353–58. The discussion is further developed in Sussman and Krivonos, *Communication,* pp. 78–79.

[9]Research summarized in Salvatore Didato, "Our Body Movements Reveal Whether We're Dominant or Submissive," Rochester *Democrat and Chronicle,* December 20, 1983, p. 1C.

[10]Baird and Wieting, "Nonverbal Communication," pp. 610, 625.

[11]Sussman and Krivonos, *Communication,* p. 83.

[12]Based on evidence presented in Ibid., p. 87.

[13]Eric H. Marcus, "Neurolinguistic Programming," *Personnel Journal,* December 1983, p. 972.

[14]Ibid., p. 975.

[15]John T. Molloy, *Molloy's Live for Success* (New York: Bantam Books, 1982), p. 32.

[16]Andrew J. DuBrin, *Human Relations: A Job Oriented Approach,* 3rd ed. (Reston, Va.: Reston Publishing, 1984) pp. 243–244.

Some Additional References

Harper, Robert G., Arthur W. Wiens, and Joseph D. Matarazzo. *Nonverbal Communication: The State of the Art.* New York: John Wiley, 1979.

Mehrabian, Albert. *Silent Messages: Implicit Communication of Emotions and Attitudes.,* 2nd ed. Belmont, Calif.: Wadsworth Publishing, 1981.

Rosenthal, Robert, ed. *Skill in Nonverbal Communication: Individual Differences.* Cambridge, Mass.: Oelgeschager, Gunn & Hain, 1979.

Patterson, Miles L. *Nonverbal Behavior: A Functional Perspective.* New York: Springer-Verlag, 1983.

Wiemann, John M., and Randall P. Harrison, eds. *Nonverbal Interaction.* Beverly Hills, Calif.: Sage Publications, Inc., 1983.

Winter, Caryl. *Present Yourself with Impact: Techniques for Success.* New York: Ballantine Books, 1983.

Chapter 7

Resolving Conflict Between Subordinates

The director of manufacturing at a company that produces peripheral equipment for computers began to observe a disruptive amount of conflict between two of his key subordinates, the managers of production and quality. He decided to intervene in this problem by conducting a three-way conference between himself and the two managers. The manufacturing manager hoped his two managers would develop a clear perception of the problem, which would lead to a resolution of the conflict.[1]

Gary Anderson (Director of Manufacturing): I've asked you two fellows to meet with me because I think your differences are getting out of hand. You're both wasting a lot of time sending angry memos to one another. And I think you're both creating morale problems. Just today one of our hourly employees told the plant personnel manager that the feuding between the production and quality (control) departments is causing production delays.

The way I want to handle this is for you two to arrive at a better understanding of the reasons behind your conflicts. I'm not going to be an arbitrator or a judge. My role is to get you guys to work things out for yourselves. From the look on your faces, it seems that I'd better give you some more structure. Tony, I'll ask you to go first. Look at Laird and tell him what he's doing that's bugging you. Be candid and thorough. We'll both remain silent while you're talking. Then Laird will get his turn.

Tony Bianco (Production Manager): Laird, I don't think I have anything against you personally. I just don't like the way you're doing a lot of things. In fact, Laird, you're getting out of hand. Let me go over the points that come to mind. At the top of my list is the fact that you're too picky. You look for defects too small for almost any customer to be concerned about. One example is that last month you wrote a report saying our high-speed printer will hit a double strike once in 150,000 strokes. Who cares? The printer sells for $3,000, not $300,000.

Another problem I see is that you act like quality is a game. You and your crew are forever playing "Gotcha." Instead of getting pleasure out of finding a zero defect product, you get your jollies out of finding defects. I hate that gleam you get in your eyes when you tell the rest of the management team about quality defects you've discovered.

I also don't like the idea of you being so sneaky and indirect. When you find a problem, I wish you would tell production first. Instead, you pussyfoot around the plant telling other people. The other departments learn of these alleged defects before we do.

Maybe the biggest problem is that you're losing perspective. In your eyes, quality is king and queen. You seem to forget that unless we produce and sell a product, there would be nothing for your department to inspect. I think you're too power hungry.

Gary: Thanks for being so candid. I can see Laird sitting on the edge of his chair, eager to let you know how he sees things.

Laird Howard (Quality Manager):   I won't dignify some of your charges with a rebuttal. Besides, the way I understand the ground rules of this meeting, right now I'm just supposed to give you my impressions of your behavior. Above all, Tony, I believe that you pay only lip service to product quality. If the president and Gary weren't so solidly behind quality, I think you would have our department report to you. You would keep it under your thumb by converting the department back to a quality-control inspection operation.

One of the reasons I think you're not really interested in quality is that you believe we don't have a quality problem until we receive a customer complaint. I remember distinctly you refused to listen to our advice on those daisy-wheel printing discs until returns from the dealers started pouring in. You told Gary you complied, but you really didn't.

And talk about power plays, you're the department that is trying to grab all the power and the glory. I have heard you downplay the importance of the quality department more than once. I heard that you tried to have the job of your department secretary upgraded one notch higher than that of our department secretary.

Tony, maybe the underlying problem is that you are too sensitive to criticism. The job of the quality department is to needle production from time to time. You're just too thin skinned.

That's all I have for now.

Gary: Now let's see how well each of you were communicating and listening. Tony, state in your own words what criticisms you heard Laird make of you. Then, Laird, you do the same.

Tony: *[smiling]* Laird thinks I'm a power-crazed fool from production. Seriously, Laird has these negatives about me. He thinks I'm not truly interested in manufacturing; I don't buy his recommendations; I want too much power for our department; and, I'm thin skinned.

Laird: Tony has some issues in relation to me that I didn't realize existed. He thinks I'm too perfectionistic; that I'm playing games with him instead of only pointing out true quality problems; that I embarrass his department by telling other departments before I notify him; and that I place too much importance on product quality.

Gary: The fact that you can both see clearly what each other thinks is a problem is a good starting point. The next step is to take action; to grant some concessions to the other side. Tony, let's begin with you. What changes can you make to decrease the conflict between you and Laird?

Tony: Since I think I pay much more than lip service to quality, I see no need for changes there. Yet, I will make a deliberate effort to never downplay the contribution of the quality department to our overall manufacturing effort. And I will try to be more open to the suggestions Laird's group has to offer.

Gary: Laird, I'd like you to react to Tony's comments, and then specify what changes you think you can make.

Laird: I would be very satisfied if Tony would make the changes he just spelled out. I don't think we're being picky, but I guess I do act a little too triumphant when we find errors. Perhaps I'm like a dentist who gets a thrill out of discovering a cavity. I will tone down a bit there. Also, I'll make certain that if we discover any quality problems, I'll discuss them with Tony first. I do feel a little guilty about having been loose tongued on that matter in the past.

Gary: I think we've made a good start toward resolving these problems. Let's all get together for lunch in about a month to review progress on these matters.

HOW TO RESOLVE CONFLICT BETWEEN SUBORDINATES

The case history just presented describes how one manager used a conceptually sound approach to resolving conflict between two subordinates. Gary's method focused on the two parties in dispute understanding each other's viewpoint, before concessions could be made and action plans drawn for resolving the conflict. Here we describe a six-part method that managers can

use to resolve a variety of conflicts between subordinates. It incorporates all
the steps taken by Gary to resolve the interpersonal dispute between Tony
and Laird. The method also incorporates many features found in several
other standard approaches to resolving conflict in organizations. In outline,
the process consists of (1) establishing a supportive climate; (2) determining
the perceptions of both sides; (3) listening without being defensive; (4)
isolating the causes of conflict; (5) determining each party's conflict resolution strategy; and (6) monitoring organizational realities and constraints.[2]

Establishing a Supportive Climate. Subordinates will be hesitant to
enlist a manager's help in resolving conflict between them if the manager is
cold, distant, and generally unwilling to listen to problems. A critical
behavior on the manager's part for encouraging conflict resolution is to
establish a climate that encourages open expression of differences of opinion. Subordinates should feel that there is nothing inherently wrong with
conflict among coworkers. Another key aspect of a climate supportive to
conflict resolution is for the manager to provide incentives for controlling
conflict. Subordinates should see more value in resolving than perpetuating
conflict. Stu, a manager in a government agency, explains his position on
this subtle issue:

> A good deal of my time is spent helping the people in my organization resolve their
> conflicts. As far as I'm concerned, not resolving conflict is a lose-lose situation.
> There's nothing to be gained by two of my department heads locking their horns
> in combat. If it appears to me that two of my people are wasting too much time in
> either fighting with or avoiding each other, I tell them something to the effect,
> "Until you two can come to terms with each other, I will not look favorably on any
> of your new proposals. Let the three of us get together, or the two of you work
> things out. Whichever course of action you choose, I want to see a decent working
> relationship between the two of you before we talk about new projects.

Determining Both Parties' Perceptions. A key ingredient to effective
conflict resolution is for the manager to understand the perspective and
perceptions of both disputants. Under conditions of intense conflict, it may
be necessary to listen to each party individually before getting them together.
Listening should be impartial, even if you believe that one side is "right" and
the other "wrong." In the process of being heard, the angry parties will
usually dissipate some of their anger. As described by the developers of this
six-part process, "Often this ability to talk about feelings and anger will lessen
the intensity of the conflict and even the conflict itself."[3] Gary Anderson
relied on this technique.

A surprising fact about interpersonal conflict is that both sides often
perceive the same situation in terms that are 180 degrees apart. Tony, the
production manager, perceived Laird, the quality manager, to be needlessly

picky about quality problems. Tony also saw Laird as a person who went out of his way to find flaws in the work of other people. Laird looked at the same situation in an opposite way. He perceived himself to be a true champion of quality, while Tony was not really interested in quality.

Listen Without Being Defensive. Although this strategy is designed for resolving conflict between others when you are the third party, it also has relevance for resolving your own conflicts. Try to hear the entire story without attempting to defend yourself or your department. Discover the source of the anger of the two people in conflict, or that of the person in conflict with you. Suppose one of the two parties begins his or her tirade in this manner, "One of the reasons Joe and I cannot get along is that we have to fight for clerical help. If this weren't such a tight-fisted department, maybe Joe and I could establish a decent working relationship." A defensive retort by you would be, "There's where you're wrong. We have a more generous clerical budget than any department our size." A response that would evoke additional conversation about the true nature of the conflict would be, "Let's hear more about that."

Another aspect of listening nondefensively is to allow both parties to fully develop their perception of the nature of the conflict. Following the technique of image exchanging, each party should also attempt to describe how the other party perceives the conflict. Laird's comments about how he was perceived by Tony, are a good example of this approach. Laird said, "Tony has some issues in relation to me that I didn't realize existed. He thinks I'm too perfectionistic; that I'm playing games with him instead of only pointing out true quality problems; that I embarrass his department by telling other departments before I notify him; and that I place too much importance on product quality."

Isolating the Cause of Conflict. The true cause of a given situation of job conflict may be so deep rooted it resists detection. Suppose Tony was really in conflict with Laird because he resented his work being second-guessed by another person at his level of responsibility. If it seems feasible, the manager should strive to isolate a cause that goes one level beneath the surface. Sometimes more than one underlying cause exists. It is possible that another contributing factor to the conflict betwen Tony and Laird is that if Tony does go along with many of Laird's suggestions, the total output of his department will suffer. Tony thus resists Laird's suggestions because he worries about not reaching his production goals.

Perhaps if Tony were encouraged to talk freely during the conflict resolution session he might candidly say, "I don't have anything personal against Laird, but I don't like being second-guessed by some expert from another department." Another comment he might make would be, "You guys are squeezing me in two directions. If my department reaches its output quota, we can't also reach the high-quality standards."

Determining Each Party's Usual Resolution Strategy. When people attempt to work out their conflicts, their behavior is typically a product of their frame of reference about conflict resolution. Many people believe, for example, that compromise is the only valid way to resolve conflict. They will assume that once the resolution sessions are completed, each side will come away with part of their demands met—much akin to negotiating the price of a new automobile. Others believe that there is always a right and wrong side to conflict. Thus they will look for a zero-sum solution in which one side gets everything. (From now on you get all the temporary clerical help and he gets nothing!)

Knowing both parties' customary mode of conflict resolution will help tell you how much relearning will be necessary to bring about a creative solution to the conflict. It is conceivable that neither compromise nor win-lose is the best approach to resolution. Many alternatives are available as described in the following paragraphs.

Selecting a Strategy. The method of resolving conflict between two people described so far can be considered a general strategy. It is also helpful to choose a specific strategy that appears most promising for the situation at hand. The final strategy selected will often represent a combination of more than one strategy. Also, you might create a strategy that is a slight variation of one of the seven described next (appeal to a third party, compromise, peaceful coexistence, integrative bargaining, domination of the other party, superordinate goals, and expansion of resources).

Appeal to a third party. Using this approach, the two parties will expect you to make a decision as to who is right and who is wrong. After listening to two subordinates complain about each other, you may decide that one side is right. One valid criticism of the appeals procedure, however, is that when the higher-ranked third party settles the dispute, the person who has lost the decision may not be psychologically committed to the decision. However, since so many people are culturally conditioned to accept a third-party judgment, the approach often works. One executive put it this way: "We're adults around here. If the president makes a decision that doesn't go our way, we live with it. Maybe next time he'll rule in our favor."

Compromise. Most people enter into negotiations or conflict-resolution sessions anticipating a compromise solution. In many instances, a workable compromise results in successful conflict resolution.[4] Suppose one worker says to the boss, "I can't concentrate because Barney plays his blasted radio all day." Barney countercharges, "It's not against company policy to play the radio, and I need the radio on to stay alert." A compromise might be for Barney to play the radio every other half hour.

Settling conflicts by compromise sometimes offers suboptimal solutions. Both sides receive something, but the real problem is not solved. Two departments may be in dispute over who is more worthy of receiving $10,000 for a new machine. As a compromise, both sides are allocated $5,000 to purchase a low-priced substitute machine. Unfortunately the $5,000 machines do not perform the job properly—thus wasting $10,000.

Peaceful coexistence. In this approach to resolving conflicts, disagreement is suppressed and commonalities are emphasized. After meeting, both parties decide it is better for the organization to avoid overt displays of disagreement. An obvious advantage of peaceful coexistence is that it leads to satisfactory work relationships between the two parties in dispute. A disadvantage is that since underlying antagonism lingers, the two parties never maximize their potential as a team. Would you want a team of orthopedic surgeons to operate on you if they were in peaceful coexistence? From your standpoint, it would be preferable for the surgical team to have resolved their differences and to be working together synergistically.

Integrative bargaining. Distributive bargaining and compromise are almost the same process—resources are distributed among the two or more people in conflict. What either side gains is at the expense of the other. Distributive bargaining encourages deception, since each side figures it will have to exaggerate its claim in order to earn a sizable share of the resources.

Integrative bargaining is an ideal state in which both parties transcend the conflict mode and move into problem solving. The philosophy is win-win. Suppose the manager of a commercial photo studio had to resolve a dispute between two photographers over who gets to use the Hasselblaad (a very expensive and desirable camera system.) An integrative solution would be to establish which kinds of assignments warranted the use of the Hasselbaad. The photographer receiving such an assignment would be authorized to use the Hasselblaad (for that assignment). The collaborative approaches to negotiation described in the previous chapter are based on a win-win philosophy.

Domination of the other party. The general procedure for conflict resolution described here usually prevents domination of one side by the other. It will be your responsibility to intervene to prevent one side bullying the other. Once when I was trying to resolve conflict between two tenants, one of the tenants offered this solution: "Throw Mary out of the building. Nobody likes her or her kids." (We were able to achieve a state of peaceful coexistence between the tenants that endured until Mary left to rent a house.)

Superordinate goals. An ideal approach to conflict resolution is for the disputants to recognize a common, overriding goal, such as helping the company make a profit or helping their hospital ward save lives. Sometimes this can be achieved by having both sides write down a list of their goals. The lists are then compared and one or more superordinate goals are identified.

In many incidents, labor and management have developed the superordinate goal of surviving under the threats of foreign competition. The unions have moderated their demands and management has exhibited some flexibility in return. A team of management writers cautions that when a crisis of this nature is over "demands for higher wages will undoubtedly return."[5]

Gary tried to help Tony and Laird see the benefits of agreement, In his opening comments, he implied that if the two men would decrease their conflict, the organization would benefit. As Gary mentioned, "I've asked you two fellows to meet with me because I think your differences are getting out of hand. You're both wasting a lot of time sending angry memos to one another. And I think you're both creating morale problems. Just today one of our hourly employees told the plant personnel manager that the feuding between the production and quality departments is causing production delays."

Expansion of resources. Basically, conflict exists because people have to compete for existing resources. Suppose two of your subordinates were in conflict because both were vying for promotion to one group leader position. Assuming economic conditions warranted it, two group leader positions could be established. The resource (group leader position) over which they were competing would have been expanded two-fold. In the process, conflict would be resolved.[6]

Monitoring Organizational Realities and Constraints. Sometimes the solution developed in the conflict resolution session may not take. Factors within the organization may surface which make your solution unworkable. Two feuding employees might decide with your approval to share overtime assignments. All of a sudden a moratorium is declared on overtime, and both parties wind up dissatisfied. Or sometimes emergencies may occur which make it necessary to postpone the conflict resolution session until the emergency situation is processed. Organizational realities and constraints may dictate that you change your solution to conflict or postpone the process until other priorities are taken care of adequately.

The Case for Collaboration and Bargaining Approaches to Conflict Resolution

The majority of conflict resolution strategies described in this chapter fall into one of two categories: (a) collaboration between two or more people in a serious attempt to settle differences among them or (b) bargaining approaches. A compelling argument for these two general approaches is that they are useful in avoiding some of the disadvantages caused by resolving conflict through power play (a general strategy in opposition to collaboration or bargaining). Power plays have been known to harm both the individual and the enterprise.[7] The use of power in resolving conflict is said to:

- Unleash aggressive behaviors and hostile feelings between those involved in the power struggle, shutting off communication and interaction. The mental health of one or both parties may be temporarily upset in the process.
- Promotes vicious gossip, which in turn distorts the valid information needed to manage successfully.
- Drives needed information underground, where it is not used for feedback and correction of counterproductive behavior.
- Sometimes subverts the organizational mission through acts of sabotage and noncompliance.
- Displaces goals because so much of the energy used in the power struggle is diverted from more productive purposes. Winning the struggle often becomes a more important end than achieving an organizational goal.

Collaboration and bargaining are also valuable because of the positive side effects to conflict they foster. Among these advantages of well-managed conflict are:

- Conflict often leads to constructive change. The two parties in conflict will often negotiate solutions that help both parties. One example is the negotiating that has taken place for safer working conditions in mines.
- Conflict revs up the energy and activity levels of people. Under conflict people tend to work harder toward achieving worthwhile goals.
- Conflict stimulates innovative thinking. When people are forced into conflict with others to obtain their share of resources, they tend to put forth more imaginative solutions to problems. One office manager told two subordinates that the company could afford one new duplicating machine this year. The department with the best suggestion for utilizing the machine for maximum benefit would get the machine. The winner was the department head who suggested running odd duplicating jobs for other companies in the same building at a slight profit.

The Case for Power Plays in Resolving Intergroup Conflict

Advocates of the power play argue that the use of force, or power plays, is often easier to accomplish than the tedious processes of collaboration and negotiation. The advocates of power play also see some specific strategic advantages to their strong arm tactics. First, by engaging in power plays, you protect your self-interest and welfare. People with whom you collaborate may not really have your interest in mind. By being uncompromising yourself, your own interests may be served best.

Second, collaboration can make you vulnerable. Collaboration and bargaining both require that you exchange information with your adversary in order to resolve a problem. For example, if you let another department head know the true size of your budget for supplies, he or she might use that information against you when negotiating for more resources.

Third, power-play strategies sometimes contribute to the joint welfare of two adversaries. When both sides push hard for their demands in an uncompromising manner, the ultimate solution may be satisfactory equilibrium, such as the aftermath of a long labor strike.

Fourth, power play is frequently well suited to decide ideological disputes. As analyzed by a conflict resolution specialist: "When values or philosophies clash, the parties are usually intransigent in their conflicting positions. They refuse to problem solve or even negotiate. The only recourse is for one to try to win at the expense of the other, and although neither may emerge victorious, both may emerge saving some face and being 'right' for having taken their stand."[8] One such ideological dispute might take place between an industrial health specialist who believed a particular product additive contributed to cancer and the product manager who believed the product to be harmless.

The Case for Not Resolving Conflict at All

Admittedly, there are many times when conflict between people is so intense that swift resolution is in order. Yet conflict can have so many functions (positive consequences) there are other times when it is more useful to let conflict run its course, or even to stimulate it. It is conceivable, for example, that the conflict described in the opening case could have motivated the production department to elevate quality just to avoid giving satisfaction to the quality department. At the same time, the quality department might have been motivated to maintain close scrutiny over production just to harass them. The net result could be better quality.

In support of the *laissez faire* position about resolving conflict, Dennis King has identified 15 potential advantages of conflict, both personal and organizational. Among the more plausible arguments especially related to conflict between subordinates are the following:[9]

- Conflict is a test of strength and power—it shows who is the stronger of the two disputants.
- Conflict can be a major source of change—a better working relationship might emerge after the conflict.
- Conflict can help surface and clarify issues and goals—for example, the relationship between the production and quality departments may have needed some improvements.
- Conflict can trigger innovation and creativity—in order to outperform one's adversary, a person is likely to search for new ways of doing things.

■ Conflict resulting in competition can improve performance—the sub-ordinates in combat may try to show each other up with high performance.

GUIDELINES FOR ACTION AND SKILL DEVELOPMENT

If your job involves dealing with people, either as a manager or an individual contributor, it is almost inevitable that you will experience interpersonal and intergroup conflict from time to time. Rather than suppress or ignore conflict, it is to your advantage to learn effective techniques to cope with or deal with conflict.

Do not expect a success rate of 90 to 100 percent in resolving conflict. When personal animosities exist between the parties, conflict is likely to erupt again. The conflict resolution technique may have to be repeated several times. In extreme situations, the only practical solution may be to physically separate the two parties.

Do not try to eliminate all conflict among subordinates but do try to resolve conflict with strong negative consequences. An optimum amount of conflict improves individual and organizational performance.

A straighforward way of improving one's skill in resolving conflict between subordinates is to practice all or part of the six-step procedure outlined in this chapter, at the next opportunity. In review: (1) establish a supportive climate; (2) determine the perceptions of both sides; (3) listen without being defensive; (4) isolate the causes of conflict; (5) determine each party's conflict resolution strategy; and (6) monitor organizational realilties and constraints. You can obtain feedback on your conflict resolution effectiveness by observing the extent to which the conflict at hand is resolved.

If an opportunity for resolving conflict on the job does not present itself soon, one might consider trying to resolve conflict among his or her children, or two relatives. The same principles of conflict resolution apply in work and personal life.

Questions and Activities

1. Would Gary Anderson have been better off just ordering Tony Bianco and Laird Howard to cooperate more fully with each other? Explain.
2. What do you see as the relationship between negotiation and conflict resolution?
3. What is your typical approach to resolving conflict with another person? Does it fit one of the tactics described in this chapter?
4. Identify a superordinate goal for two opposing attorneys in a criminal case.

5. Which strategy described in this chapter could readily include the use of money as a vehicle for conflict resolution?

6. What is the difference between the approach to resolving conflict taken by Gary Anderson, versus the role taken by a judge or arbitrator?

7. Get three people together to role play the scenario of a manager trying to resolve conflict between two subordinates over an important issue. Either develop a new scenario or use the opening case in this chapter as material for the role play.

Notes

[1]The original source of this technique appears to be Edgar H. Schein, *Process Consultation: Its Role in Organization Development* (Reading, Mass.: Addison-Wesley, 1969), pp. 71-72.

[2]The six-part process described here is based on Lyle Sussman and Paul D. Krivonos, *Communication for Supervisors and Managers* (Sherman Oaks, Calif.: Alfred Publishing, 1979), pp. 187-91.

[3]Ibid., p. 189.

[4]New data on the widespread use of compromise is found in M. Afzalur Rahim, "A Measure of Styles of Handling Interpersonal Conflict," *Academy of Management Journal*, June 1983, pp. 368-376.

[5]James L. Gibson, John M. Ivancevich, and James H. Donnelly, Jr., *Organizations: Behavior, Structure, Processes*, 4th ed. (Plano, Tex.: Business Publications, 1982), p. 217.

[6]Stephen P. Robbins, *Management: Concepts and Practices* (Englewood Cliffs, N.J.: Prentice-Hall, 1984), p. 400.

[7]The following list is paraphrased from C. Brooklyn Derr, "Managing Organizational Conflict: Collaboration, Bargaining, and Power Approaches," *California Management Review*, Winter 1978, pp. 76-82.

[8]Ibid., p. 80. (The three preceding points are from pp. 79-80.)

[9]Dennis King, "Three Cheers for Conflict!" *Personnel*, January-February 1981, pp. 15-21.

Some Additional References

Brown, David L. *Managing Conflict at Organizational Interfaces.* Reading, Mass.: Addison-Wesley, 1983.

Culbert, Samuel A., and John J. McDonough. *The Invisible War: Pursuing Self-Interest at Work.* New York: John Wiley, 1980.

Fisher, Cynthia D. and Richard Gitelson. "A Meta-Analysis of the Correlates of Role Conflict and Ambiguity." *Journal of Applied Psychology*, May 1983, pp. 320-333.

Howat, Gary and Manuel London. "Attribution of Conflict Management Strategies in Supervisor-Subordinate Dyads." *Journal of Applied Psychology*, April 1980, pp. 172-175.

Stimac, Michele. "Strategies for Resolving Conflict: Their Functional and Dysfunctional Sides." *Personnel*, November-December 1982, pp. 54-64.

Appendix to Chapter 7

The Job Conflict Questionnaire*

To help you develop an appreciation of the symptoms of job conflict, complete the questionnaire shown. Apply it to a place you presently work or have worked in the past. As with many other questionnaires or checklists that you complete for study or research purposes, candor is important. As before, we are not dealing with a scientifically validated instrument.

Directions: Check each of the following statements "mostly agree" or "mostly disagree" as it applies to your place of work.

	Mostly agree	Mostly disagree
1. A few of our departments do not talk to each other.	_____	_____
2. You frequently hear bad things said about other departments.	_____	_____
3. We seem to have more security guards than do most places.	_____	_____
4. You find a lot of graffiti about management in the restrooms.	_____	_____
5. People are fearful of making mistakes around here.	_____	_____
6. Writing nasty memos takes up a lot of our time.	_____	_____
7. A lot of people at our place of work complain about ulcers or other psychosomatic disorders.	_____	_____
8. We have considerable turnover in management.	_____	_____
9. We have considerable turnover among employees.	_____	_____
10. "Finger pointing" and blaming others happens frequently around here.	_____	_____

12. You can almost feel the tension in some
    departments.   _____   _____
13. A widely used expression around here is
    "They are a bunch of fools."   _____   _____
14. We have had several incidents of vandalism
    and sabotage during the last year.   _____   _____
15. We have a lot of bickering over such mat-
    ters as who should do what job.   _____   _____
16. Many people around here say, "That's not
    my job," when asked to do something out
    of the ordinary.   _____   _____
17. Some departments in the organization are
    practically hated.   _____   _____
18. Our organization seems more like a roller
    derby than a team.   _____   _____
19. People rarely help you out because they
    actually want you to look bad in the eyes of
    management.   _____   _____
20. We disagree more than we agree in our
    office (or factory).   _____   _____

Interpretation of Scores. Use this questionnaire primarily as a guide to sensitizing you to the presence of interpersonal and intergroup conflict in a job environment. However, as a measure of conflict, you might use this rough scoring system: if you agreed with 15 or more statements, it probably indicates that you work in a conflict-ridden environment. If you agreed with three or less items, it could mean that too little conflict exists; perhaps people in your company are in danger of becoming too complacent. Scores from 4 to 14, those outside of the extremes, probably indicate that your organization is a mixture of conflict and cooperation. Most work organizations fall into this category.

Chapter 8

The Prevention and Control of Sexual Harassment

The public accounting firm in the case described had not paid much attention to the potential problem of sexual harassment of its employees. Then an incident involving one of its senior auditors and a young CPA triggered the partners into recognizing the importance of two actions. First, establishing a formal policy about sexual harassment within their firm; second, developing a program for its prevention and control.

Brett, the manager of auditing services at Browntree, Gibbons, O'Shea, and Cohen, thought to himself as he looked at his office calendar, "It's time to plan a trip to the Des Moines subsidiary of my major client. It's something I should have done two weeks ago. What a coup if I could get Kathy to go with me. She's real sharp both professionally and personally."

Brett then left an electronic mail note for Kathy that she would most likely access the first thing next morning. It read, "Kathy, please see me right away. We have a key audit assignment that requires our immediate attention." As he entered his message into the computer, Brett felt both excitement and anticipation. He began to visualize how pleasant it would be travelling to Des Moines with Kathy.

As Brett hoped, Kathy showed up at his office the next morning promptly after the start of the working day. In her usual eager way of presenting herself, Kathy asked Brett, "What's up? My display screen tells me there is something big brewing."

"Kathy, here's what I have in mind. United Metals has been asking us to conduct an audit of their Des Moines subsidiary. Although they won't say it directly, I think they suspect that some shoddy financial reporting is taking place in Des Moines. We need to visit them the first three working days of next month. I'm assigning you to be my partner on this audit team. Please free up your calendar. My secretary will make the necessary arrangements."

"You mean that you and I will be working at the Des Moines subsidiary at the same time for three days?"

"Yes, Kathy that's right. Are you surprised?"

"A little surprised, Brett. Especially because a couple of the other juniors in the office have done more work for United Metals than I have."

"It's a question of scheduling. Besides that, you're so sharp that I want the chance to get to know you better professionally. We'll have to leave that Sunday night. I'll be happy to pick you up at your apartment. No sense in both of us leaving cars at the airport for four days. And I only live about four miles from you."

During the flight to Des Moines, Kathy asked Brett a series of questions about auditing procedures used at United Metals, and possible red flags to look for in conducting their audit. After answering several questions perfunctorily, Brett commented, "Kathy, I'd like to save professional conversation for the time we're actually on the client premises. This is a fabulous opportunity for us to get to know each other personally. I want to learn more about you as a human being. Forget the shop talk for now. Here's the service cart coming down the aisle. What are you drinking?"

After the two had checked into the hotel, Brett urged Kathy to have dinner with him. Kathy said she preferred to have a sandwich sent to her room because she was tired from the trip, and also that she wanted to feel fresh and alert for a potentially demanding audit. Begrudgingly, Brett conceded, but nevertheless telephoned Kathy at 10 that night, requesting that they have a drink together. Kathy said that she was ready to retire for the night, but would take a raincheck.

Monday night, Brett and Kathy had dinner with the president and two financial executives of the United Metals subsidiary. It was 10:15 P.M. before the last cordial was served and the check paid. After Brett and Kathy returned to their hotel, Brett asked Kathy if she could be talked into having a nightcap. Kathy refused politely, explaining that she was emotionally and physically exhausted after a day of intense work.

As the next workday drew to a close, Brett motioned to Kathy to meet with him in the conference room they were using as an office. "Kathy, I have a surprise for you. We don't have to be entertained by our clients this evening. Instead, you and I are going to take a well-deserved break. We're going out to dinner at one of the city's best restaurants. We need to go over some important impressions I've been making about the true financial condition of United Metal's facility here."

With an air of reluctance, Kathy responded, "If you think it's necessary to call a business meeting for tonight, I'll comply. But I do think it would be a little more convenient to eat in the hotel restaurant. It would save time and money."

"I'll worry about the money. This evening is on me," said Brett.

As they sat down to dinner, Brett ordered champagne. In response to the quizzical look on Kathy's face, Brett said, "As I have tried to explain to you before, I really like you. It goes beyond just an admiration of your professional skills. I find you to be an alluring and exciting young woman. In this day and age, there is nothing wrong with an established businessman having a personal relationship with a beautiful young woman."

Backing away from the table slightly, Kathy said in an unappreciative tone, "Brett, let me remind you. We are on a business trip. I am not your date. You are my boss, and I respect that. But you are not my boyfriend. There is a big difference."

"I'm not talking about you leaving your boyfriend for me. I just want to have a discreet, but meaningful personal relationship with you that goes far beyond the usual mentoring relationship. I care for you and I want to get emotionally and physically involved with you."

"Brett, are you drunk? This is a business trip. I have never given you any indication that I want more than a superior-subordinate relationship with you. Either you stop your verbal advances or I'll skip dinner."

"Okay, okay, let's talk about Browntree, Gibbons, O'Shea, and Cohen," muttered Brett. After the entree dishes were cleared, Brett returned to the earlier topic. "Maybe, I'm not making myself clear Kathy. If you want to stay on good terms with me, and you want to get ahead in our firm, you and I are going to spend some intimate time together tonight. The situation is ideal. Nobody else will ever know."

Kathy rose from her chair and quickly left the restaurant. Conversation between them was kept to an absolute minimum the next morning and during the trip back home the following afternoon.

The second day back from the trip, Brett found a message on his display terminal stating that Mr. Browntree wanted to see him at his earliest possible convenience. After Brett was seated in Browntree's office, the latter initiated the conversation.

"Brett, we have something of grave consequence to talk about. Kathy has told me all about the uncomfortable pressures you placed on her during the United Metals trip. Based on what she told me, the firm finds you guilty of sexual harassment toward one of our employees. We are totally shocked by your behavior. What can you say in your defense?"

"I may have been a little forward toward Kathy, but I am not guilty of sexual harassment. I never touched her physically. Not even a kiss. I think I am guilty of poor judgment, but not sexual harassment."

Browntree replied, "Sexual harassment, according to its legal definition, includes verbal threats and intimidation. Your suggestion to Kathy that she comply with your wishes if she wanted to advance in the firm is reprehensible."

"The firm and Kathy both have my apologies. I will prepare a written apology if you think it would be appropriate. And you have my promise that it will never happen again. Does that close this matter?"

"By no means," said Browntree. "I am recommending to the other partners that you be placed on probation for six months and that your profit-sharing bonus be denied you this year."

Squirming uncomfortably in his chair, Brett commented, "This is the most embarrassing thing that has ever happened in my career. How am I going to explain it to my wife? What will happen if the other employees and my clients learn of this incident? It could ruin my careeer."

"I wish you had those concerns before you intimidated Kathy," said Browntree as he rose from his chair to end the meeting.

ELEMENTS OF AN EFFECTIVE PROGRAM OF PREVENTION AND CONTROL

The CPA firm described spontaneously handled an incident of sexual harassment involving a senior male employee making unwanted sexual advances toward a junior female employee. Many organizations today rely less on spontaneous judgment and more on formalized procedures in managing sexual harassment. These formalized procedures have arisen in response to the related forces of government involvement in the problem, and a growing awareness of sexual harassment in the workplace.

Below we describe the elements of an effective program for the prevention and control of sexual harassment based on experience in a variety of work organizations. The program is designed to deal with the many varieties of sexual harassment (presented in decreasing order of frequency): males against females; males against males; females against males; and females against females.

Be Aware of the Meaning of Sexual Harassment

An effective program of prevention and control begins with an agreed-upon definition of the problem. The definition of sexual harassment provided by the Equal Employment Opportunity Commission (EEOC) is widely accepted because it has legal stature. It defines the problem as

> Unwelcome sexual advances, requests for sexual favors, and other verbal or physical conduct of a sexual nature when (1) submission to such conduct is made either explicitly or implicitly a term or condition of an individual's employment, (2) submission to or rejection of such conduct by an individual is used as the basis for employment decisions affecting the individual, or (3) such conduct has the purpose or effect of unreasonably interfering with an individual's work performance or creating an intimidating, hostile, or offensive working environment.[1]

The American Federation of State, County, and Municipal Employees has developed a definition of sexual harassment, not necessarily linked to adverse job actions taken against the employee who refuses to comply with the harasser. According to the union (AFSCME):

> Sexual harassment encompasses a wide range of unwanted, sexually directed behavior including rape, other physical or verbal abuse. It may or may not be accompanied by threats of adverse job actions or promises of raises and promotions. However, all sexual harassment constitutes discrimination because it subjects the worker to adverse employment conditions having nothing to do with job performance or qualifications.[2]

An advantage of this definition is that it encompasses unwanted sexual advances among co-workers. A case in point is the complaint made by many female production employees that they are harassed by male co-workers who fondle them, make verbal suggestive remarks toward them, and even use "flashing" as a form of humor on the job.

It may prove helpful to supplement the two legalistic definitions with the informal, comprehensive definition provided by the Working Woman's Institute:

> Sexual harassment is any unwanted attention of a sexual nature from someone in the workplace that creates discomfort and/or interferes with the job.[3]

Establish a Policy about Sexual Harassment

A large number of private, public, and nonprofit organizations have developed formal policies about sexual harassment. Such policies make a major contribution to the prevention and control of sexual harassment, particularly if they are widely disseminated throughout the organization. It will be helpful to examine two representative policies dealing with the issue under discussion.

Here is a policy statement following the often-used approach of linking sexual harassment policy to the law:

The Equal Employment Opportunity Commission (EEOC) has issued guidelines setting forth the Commission's interpretation regarding sexual harassment as a violation of Title VII of the Civil Rights Act of 1964. These guidelines are consistent with our long-standing policy that conduct creating an intimidating, hostile, or offensive working environment will not be tolerated and those violating this practice may be subject to disciplinary action up to and including discharge. To make sure employees are aware of management's position toward sexual harassment, the following should be considered:

1. Review policies to determine if sexual harassment is adequately identified as unacceptable conduct.
2. Examine the need for additional communication.
3. Encourage employees to discuss their sexual harassment concerns with supervision.
4. Include in supervisory training programs a discussion of sexual harassment and the need for supervision to take timely corrective action when the problem exists.[4]

A broader approach to policy making in this area suggests that a policy statement on sexual harassment should also encompass racial, ethnic, and religious harassment since the same concepts of liability apply. A sample company policy of this nature is:

Since the founding of *(name of firm)*, it has been our policy to provide all employees with a work environment free of any form of discrimination, including sexual harassment.

In addition, The *(State)* Fair Employment Practices Act and Title VII of the 1964 Civil Rights Act prohibits discrimination on the basis of race, color, sex, national origin, religion, and pregnancy. Under both of these laws, it is illegal for an employee to engage in unwelcome sexual advances, requests for sexual favors, verbal or physical conduct of a sexual nature, or any other verbal conduct that might be construed as a racial, ethnic, or religious slur.

Such behavior, regardless if committed by a supervisor or co-worker, will be considered employee misconduct and will be subject to employee disciplinary action, up to and including termination.

Any questions regarding corporate policy, state or federal law or complaints regarding any form of harassment should be addressed to our vice president of human resources or the president of the firm.[5]

A logical corollary of a formal policy against sexual harassment is to treat employees equitably, thus reducing chances of a sexual harassment complaint. An example would be for a male supervisor not to give preference to a female subordinate when making assignments that involve long periods of working alone together (such as done by Brett in choosing Kathy for the trip to Des Moines). "Equitably," however, does not mean that males should avoid choosing females to accompany them on business trips, or vice versa.

Adopt Sanctions

Policies against sexual harassment will be strengthened to the extent that policy violators are punished. Donald J. Petersen and Douglass Massengill recommend that the penalties for sexual harassment be made a part of regular company rules. They note that a major-minor system of rule violations is used in many organizations. Major rule violations lead to discharge for one offense, but lesser offenses lead to lesser sanctions such as verbal warnings, written warnings, and suspensions. For blatant sexual harassment such as rape or attempted rape (a major rule violation), discharge may be the appropriate response. For lesser acts of harassment, the harasser may receive a smaller penalty based on the nature of the offense, and the schedule of the organization's penalties.[6]

In support of this reasoning, the EEOC guidelines suggest considering each case on its own merits. Thus, the penalty imposed on Brett—probation and the forfeiture of one's year bonus—would seem stiff but not inappropriate.

Develop Mechanisms for Investigating Complaints

For a program of sexual harassment and control to be effective, it is important for the organization to encourage the complaining employees to protest through formal channels developed for that purpose. Petersen and Massengill found that 40 of the 68 *Fortune* 500 firms responding to their survey had a formal complaint procedure. Those firms with a formal complaint procedure (for harassment) were more likely to have dealt with such a problem than those without a formal procedure (74 percent versus 29 percent).[7]

A related study showed that if clear organizational policies against sexual harassment are developed, information about sanctions disseminated, and standard procedures for dealing with incidents of harassment are developed, a predictable trend occurs. At first there is an increase in the number of complaints of sexual harassment by employees. However, if the anti-harassment policies are maintained, complaints will begin to decline.[8]

The four more frequently used formal complaint channels are these:

1. Arrange appointment with top-level director of human resources.
2. Open door policy—bring in complaint anytime to top level manager without having to go through the chain of command.
3. Follow chain of command in making complaint.
4. Contact equal employment opportunity (EEO) manager.[9]

Develop Mechanisms for Handling the Accused

It has already been suggested that the individual accused of sexual harassment should receive sanctions that are commensurate with the particular offense. Jeanne Bosson Driscoll notes furthermore that a person accused of harassment must be assured of a fair and thorough investigation that protects his or her individual rights. This is particularly true given the current emotional climate surrounding sexual harassment.[10] It must also be recognized that not every complaint of sexual harassment is valid. One problem is that some instances of sexual harassment are based upon subjective interpretations of what constitutes harassment. At one college, a woman student complained that she was sexually harassed by one of her professors. The substance of the complaint was that the professor said to her, "I've always admired beautiful and intelligent young women. If I were much younger, I would like to marry someone like you." (Bad judgment, yes; harassment no!)

Another reason for carefully investigating complaints of harassment is that these complaints are sometimes used as a form of blackmail. A male maintenance worker in an office building told his boss (a male), "If you don't get me a raise, I'm going to tell the company that you refused to get me one because I wouldn't have sex with you." The worker did bring forth the complaint, but it was later dismissed as frivolous.

Driscoll reports that employees who are cited as acting in a manner that another employee perceives as sexually harassing, may require assistance to understand the other's point of view. They may also need personal counseling to obtain further insight into how to control their behavior. If termination is required, outplacement may be advisable.[11] (Outplacement is a formal program of helping an employee find a new job or career, with the assistance of professional counseling.) In short, the sexual harasser should be granted the same due process granted employees charged with other offenses.

Develop Mechanisms for Handling Victims of Harassment

Employees who feel sexually harassed may require counseling support and assurance that the organization will protect their rights as well as investigate all allegations. Some employees are reluctant to make formal charges of harassment out of fear of reprisal. The harassment victim should also be assured that appropriate disciplinary action will be taken. It may also be necessary to help the harassed persons realize that they are not responsible for the actions of the initiator. Victims of harassment often feel guilty for somehow having encouraged such behavior on the part of their harasser.[12] For instance, the harassed individual is sometimes accused of having acted in a sexually provocative manner toward co-workers and superiors.

In some cases, the feelings of the harassment victim are similar to those experienced by rape victims. Driscoll observes that "The combination of rage and guilt can be long-lasting and can affect one's ability to be productive. Counseling should be provided to help the victim sort out those feelings and gain understanding of the situation and the feelings it generated."[13]

Provide an Appropriate Training Program

A comprehensive strategy for preventing sexual harassment is to provide appropriate training at all levels in the organization. As mentioned in one of the policy statements above, the topic should be introduced in supervisory training programs. These programs should communicate the type of information presented in this chapter, such as definitions of sexual harassment, company policy statements on the issue, EEOC rulings about harassment, and the rights of both the accused and victims. An underlying purpose of the training program is to increase the level of awareness about the problem throughout the organization.

Another major purpose of a sexual harassment training program is to overcome the credibility problem surrounding the subject. George K. Kronenberger and David L. Bourke report that many male employees cannot believe that their language, attitudes, and jokes can be construed as sexual harassment. The training program, therefore, has to be quite specific and well planned. Kronenberger and Bourke suggest that the following should be incorporated into an EEOC training program about sexual harassment.[14]

Moderately Technical Level. The program should present a brief description of relevant federal and state or provincial law. Yet, if the discussion enters into great detail, the audience may become confused and alienated. Human resource specialists and company lawyers can be consulted for more legal detail when it is needed.

Corporate Policies. The training program on sexual harassment may present a timely opportunity to reaffirm existing corporate policies on equal employment opportunity and training. The message can be communicated that concern about sexual harassment fits into existing concern about decreasing discrimination in the workplace.

Judicial Examples. Actual judicial actions should be presented to emphasize the legal implications of the issue and to show how the courts are likely to view acts of sexual harassment. A representative case used in these training programs is *Miller vs. Bank of America.* Its essential points are as follows:

> Margaret Miller alleged that she was discharged from the Bank of America because she refused her supervisor's demands for sexual favors. The bank argued that it had established (1) a policy prohibiting sexual harassment, and (2) an inhouse grievance mechanism. Therefore, Bank of America contended that it was not liable for its supervisors' actions. The Ninth Circuit Court of Appeals ruled that despite the administrative policies and mechanisms, Bank of America was still liable because supervisors were acting as its agents.

Miller is considered a value training case because it shows that human resource specialists and managers from other functions must take affirmative action to stop acts of sexual harassment and that concerted action is necessary to limit company liability.[15]

Corporate Examples. If it can be done with sensitivity and confidentiality, it is helpful to review company cases of sexual harassment. Such cases are more readily used in large organizations where the participants may not be aware of the case under discussion.

Extent of Employee Involvement. Ideally, all employees should participate in the program. At a minimum, all first-level managers should attend the training program. Those employees who do not attend the program should be made aware of its major aspects. Supervisors can conduct staff meetings to disseminate some of the information, particularly the EEOC guidelines and company policy.

Competent Trainers. To enhance credibility, the training program should be administered by employees with sufficient company experience and adequate background in EEO matters so that all questions can be answered authoritatively. Training of this type can sometimes be conducted externally. Among the sources are management consultants and education associations (such as the American Management Association) who sometimes offer programs on the prevention and control of sexual harassment.

Specific Techniques on Dealing with Acts of Harassment. Although the program just presented is of merit, it may need to be supplemented with specific techniques for controlling the sexual harassment of one individual by another. At times the discussion of specific strategies will suffice, but at other times role-plays may be more effective. Following are two specific suggestions for dealing with harassers that have been incorporated into training programs:

The easiest way to deal with sexual harassment is to nip it in the bud. The first time it happens respond with a statement of this type: "I won't tolerate this kind of talk." "I dislike sexually oriented jokes." "Keep your hands off me."

A woman's best defense against harassment is a polite, nonthreatening, "No." That is particularly true for verbal harassment unconnected to receiving preferred treatment on the job. Sometimes ordinarily sensitive men will engage in this kind of talk or action, unaware that they are being offensive. If the man persists despite receiving a repeated "No," the woman should consider a surprise act of physical retaliation. Suppose the man continues to pat the woman's rump from time to time. The woman might try punching *him* in the rump. The shock effect may very well work.[16]

THE CASE FOR AND AGAINST FORMAL PROGRAMS RELATING TO SEXUAL HARASSMENT AND CONTROL

There are several pressing reasons why organizations should embark upon a formal program of preventing and controlling sexual harassment. One primary consideration is humanitarian: Sexual harassment has been characterized as the most widespread problem women face in the workforce. It has been estimated that up to 88 percent of employed women are sexually harassed in one form or another.[17] Another justification for such programs is that they have a large potential for being cost-effective. A survey of more than 17,000 federal employees, conducted by the Merit Systems Protection Board, concluded that sexual harassment cost tax payers $205 million during a two-year period in sick leave, lost productivity, and turnover.[18]

Employer liability for acts of sexual harassment committed by employees is another reason top management should favor programs of sexual harassment prevention and control. Several major court cases have supported the EEOC position that the employer is responsible for sexual harassment by its employees—even if they were forbidden by the employer and regardless of whether the employer knew or should have known of their occurrence.[19] The governing legal principle states: "The fact of delegation of authority to the supervisor by the employer makes the employer responsible for any exercise of that authority in violation of Title VII."[20]

The case against formal programs of this nature does not dismiss the significance of sexual harassment in the workplace. It simply argues that mature adults should take responsibility for their own behavior without external control exerted by both the employer and government. If an employee is harassed by another, the former should handle it in the way that he or she would handle another employee who violated his or her rights in any other way. The harassment victim could retaliate directly by filing a complaint with the employer or police.

It can also be argued that an astute individual should be able to prevent a potentially harassing situation from progressing too far. You will recall that Kathy, the young CPA, handled herself quite well. The tips about warding off harassment mentioned in the training program above could be implemented by any person with good intuition and interpersonal skills.

GUIDELINES FOR ACTION AND SKILL DEVELOPMENT

Although the elements of an effective program for the prevention and control of sexual harassment presented above should be interpreted as action steps, a few summary tips are in order (one for the organization, one for the supervisor, and one for the trainer).

Based on his review of legal cases, Robert H. Faley advises that the most significant thing an employer can do is to take the problem of sexual harassment seriously. Top management should demonstrate by its actions a genuine concern for the sensitivity to the issues.[21]

The best preventive measure the supervisor can take is to avoid harassing behavior. The *appearance* of innocence can sometimes be as important as actual innocence. A survey showed that male supervisors should avoid placing themselves in compromising situations such as driving female employees home after work, engaging in sexually suggestive conversations, and having unnecessary "business dinners."[22]

Because sexual harassment is a sensitive and ambiguous subject, the person conducting a training program about it should try to know the audience and not be viewed as condescending or dogmatic. An improper attitude may alienate the group and render the program ineffective.[23] Humor should be used sparingly and with sensitivity. A tasteful joke can relieve tension, while a tasteless joke will be interpreted as a sexist slur and alienate members of the audience.

Based on the author's experience, here is a joke that relieves tension without engendering anger and resentment: "Recent data indicate that many young men employees are filing complaints that they are being sexually harassed by their women bosses. My suspicions are that some of these complaints are valid, but in most cases the men are either bragging or dreaming."

Questions and Activities

1. How fair do you think Browntree was in his handling of Brett?
2. Can you offer Kathy any constructive criticism for the way she handled the situation with Brett?
3. What do you see as the conceptual link between conflict resolution, and the prevention and control of sexual harassment?
4. Is the attention management is paying to sexual harassment a fad? Or is it likely to be a permanent concern? Explain.
5. Identify two suggestions made in this chapter that deal more directly with the prevention (rather than the control) of sexual harassment.

6. According to any of the definitions of sexual harassment presented in this chapter, is telling sexually oriented jokes to another employee a form of sexual harassment? Explain.

7. Interview a couple of managers or human resource specialists to obtain their answers to the following: Identify three sexually oriented statements or actions that are (a) clearly a form of sexual harassment, and (b) clearly not. Also give your answers.

Notes

[1] Equal Employment Opportunity Commission Guidelines on Sexual Harassment, April 10, 1980. (29 C.F.R. No. 1604.11 [a])

[2] Quoted in *Sexual Harassment and Labor Relations: A BNA Special Report*, Washington, D.C.: The Bureau of National Affairs, Inc., 1981.

[3] Quoted in Kay Bartlett, "Is Sexual Harassment in the Work Place the 1980s Glamour Cause?" Associated Press story printed in Rochester *Democrat and Chronicle*, February 28, 1982, p. 1C.

[4] Donald J. Petersen and Douglass Massengill, "Sexual Harassment—A Growing Problem in the Work Place," *Personnel Administrator*, October 1982, p. 83.

[5] Adapted from George K. Kronenberger and David L. Bourke, "Effective Training and the Elimination of Sexual Harassment," *Personnel Journal*, November 1981, pp. 882–883.

[6] Petersen and Massengill, "Sexual Harassment," p. 87.

[7] Ibid., p. 84.

[8] Ibid.

[9] Ibid.

[10] Jeanne Bosson Driscoll, "Sexual Attraction and Harassment: Management's New Problems," *Personnel Journal*, January 1981, p. 36.

[11] Ibid.

[12] Ibid.

[13] Ibid.

[14] George K. Kronenberger and David L. Bourke, "Effective Training and the Elimination of Sexual Harassment," *Personnel Journal*, November, 1981, p. 880.

[15] Adapted from ibid., p. 881.

[16] "Abusing Sex at the Office," *Newsweek*, March 10, 1980, p. 82.

[17] Data summarized in Robert H. Faley, "Sexual Harassment: Critical Review of Legal Cases with General Principles and Preventive Measures," *Personnel Psychology*, Autumn 1982, p. 584.

[18] Survey reported in Bartlett, "Is Sexual Harassment in the Work Place," p. 1C. Dollar figure adjusted to curent value.

[19] Elizabeth C. Wesman, "Shortage of Research Abets Sexual Harassment Confusion" *Personnel Administrator*, November 1983, p. 62.

[20] Nancy Fisher Chudacoff, "New EEOC Guidelines On Discrimination Because of Sex: Employee Liability for Sexual Harassment Under Title VII," *Boston University Law Review*, March 1981, p. 542. Quoted in ibid.

[21] Faley, "Sexual Harassment: Critical Review," p. 597.

[22] Petersen and Massengill, "Sexual Harassment—A Growing Problem," p. 86.

[23] Kronenberger and Bourke, "Effective Training," p. 880.

Some Additional References

Collins, Eliza G. C. "Managers and Lovers." *Harvard Business Review*, September-October 1983, pp. 142–53.

Cunningham, Susan. "Suit Leads to Study of Sexual Harassment on the Job." American Psychological Association *Monitor*, January 1984, p. 10.

Diamond, Robin, and Lynn Feller. *Sexual Harassment Action Kit*. Washington, D.C.: American Psychological Association, 1981.

Josefowitz, Natasha. "Sexual Relationships at Work: Attraction, Transference, Coercion or Strategy," *Personnel Administrator*, March 1982, pp. 91–96.

Part 3

Improving the Functioning of Work Groups

The three techniques, methods, and programs of applied management described in the next three chapters focus primarily on the small work group. It is important to recognize that distinctions among individual, group, and organizational level are not absolute. Obviously, a small work group is composed of individuals, and the larger organization is composed of both individuals and small groups. Also, small group techniques such as quality circles are used to enhance organizational effectiveness.

As with any of the behavioral-science based techniques presented in this book, those described stem from a core of theory and research. Chapter 9, Conducting an Effective Meeting, is derived from both social psychology and organizational communications. Chapter 10, Building Teamwork, is based on a number of sources. The discussion of managerial strategies for building teamwork is based on group dynamics or small group psychology. The discussion of autonomous work groups describes an approach to organization design based on sociotechnical systems, an attempt to inter-relate principles of organization structure with principles of work motivation (particularly with respect to the satisfaction of human needs).

Chapter 11, Quality Circles, describes a program aimed at improving the quality of goods and services by way of soliciting employee suggestions. It is a currently popular, yet increasingly controversial, technique rooted in the canons of participative management.

Chapter 9

Conducting an Effective Meeting

The executive staff of a building maintenance company held a meeting to deal with a major decision facing the company: whether to locate their expanded company headquarters downtown or in a suburban office park. The executives used a combination of intuition and common sense to guide the conduct of the meeting.

Building Maintenance, Inc., a firm of 325 full- and part-time employees is engaged in the cleaning and general maintenance of offices and shopping plazas. Starting as an operation of "one man and one van" about 10 years ago, BMI has grown into the largest firm of its kind in its region. Bud, the founder and president of BMI, is the major shareholder of this privately held firm. The other four members of the executive team are also major shareholders. At present, the company is headquartered in an old office building scheduled for demolition.

The pending demolition has forced the firm to face a relocation decision. Bud has called a 10 A.M. meeting of the executive team to address this problem. Two days before the meeting he sent a memo announcing the meeting (see Exhibit 9–1).

The morning of the meeting, Bud rushed into his office at 10:10. Karen, Liz, Marty, and Nick were already seated.

Bud: Sorry to be a few minutes late. I got tied up at the bank, talking to a loan officer. You know how much detail those bankers can sometimes demand. The reason I called us together is to decide where to locate our new offices. I assume you've given some thought to this matter already.

Let me go over the alternatives I see. We can either relocate to some

Exhibit 9-1
Memo Used by Business Owner to Announce Meeting

BUILDING MAINTENANCE INCORPORATED
"Your cleanliness is our business."

TO: The Executive Team (Karen, Marty, Liz, and Nick)
FROM: Bud
DATE: March 13th
SUBJECT: Office relocation

Demolition Day is fast approaching. Let's meet in my office, March 15th at 10 A.M. to wrestle with this problem. We've got to relocate someplace. Put on your thinking caps and be prepared to reach a quick decision.
See you then.

---

decent space in one of the newly refurbished downtown buildings, or we can get some slightly better space in a suburban park. Karen, as our financial officer, you must have some relevant facts and figures.

Karen: As you requested a few weeks ago, Bud, I have looked into a variety of possibilities. We can get the decent downtown space you describe at about $21 per square foot. And, we can get first-rate accommodations in a suburban office park for about $22 per square foot. Relocation costs would be about the same. So it's a wash with respect to rental fees.

Bud: Now, we've heard it from the financial side. Marty, from your vantage point as sales director, where do you think we should relocate?

Marty: That's what I like to see, a business owner who puts the customers up front at all times. I agree strongly that the demands of our customers should always carry the heaviest weight with respect to any internal decision we make. Too many large organizations fall victim to the trap of letting bureaucracy overshadow their concern for the external environment. At least, I read something to that effect in a business magazine.

Customers are influenced by image. So long as we have a good image, I think the customer will be satisfied. By the way, we are doing something that is negatively affecting our image to customers. Our order clerks are just too rude over the phone. I think these gals should have proper training before we turn them loose on the customer phone. Remember, all we sell is service. Lots of other companies have good brooms, vacuum cleaners, and power-cleaning equipment. Our only edge is the good service we offer customers.

I'm glad I had the chance to make this point.

Bud: Liz, what is your position on this relocation decision?

Liz: As employment director, I have a lot to say about relocation. I agree with Marty that customer service should receive top weight in any decision we make about relocation. Customer service, of course, is a direct result of having an efficient crew of maintenance employees. A suburban office park may sound glamorous, but it could be a disaster in terms of getting help. Maintenance workers know how to get downtown, and can afford to get downtown. The vast majority of them live in the city and they are dependent on mass transit to get to work.

You typically need private transportation to get to an office park. The vast majority of our permanent and temporary employees do not own cars. And many of them that do own cars, usually can't afford to keep them in good repair. Many of the temporary help can only put gas in their cars on payday.

So if we relocate to a suburban park, we'll have to rent a small employment office downtown anyway.

Bud: So you're telling us that maybe we should choose both alternatives. We should open an employment office downtown and move the executive office to a suburban office park.

Liz: I agree with part of your reasoning, Bud. Yet, I think you're putting words in my mouth. I'm less concerned about where we put the executive office. My big worry is to have a location that makes it possible for us to hire the employees we need.

Karen: Now, we're introducing a third alternative. We could have two offices downtown. One for the executive and clerical staff, and one for recruiting and selecting help.

By the way, who was supposed to bring the coffee and pastry to this meeting? How can you make a big decision without refreshments?

Bud: Nick, what do you think? Which location would be best for you as director of maintenance operations?

Nick: I'm not in the office too much. I spend most of my time in the field overseeing our supervisors and their crews. Most of our help never see the office after they are hired unless they have a major problem. They report directly to the site. To them their place of work is the building or shopping plaza where they are assigned. Other things are more important than location.

One of the important things we should be considering is a big holiday party this year. Our biggest competitor holds a once-a-year party that every employee gets invited to. It's a real morale builder. I think it's cost effective in terms of how much turnover it reduces. Some of the cleaning help stay on for a couple of extra months just to attend the party.

So far nobody has mentioned the color and furnishings of the new offices. To me, office decor is as important as location.

Karen: Nick, do you have any figures to prove the cost-effectiveness of an annual company party? It can run about $20 for each person in attendance. We can expect that more than two-thirds of the employees will bring a guest.

Nick: So what? You can't put a dollar figure on morale.

Marty: It looks like you folks have got the major issues out on the table. I really don't care where we locate so long as the needs of the customer come first. I'm eager to know what you folks decide. But right now I have to run. I have a luncheon appointment on the other side of town that could mean a big shopping-plaza contract for us. As I said before, I'm more concerned about customers than internal bureaucracy.

Bud: Good luck with the sales call, Marty. However, I suspect you could have scheduled that luncheon for another day. This is a pretty important topic. I'd like you to stay five more minutes.

Nick: Bud, you're the boss. What do you think should be our relocation choice? We'll go along with any sensible decision.

Bud: It seems that it's premature for us to reach a decision on this important matter today. Maybe we should call in an office location consultant to help us decide what to do. In the meantime, let's talk some more about the office party. I kind of like that idea.

SUGGESTIONS FOR CONDUCTING A PRODUCTIVE MEETING

The BMI meeting illustrates an event that is repeated innumerable times every working day: many meetings fail to accomplish their intended purpose because they are conducted poorly. Here we describe a wide range of suggestions for conducting productive meetings, based on a mixture of experience, common sense, and research. A meeting in this sense is any gathering of people with a purpose in mind, including staff meetings, committee meetings, task force meetings, strategy sessions, and meetings called for the purpose of practicing participative management. The common thread to all these meetings is that the group is trying to solve some type of problem, and therefore either make a decision or lay the ground for making one.

As you review the suggestions for conducting meetings, relate them to the BMI meeting. The vignette was purposely chosen because it violates so many principles and practices of importance in conducting a productive (or effective) meeting. The suggestions are divided into two general categories: those dealing more with (a) the structure and process of meetings, and (b) the people present at the meeting. Although most of the suggestions are aimed at the leader, many of them can be applied to other participants at the meeting. For example, the leader should strive to keep others from going off on tangents. At the same time, each person should share the responsibility of staying on track. Additionally, one participant can sometimes help another stay on track by making a polite request to that effect.

Dealing with Structure and Process

The structure of a meeting includes organization and agenda, timing, and physical arrangements. In this context, process refers to activities such as drawing up minutes, providing summaries, and directing effort toward surmountable problems. The 17 suggestions presented in this section reflect and summarize contemporary thinking about improving structure and process to make meetings more productive.

Have a Valid Reason for Calling a Meeting. Many meetings are unproductive simply because there was no valid reason for calling them. A meeting is justified primarily when there is a need for coordinated effort or interaction on the part of participants. If straightforward, factual information needs to be collected or disseminated, memos can be substituted for meetings. Peter A. Turla and Kathleen L. Hawkins make this analysis:

> Before calling a meeting, assess whether the time invested in the meeting is going to equal or exceed the dollar yield. Do you need advice from all the people who will attend? Do you need group involvement to make a decision or solve a common problem? Do you need a group vote to approve new policies?[1]

Based on the above criteria, Bud was certainly justified in calling a meeting to decide about the new office location.

Have a Specific Agenda and Stick to It. Few people in a work setting would deny the importance of having an agenda, distributing it in advance of the meeting, and staying on track. Yet, this could be the most frequently violated principle of conducting a productive meeting. The agenda should be distributed about 24 hours prior to the meeting, even though the meeting and its general purpose should be announced much sooner. If the agenda is distributed too early it may be lost or forgotten. Most people can prepare themselves for a meeting within 24 hours.

An agenda should, if possible, include at least one agenda item of high potential interest to each participant. An exciting agenda item adds a spark to the meeting that may spill over to other topics to be discussed. Examples of almost universally exciting agenda items include discussions of cash bonuses, salary increases, and layoffs.

Decide Carefully Who Should Attend. Considerable time is wasted in meetings because planners do not carefully select participants. The skills, authority, and motivation of the participants should be appropriate for the task at hand. Barbara C. Palmer and Kenneth R. Palmer note that if you are orchestrating a group responsible for identifying and evaluating alternatives for toxic waste disposal you would not want morticians, librarians, and driver education teachers involved, but chemists, botanists, biologists, physicians, and possibly urban planners.[2]

Another source of low productivity is the failure to invite people who are prepared or authorized to act, as opposed to those who cannot or choose not to make decisions. Inviting people to the meeting who regard attendance as a punishment rather than a reward can also contribute to an unproductive meeting.

It may also be important to invite to the meeting those people whom you are trying to convince, or whose cooperation you need. As one manufacturing manager commented, "I always invite representatives from finance and engineering to our key planning meetings. It helps explain to them some of the problems we face in making a product."

Schedule the Meeting at a Convenient Time and Location. To minimize the risk of poor attendance, schedule a meeting at a time and location that will make it feasible for most people to attend.[3] Perhaps Bud should not have scheduled a meeting so close to lunchtime, knowing that the sales director would most likely have scheduled a business lunch. A preferred meeting time for most busy managers and professionals is at the start or toward the end of a working day. When the people required or invited to attend a meeting are from dispersed locations, it is helpful to choose a central site.

A related consideration is that some geographic locations are easier to reach than others, whether or not they are centralized. Time lost on ground transportation in major cities has become a concern for many business people. For this reason, many business conferences today are held at hotels located adjacent to airports. Teleconferencing is growing in popularity as a way of cutting down time spent traveling to meetings. However, the teleconference location must also be chosen with care.

Start and Stop the Meeting on Time. Meetings that are held to their designated starting and stopping time contribute to an organizational culture of professionalism. When a meeting starts late, the prompt attendees are penalized and the latecomers are rewarded. A precedent may then be established for people to arrive habitually late for meetings. Short time limits should be set on meetings whenever possible (perhaps 45 minutes to one hour). The underlying reason is that meetings follow Parkinson's Law: They tend to expand (or contract) to fill the allotted time.[4]

Recently some attention has been paid to *standup* meetings as a way of shortening their length.[5] If people are forced to stand, they are more likely to feel uncomfortable and will move quickly through the agenda to minimize discomfort. However, there are several real problems with standup meetings. Attendees cannot take notes comfortably; they may feel so awkward that their attention will be diverted; and, the meeting may not be taken seriously because it departs so far from standard business practice.

Direct Effort toward Surmountable Problems. Many meetings are ineffective because participants spend time discussing "who is to blame for the problem," or "what should have been done to avoid the problem."[6] Rather than try to change the past, it is better to invest energy and time into dealing with how things can be improved in the future. To the credit of the BMI team, at least they did not spend time bemoaning the fact that they had rented space in a building so old that demolition in the near future was inevitable.

Keep Comments Brief and to the Point. One of the major challenges facing the meeting leader is keeping conversation on track. Marty's well-intended comments about responding to customer needs is a good example of tangential discussion during a business meeting. One way for the leader to keep comments on target is to respond only to targeted comments. Another method is to ask the participant, "How does your comment relate to the agenda?" As a last resort, the leader might have to respond sternly, "You've made your point about that issue, but now we have to get back to the purpose of the meeting."

Participants, too, have an obligation to keep their comments focused on the problem at hand. Aside from lowering the productivity of meetings, irrelevant comments annoy other members. Participants can also play a leadership role by subtly asking other participants to avoid tangents.

Despite the importance of not making irrelevant comments, a meeting should allow some room for spontaneity and the introduction of important ideas that might be dealt with at a future meeting. A major underlying purpose of some meetings might be to foster informal discussion.

Provide Summaries for Each Major Point. An effective way of keeping a meeting focused on important issues is for the leader to provide summaries of each major point after they are made. Doing so provides structure to the meeting and gives members the feeling that something specific is being accomplished. Instead of concluding that it was premature to reach a conclusion, Bud might have summarized the several different viewpoints offered about where the new office should be relocated. The group could then have possibly rexamined their thinking.

Repeat or Restate Unclear Comments. Participants at a meeting often mumble or present their ideas in an unclear manner. The leader can play a valuable role in repeating or restating these comments so that they can be understood by other group members. If the leader does not understand either, the participant can be asked to "Please restate your point. Some of us did not follow you."

Set Up a Physical Structure That Encourages Communication. A circular, semi-circular, or elliptical arrangement of members encourages verbal interaction. In contrast, a typical classroom arrangement discourages two-way communication among participants. A provocative analysis of ways that physical seating arrangements and layouts influence interaction at meetings is presented in Figure 9-1.

Use Parliamentary Procedure Only for Legalistic Meetings. Parliamentary law, as exemplified by *Robert's Rules of Order*, provides specific rules for conducting a meeting including such items as when motions can be introduced, who can second a motion, and what proportion of members have to vote affirmatively on a motion for it to be passed. These rules tend to discourage informal interaction, spontaneity, and creativity. Also, they tend to create a dreary, somber atmosphere that often detracts from group effectiveness.

Nevertheless, parliamentary procedure does have its place. Legislation (the making of rules and laws) usually requires the assistance of rules of order.[7] To illustrate, the boards that oversee the activities of licensed professionals in the United States and Canada conduct their meetings according to parliamentary procedure. At these meetings, rules sometimes are formulated that govern the behavior of self-employed professionals (such as specifying the amount of job experience an engineer must have before being qualified to obtain a license).

Use Handouts Sparingly. Most people attending a meeting expect to receive at least one handout summarizing an important issue related to the central topic. With the almost universal availability of photocopying machines, the distribution of handouts at meetings has reached the point that many participants suffer from communication overload. Another problem with distributing handouts at a meeting is that it leads to participants' reading the handouts rather than listening to each other or making spoken contributions.

Take Minutes and Distribute Them Promptly (if Necessary). A relatively small percentage of meetings require minutes. Yet minutes are necessary under conditions such as:

1. Policy affecting a large number of people or organizations is being formulated.
2. A high volume of business is being transacted.
3. A continuing need to consult the record of the group's activities is anticipated.
4. Follow-up implementation activities are assigned at the meeting.[8]

Figure 9–1
Alternative Meeting Room Layouts

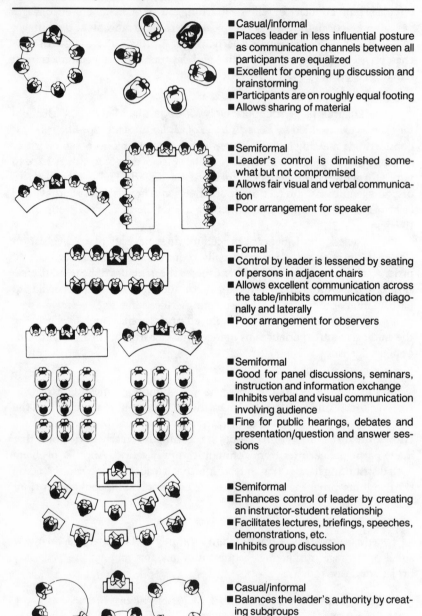

- Casual/informal
- Places leader in less influential posture as communication channels between all participants are equalized
- Excellent for opening up discussion and brainstorming
- Participants are on roughly equal footing
- Allows sharing of material

- Semiformal
- Leader's control is diminished somewhat but not compromised
- Allows fair visual and verbal communication
- Poor arrangement for speaker

- Formal
- Control by leader is lessened by seating of persons in adjacent chairs
- Allows excellent communication across the table/inhibits communication diagonally and laterally
- Poor arrangement for observers

- Semiformal
- Good for panel discussions, seminars, instruction and information exchange
- Inhibits verbal and visual communication involving audience
- Fine for public hearings, debates and presentation/question and answer sessions

- Semiformal
- Enhances control of leader by creating an instructor-student relationship
- Facilitates lectures, briefings, speeches, demonstrations, etc.
- Inhibits group discussion

- Casual/informal
- Balances the leader's authority by creating subgroups
- Facilitates lectures, briefings, speeches, panels, and demonstrations
- Allows group discussion and work

Figure 9–1
(Concluded)

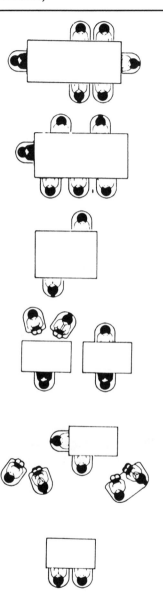

- Casual/informal
- Participants are on an equal footing
- Facilitates cooperation
- Inhibits visual and vocal communication
- Allows sharing of materials

- Casual/informal
- Participants are on an equal footing
- Allows visual and vocal communication
- Allows sharing of material

- Formal
- Allows good visual and vocal communication
- Establishes adversarial or superior/subordinate relationship (especially if a desk is involved)
- Restricts ability to share materials
- Creates psychological barrier between participants

- Casual/informal
- Permits independent activity/work and limited communication
- Participants are on an equal footing
- Makes sharing of materials difficult

- Formal
- Allows fair visual and verbal communication (head chair will receilve most communication)
- Leader/follower or boss/employee relationships established
- Allows some sharing of materials

- Formal
- Establishes psychological distance between participants and leader
- Nuclear group lessens authoritative posture of leader at opposite end of table
- Established leader/follower, boss/subordinate or adversarial relationships
- Restricts sharing of materials

Source: Barbara C. Palmer and Kenneth R. Palmer, *The Successful Meeting Master Guide* (Englewood Cliffs, N.J.: Prentice-Hall, 1983), pp. 92–93. Reprinted with permission.

An effective practice is to prepare minutes that reflect an informal summary of the meeting, much like an extension of the agenda items. The minutes should be distributed within several days of the meeting to help dramatize their importance. Minutes of meetings held weeks ago tend to receive little attention from busy people.

Avoid Interruptions Except for Emergencies. A real danger in holding a meeting near the work area of most of the attendees is that the meeting is likely to be interrupted for routine phone calls and requests for minor information. One meeting was interrupted because an administrative assistant wanted to know if her boss preferred mustard or mayonnaise on his roast-beef sandwich. When minor interruptions are tolerated, it creates the impression that the subject matter of the meeting is not as important as routine events taking place outside the meeting.

Conclude on a Positive Note. After the agenda is completed, or if the time deadline is near, the meeting should conclude on a positive note. The participants should leave with a feeling of having accomplished something worthwhile. If there has been much disagreement and not much visible progress, the leader should point out what went right in the meeting. For instance, Bud might have concluded, "Although we haven't agreed on anything specific yet, at least we have established what the major factors are in choosing a location for our new office."

Dealing with People

Our mention of people so far in this chapter has focused on the human aspects of improving the structure and processes of meetings, such as taking into account personal convenience in scheduling a time and place. Below we describe 16 tactics that deal more directly with managing the people present at a meeting. The distinction we make between structure and process versus people is done more for convenience than in the interests of scientific rigor. An alternative would be to classify our discussion into formal versus informal aspects of conducting a meeting.

The Leader Should Be Both Task-Oriented and Relationship-Oriented. Without effective leadership, most meetings are doomed to low productivity. For most situations, effective leadership style is characterized by a high concern for both the task and members. A high task orientation is necessary to keep the group moving toward accomplishing the goals of the meeting. A high relationship orientation is required to provide the kind of emotional support that encourages group interaction and creativity. A keen sensitivity to people is also necessary in running a meeting because of the many subtle interactions taking place (such as members dragging their heels when they disagree with a given proposal).

The Leader Should Share Power and Act as a Collaborator. In order to encourage constructive ideas, the leader can share power and act as a collaborator with members. In most meetings, the leader makes many statements that inhibit creative responses from participants. Accepting ideas from participants tends to spur creativity. Considerable skill is required to constructively modify or resist suggestions from the group without inhibiting imagination or further contributions. Extraneous concerns and flaws should be acknowledged as subproblems to be worked on, but the group's energy should be focused on building a solution.[9] Here is an example of what Bud could have done in this regard:

> Liz: So if we relocate to a suburban park, we'll have to rent a small employment office downtown anyway.
>
> Bud: Your point about the problems our labor pool would have in getting to a suburban location is a good one. I therefore understand what you mean about maintaining a downtown employment office. I agree that our labor force must be given top consideration. But I'm looking for a solution that will give us one cohesive, central office. We'll keep your point in mind.

Create a Good Atmosphere for a Group Discussion. The leader plays a major role in creating an atmosphere that fosters group discussion. Behaviors that accomplish this include listening to ideas, giving verbal reinforcement for the expression of worthwhile ideas, being tolerant of mistakes made by participants, and smiling frequently. An ability to accept criticism from group members also contributes to a free discussion.

A poor atmosphere for group discussion is created by the opposite of behaviors just mentioned. The person who approaches the meeting with arrogance and self-righteousness, attempting to dominate others and impress them, will also inhibit group discussion.[10]

Listen Carefully to Members. Listening to members serves important functions in addition to creating an atmosphere for group discussion. It enables the leader to gather information that could be vital in solving the problem facing the group. Active listening will also help the leader gauge how well his or her ideas are being accepted. If, for example, one or more participants change the subject after the leader contributes an idea, that idea requires further development and selling.

Strive for Balanced Contributions by Members. To effectively lead a meeting, the leader must gently curtail the participation of domineering and garrulous members. Equally important, the leader has to coax more reticent members to contribute their ideas. A simple, but effective method of drawing people out is to ask their opinion about agenda items. Asking for factual answers is less helpful in encouraging a balanced contribution for this reason: the person may not know the answer and therefore become more inhibited out of embarassment.

Give Participants the Opportunity to Assume a Leadership Role. Yet another way of creating a give-and-take atmosphere and encouraging a balanced contribution from members is for the leader to encourage others to take over some leadership activity. One way of accomplishing this end is to turn over a portion of the meeting to a member who is responsible for a particular agenda item. When that agenda item is processed, the leader can take the leadership role back gently. A less formal way of encouraging leadership behavior among members is to express appreciation for meritorious suggestions volunteered by them.

Encourage Candid Comments. A dull, ceremonial meeting is characterized by participants offering only polite, psychologically safe comments. In contrast, an exciting, results-oriented meeting is characterized by members contributing candid opinions about agenda items and related topics. You will recall that Liz, the employment director, offered candid comments about the importance of having a downtown office to accommodate maintenance workers. Without her contribution, the concept of a suburban office location would have gone unchallenged. The leader can encourage candid comments by not acting defensively or showing displeasure when an initial open comment is made.

Suppose a group member makes the comment, "It doesn't matter what machine we purchase. The real problem behind our low productivity is a group of top managers who are operating in the Dark Ages." To encourage additional candid comments, yet still preserve a sense of discipline, the leader might respond: "Okay, the way you see things, if we want to improve productivity, we must examine corporate policy and top management practices. Do you have any specific suggestions I can carry forward?"

Nonverbal Communication Should Be Used Freely. Another way of keeping a meeting vital is for members to make ample use of nonverbal communication to supplement their verbal communication. Without these silent messages, the meeting can take on a stiffness much like a meeting governed by parliamentary law. All the forms of nonverbal communication described in Chapter 6 would be relevant here, since meetings are a natural setting for such communication. The leader can encourage nonverbal behavior by serving as a model. Among the silent messages widely used in meetings are table thumping, smiling, finger-pointing, and leaning forward toward the person making a point.

Members Should Be Tolerant of Divergent Views. The group leader plays a key role in creating an atmosphere that encourages diverse viewpoints. Participants can play an equally significant role by showing tolerance for extreme viewpoints and controversial opinions. Toleration can be communicated by subtle behaviors such as a nod of approval or a wink after another participant has expressed an extreme viewpoint. The nod, wink, or similar behavior does not necessarily imply agreement, but it does imply acceptance of divergent views.

Encourage Group Interaction. We mentioned the importance of the leader's encouragement of group discussion. Similarly, the leader should encourage group *interaction*. A meeting loses the advantage of two-way communication when all communication pathways are between the leader and members. It is more effective for the participants to react to each other's comments. At times, tactful challenges are in order. When Nick, the director of maintenance operations, took off on a tangent about the importance of the company party, another member of the team might have said, "Nick, I can't disagree with the importance of the party, but let's deal with the problem of office location."

Although group interaction is welcome, whispers and other side comments should be discouraged. The most effective technique of quelling whispering is for the leader to stare in silence at the whisperers until they stop.

Translate Jargon for Outsiders. Jargon generally receives negative commentary, yet it serves the useful purposes of shortening communication and fostering a feeling of group-belonging. The jargon of one technical group may be unfamiliar to an outsider attending the meeting. Rather than trying to eliminate jargon, we suggest that the terms be defined for outsiders. This has the advantage of making the meeting more informative for the outsider. For instance, in one meeting a computer scientist referred to "32-bit architecture." With a smile, he turned to the noncomputer people in the meeting and commented, "That's hacker's jargon for how much data the computer can store. And by the way, a hacker is simply a computer freak."

Strive for Consensus, Not Total Acceptance. Few groups composed of assertive individuals will arrive at total agreement on most agenda items. It is more realistic to strive for consensus—a state of harmony, general agreement, or majority opinion with a reasonable amount of disagreement still present. When consensus is achieved, each member should be willing to accept the plan because it is logical and feasible. The following suggestions made by Francis X. Mahoney are designed to help the leader achieve consensus:

1. Accept the idea that "there's more than one way to skin a cat."
2. Encourage the team members to clarify and build on one another's ideas. Encourage the entire team to be sure that everyone's ideas are heard.
3. Avoid vigorous or heated arguments in favor of one person's position, especially your own. Encourage the team not to let itself be railroaded by one or two people.
4. Avoid easy ways out—such as majority vote, averaging, and coin flipping—unless the issue is virtually meaningless. Such selection methods may leave team members with strong differences of opinion. Then you have no consensus at all.
5. Shoot for win-win solutions (or plans) if at all practicable. This means that everyone feels reasonably comfortable with what is going to happen. This is where you should be when you believe that you have a consensus.[11]

Participants Should Delay the Expression of Strong Emotion. Recent experiments suggest that the expression of emotion about decision problems should be delayed until after alternatives to the problems have been generated. Two dysfunctional consequences are associated with the early expression of strong emotion: a reduction in group energy and a narrowing of the range of accepted ideas. High levels of emotion will sometimes hinder the capacity of the group to think clearly about the task at hand, and also foster misunderstanding and poor communication within the group.[12] An example of such early display of emotion would be cheering when the first acceptable tentative solution to the problem at hand arises. The leader should help restrain emotion from members until additional alternatives have been explored.

Avoid Distruptive Behavior. The leader also may have to act as suppressor when participants engage in behavior that has a debilitating effect on meetings. According to Palmer and Palmer, the most frequent behaviors of this kind are: inept humor, personal anecdotes, domination of the discussion, switching topics in midstream, side conversations, unconstructive cynicism, repetition of arguments, and insistence on questioning decisions already made by the group.[13] In all these instances, the disruptive person may have to be dealt with assertively by the leader (or other members).

Manage Conflict as Needed. Healthy, open discussion inevitably brings about interpersonal conflict. Instead of trying to suppress or ignore this conflict, the leader should consider dealing with it openly. An interpretation of the difference of opinion between the two participants can be helpful in turning the conflict into a constructive force.

Provide Refreshments when Motivation Is a Problem. A cultural fact of organizational life is that many people expect refreshments at meetings. When participants, or their organizations, pay to attend meetings (such as conventions, professional meetings, and trade shows) refreshments are mandatory. For briefer, on company premises meetings, refreshments are optional. Yet, many people expect to be offered food and beverage during the meeting. Since eating and drinking take time away from the meeting, and do cost some money, refreshments should not be served indiscriminately. As a rule of thumb, since the lack of refreshments can dampen satisfaction and motivation, they should be served primarily when satisfaction and motivation are potential problems. Following this logic, refreshments are mandatory at Saturday morning meetings!

The Argument For and Against Following Suggestions for Conducting Effective Meetings

Although all of the suggestions presented in this chapter may not work all of the time, they have high potential for being cost effective for two reasons. First, managers spend a substantial amount of time in meetings, perhaps up to two-thirds of their average workday. Second, it has been estimated that about half of time spent in meetings is wasted.[14] This waste can be translated into two types of costs. One is the cost attributed to the salaries and benefits paid to the participants while they are attending the meeting (computed as the hourly salary, plus benefits multiplied by the time spent attending and traveling to and from the meeting.) The other are the opportunity costs— productive work the people might have done if they had not been at the meeting.

One argument for ignoring the suggestions in this chapter is that if rational people want to make meetings more effective, they will. Perhaps the time wasted in meetings is really functional. The gabbing and ceremonial activity that takes place in a meeting relieves tension and helps build a sense of camaraderie among workers. Another argument in opposition to these suggestions is that the time wasted in meetings is not a real cost, owing to Parkinson's Law. After people have wasted time in a meeting, they scurry to finish up their day's work. If they did not attend the meeting, they would work at a more leisurely pace the remainder of the day.

GUIDELINES FOR ACTION AND SKILL DEVELOPMENT

To improve the productivity of the meetings you chair and/or attend, use the suggestions made in this chapter as a checklist of steps that can be taken or factors that can be considered. Not all of these suggestions will be applicable to every meeting. The major points in the chapter are summarized below to assist you in using them as a checklist.

Checklist for Improving the Productivity of Meetings

	Do It Now	Should Do It	Not Appl.
Dealing with Structure and Process			
1. Valid reason for meeting.	___	___	___
2. Stick to specific agenda.	___	___	___
3. Select attendees carefully.	___	___	___
4. Convenient time and place.	___	___	___
5. Stop and start on time.	___	___	___
6. Work on surmountable problems.	___	___	___
7. Brief and pointed comments.	___	___	___
8. Provide summaries for key points.	___	___	___
9. Repeat, restate unclear comments.	___	___	___
10. Physical structure for communication.	___	___	___
11. Limited use of parliamentary procedure.	___	___	___
12. Use handouts sparingly.	___	___	___
13. Send minutes soon after meeting.	___	___	___
14. Minimize interruptions.	___	___	___
15. Conclude on a positive note.	___	___	___
Dealing with People			
1. Task- and relationship-orientation.	___	___	___
2. Power-sharing leader.	___	___	___
3. Group discussion atmosphere.	___	___	___
4. Listen carefully to members.	___	___	___
5. Balanced contributions by members.	___	___	___
6. Participants given a chance to lead.	___	___	___
7. Encourage candid comments.	___	___	___
8. Free use of nonverbal communication.	___	___	___
9. Tolerance of divergent views.	___	___	___
10. Encourage group interaction.	___	___	___
11. Translate jargon for outsiders.	___	___	___
12. Strive for consensus.	___	___	___
13. Delay expression of strong emotion.	___	___	___
14. Avoid disruptive behavior.	___	___	___
15. Manage conflict as needed.	___	___	___
16. Serve refreshments if needed.	___	___	___

The checklist just presented can be used for skill building. During meetings you attend or chair, make a serious attempt to practice the applicable behaviors outlined in the checklist. For instance, if you think group discussion is very important in your meeting you would take note of point 10, "Physical structure for communication." In referring back to Figure 9–1, you would then choose the "casual/informal" seating arrangement. Another example of how this checklist can be used for skill building, would be the application of point 8, "Provide summaries for key points." If you chair a meeting, remember to stop at certain checkpoints to provide oral summaries of key topics. If your summaries seem to add to the productivity of the meeting, you will most likely incorporate summaries of key points into your repertoire of skills.

An important general skill to develop in conducting a meeting, is to find a way to keep people listening. Even at high levels in organizations, many people daydream, whisper, or work on other matters while attending a meeting. A powerful antidote to this problem is to frequently ask people their opinion about issues that surface. Rather than risk being embarassed by not having heard the issue, most attendees will stay alert. Another antidote to the problem of nonlisteners, is for the meeting leader to confront the daydreamer or whisperer with a comment such as, "Are you with us?"

Questions and Activities

1. Why do so many people say they hate meetings?
2. Identify one or two political reasons for conducting meetings.
3. For which of the standard functions of management (planning, organizing, leading, controlling, and so forth) are meetings used?
4. How would you handle the situation if your boss went off on a tangent during a meeting and you believed that this behavior was lowering the productivity of the meeting?
5. Organizations sometimes send key personnel to a "retreat" for purposes of formulating strategy or dealing with other important matters. Why are such retreats likely to be more productive than meetings held on organizational premises?
6. For what purposes do you think standup meetings are best suited?
7. Use the Checklist for Productive Meetings to analyze the next meeting you attend. If time permits, bring your findings back to class.

Notes

[1]Peter A. Turla and Kathleen L. Hawkins, "Meaningful Meetings," Success, June 1983, p. 40.

[2]Barbara C. Palmer and Kenneth R. Palmer, The Successful Meeting Master Guide (Englewood Cliffs, N.J.: Prentice-Hall, 1983), p. 31.

[3]Ibid., p. 31.

[4]Turla and Hawkins, "Meaningful Meetings," p. 40.

[5]Stan Kossen, *The Human Side of Organizations*, 3rd ed. (New York: Harper & Row, 1983), p. 110.

[6]Gary Dessler, *Human Behavior: Improving Performance at Work* (Reston, Va.: Reston Publishing Company, 1980), p. 277.

[7]Palmer and Palmer, *The Successful Meeting*, p. 107.

[8]Ibid., p. 164.

[9]The concept and example here are both based on George M. Prince, "Creative Meetings through Power Sharing," *Harvard Business Review*, July–August 1972, p. 53.

[10]Palmer and Palmer, *The Successful Meeting*, p. 33.

[11]Francis X. Mahoney, "Team Development, Part 4: Work Meetings," *Personnel*, March-April 1982, pp. 52–53.

[12]Richard A. Guzzo and James A. Waters, "The Expression of Affect and the Performance of Decision-Making Groups," *Journal of Applied Psychology*, February 1982, pp. 67–74.

[13]Palmer and Palmer, *The Successful Meeting*, pp. 128–129.

[14]Turla and Hawkins, "Meaningful Meetings," p. 40.

Some Additional References

Bradford, Leland P. *Making Meetings Work: A Guide for Leaders and Group Members*. San Diego, Calif.: University Associates, 1980.

Dunsing, Richard J. *You and I Have Simply Got to Stop Meeting this Way*. San Diego, Calif.: University Associates, 1983.

Guzzo, Richard A. *Group Decision Making in Organizations*. Reading, Mass.: Addison-Wesley, 1983.

Klein, Alan F. *Effective Groupwork: An Introduction to Principle and Method*. Chicago: Follett, 1983.

Schindler-Rainman, Eva and Ronald Lippitt, in collaboration with Jack Cole. *Taking Your Meetings Out of the Doldrums*. San Diego, Calif.: University Associates, 1982.

Chapter 10

Building Teamwork

An electronics firm was experiencing quality problems with their line of TV receivers, and a related problem of low job satisfaction among its production workers and supervisors. To remedy these problems, the firm decided to reorganize its assembly-line operation into small work teams, called autonomous work groups (or semiautonomous work groups).

"Let's review quickly why we are getting together today," said Jack Ross, manufacturing vice president of Chartwell Electronics. With him were Dave Cooper, general manager of Chartwell's Yellow Junction plant, and Meryl Butwid, corporate industrial engineering consultant.

We've hashed over this same problem many times during the last several years. I've listened to dozens of suggestions, I've read many industry studies, and I've made some of my own observations. Now we are ready to act before we lose an important segment of our business.

For the last few years we have been in trouble with our line of TV sets. Our price is still competitive, but just barely. We get a lot of squawks from retail outlets that our sets are coming back to the store for refund or replacement. I have to admit, some shoddy merchandise has been getting through. I'm not so sure I would give my own mother a Chartwell TV for a present if she didn't have ready access to a service center. During the last six months, our share of the market declined 25 percent. Our sales were down 15 percent, while industry sales as a whole were down only 7 percent.

Meryl, will you go ahead and tell Dave and me your latest analysis of the problem?

Meryl: I want to point out that Dave and his staff members are in essential agreement with my diagnosis of the problem. They may not all agree on my solution, but at least we have a consistent viewpoint of the nature of the beast. We have a growing epidemic of the blue-collar blues, not just in the Yellow Junction plant, but all over. Many of our workers, perhaps one half to two thirds, are burned-out. They've lost whatever spark of enthusiasm they once had for their jobs. Our supervisors are becoming discouraged dealing with so many technical and morale problems.

It's rumored that many of our workers themselves believe we are producing inferior TV sets. A joke circulating around our plants these days is that if you want to enjoy Super Bowl Sunday, visit a friend who owns a competitor's TV. Because our production jobs are so boring, our problems with turnover, absenteeism, and tardiness have increased sharply.

We know there must be a better way. The better way we have formulated is the team approach to job enrichment. Some call it job redesign, but the latest buzz word is *autonomous work groups*. The team approach to production work has been used in Europe since the mid-1960s.[1] The sociology behind it is that many workers feel alienated because their work lacks challenge and meaning.

The concept is quite simple. Teams of from 8 to 12 workers will cover a full set of tasks, and team members will decide which people will perform which tasks. It will be as if we have 10 small TV-making shops in the plant instead of one large assembly line. It's like setting scientific management back 100 years. We'll have small groups of generalists, rather than a large number of employees performing specialized, narrow tasks. I know that Dave would have some comments about the reorganization and retooling necessary to convert from a traditional assembly to autonomous work groups.

Dave: I've studied the situation carefully including getting loads of input from our manufacturing engineering department. We're talking about a couple of hundred thousand dollars worth of revamping for just one assembly line. We would have to rearrange work stations. We'd have to tear down some partitions. We'd have to select and train the right people. We'd have one line out of operation for three months during the tooling-up process.

An analysis performed by Meryl and the plant staff suggests that we should start small. Our worst problems are with the portable black and white TV sets. Maybe that's because the production of those sets is so routinized. About one half the Yellow Junction capacity is devoted to the manufacture of our black and white portables.

Another solid reason for beginning this experiment at Yellow

Junction is that the union there is so cooperative. Nick Langdon, the local president, is willing to let us try this for one year before we negotiate the new job structure into the next labor agreement. Nick says his senior people are frightened that the Yellow Junction plant might close. We've already had one small layoff due to a softened demand for our TVs.

Jack: It sounds like we have our experiment with autonomous work groups pretty well planned. I'd say let's get moving with the project. We'll start committing resources to the project right away. I'd like to see the system on line by January 1.

Nine months later, Jack and Dave made one of their regular visits to Yellow Junction to evaluate progress on the project and offer whatever advice and support they could offer. Meryl Butwid was on site, working with a behavioral science consultant. She offered the visitors a brief explanation of the current status of the project:

Meryl: We've been in full operation for about two months. The format seems to be working. In essence, each group of nine workers has total responsibility for the assembly task. The team also deals directly with staff groups such as purchasing and quality control. We use a team leader but not a supervisor. Some of our supervisors have been selected as team leaders. Others chose to take staff jobs or work as assemblers on the color TV line until a supervisory position opened over there.

It's too soon to tell for sure, but team spirit is high, attendance is up, and our quality department says manufacturing defects are way down. The number of units shipped in a week is slightly behind the assembly line format. Ken Phillips, the psychological consultant who's been advising us on this project, has a few comments.

Ken: I think we're going to get the increase in quality and morale that you are seeking. But it will take awhile. Not every employee who volunteered to work on a team has the immediate skills necessary to perform as a team member. Some people lack the confidence necessary to handle all the responsibility. We're asking people to become TV makers instead of specialists in putting together some miniscule part. It's much like asking somebody to change part of their self-image.

We're also asking people to become responsible members of a team. If they are out one day, they have to feel somewhat guilty about letting the team down. The assembly line is so much more depersonalized. Another big change is that young inexperienced employees are now working as co-equals with higher paid, more senior employees. Dealing with the status difference makes some people feel awkward. One gal told me that she had to bring a part back for rework to an older woman. That woman happened to be her occasional babysitter when she was six years old. That's heavy stuff for a 20-year-old raised in Yellow Junction.

On one of my trips here, I had my hair trimmed at the local barber shop. I heard a comment that makes me think autonomous work groups will be around a long time. One older man said to another, "If you're looking for a spiffy wedding present for your daughter, why not get her a Chartwell portable TV made at Yellow Junction? These days they outperform the Japanese models."

HOW TO ENCOURAGE TEAMWORK AND GROUP EFFECTIVENESS

The formation of autonomous work groups represents an organization-design approach to encouraging teamwork. A manager can also use informal, day-by-day methods to foster teamwork, high morale, group cohesiveness, and group effectiveness. In this section, we will summarize a variety of tactics and strategies to achieve these ends. Common sense and judgment must be used to choose which of these 21 strategies or tactics will probably best fit a given circumstance.

Develop a Norm of Teamwork. An overall strategy the team leader should use to promote teamwork is to cultivate the attitude among group members that working together effectively is an expected standard of conduct. (A group norm is defined as an informal rule adopted by a group to regulate and regularize group members' behavior.) [1] A direct way of accomplishing this end is for the leader to make explicit statements about the desirability of teamwork. Normative statements about teamwork made by powerful group members can have a similar effect. The manager of an information systems department at a food manufacturing company used the following comments (with good results) to help foster a norm of teamwork:

> My boss is concerned that we are not pulling together as a cohesive team. And I can see some merit in his argument. We are performing splendidly as a group of individuals, but I see a need for an improved united effort in our group. We need to share ideas more, to touch base with each other, to pick each other's brains more. From now on when I evaluate performance, I'm going to give as much weight to group effort as I do to individual contribution.

Promote Pride. A related approach to developing teamwork is for the leader to promote the concept that team members should be proud to belong to the group. Joe Paterno, the Penn State football coach, has a winning percentage of about 83 percent, overshadowing all active coaches who have been around a decade or more. He attributes a good share of the success of his teams to group pride. He explains it in these terms:

You start with the idea that you build some pride. You make people feel that they're with a special company, a special institution, that's worth making sacrifices for. If you're the kind of guy that we call the "we and us" people that can work with the group, by being unselfish, benefits will accrue to you.

Paterno also notes that pride helps the leader accomplish his or her mission: "If you have pride in your organization, you can get people to do anything."[2] The challenge to the manager is to translate this platitude about pride into action. One important business example is the pride in their organization experienced by technical and professional employees of Apple Computer. This pride is one of the reasons a large proportion of these professional and technical personnel are willing to work up to 70 hours per week without complaining or asking for extra compensation. Their pride in being a member of the Apple organization helps them believe that they are part of a very important mission—advancing the computerization of society.

Paterno, of course, is dealing from strength when he uses the concept of pride to foster teamwork. Group members, and potential group members, readily develop pride in belonging to a high-status group like the Penn State football team. A losing team in athletics or in business has a difficult time instilling pride in the organization. The teamwork concept under scrutiny can be summarized in this fashion: Pride leads to teamwork and group success, and group success fosters pride leading to improved teamwork and more success.

Make the Task the Boss. Teamwork is fostered when group members pull together toward a common goal. One way of accomplishing this is to make the "task the boss," a concept illustrated by the training film, "Task Oriented Team Development."[3] The underlying premise is that an agreed-upon goal, rather than the leader per se, directs the team. This idea complies with the generally accepted principle of group dynamics that working toward a common goal enhances group effectiveness. An important contribution of the leader is to help the group realize the path toward goal attainment. A basic example of the latter would be for the leader to fight for appropriate support services for the group.

A practical way of helping the group realize a common goal is to conduct group meetings devoted to goal setting and strategy (long-range goals and plans). The hoped for outcome of such meetings would be an awareness by group members of common goals. Three useful discussion questions for goal-setting meetings are:

1. Where are we headed as a group?
2. Who are we?
3. What are we trying to accomplish?

Choose an Appropriate Leadership Style. Effective work groups are characterized by an approach to leadership appropriate to the particular situation. If a leader were asked to supervise a group of unsure, poorly trained, and inexperienced workers, the leader would have to supply a large amount of emotional support and careful directions. Small groups usually require a leader who is directive and task oriented.[4] Groups need definite guidelines to perform their task and usually require occasional assistance from the leader. Nevertheless, an effective small group leader does not neglect the feelings and emotional needs of group members. For example, an effective leader is usually a good listener.

Respect and Accept the Informal Leader. Most work groups have one member who is perceived by the other group members as having leadership qualities. Often this informal leader acts as the spokesperson in matters of importance to the group. The informal leader is also influential in swinging group opinion. A formal leader who respects the role of the informal leader stands a good chance of establishing and maintaining the support of the group. In contrast, a manager who acts resentful of this role may lose the confidence and support of the group.

A note of caution: You must proceed tactfully in trying to cultivate the informal leader. If it appears that you are trying to bribe the informal leader to sway the group toward your way of thinking, the process may backfire. The informal leader might inform the group of the bribe attempt.

Encourage and Provide Emotional Support. An effective work group provides emotional support to members. Such support can take the form of verbal encouragement for ideas expressed, listening to a group member's problems, or even providing help with a knotty technical problem. The leader can provide such support and also encourage other members to help each other.

> Jimbo, a pressroom supervisor, well respected for his leadership capabilities, used a straightforward method of encouraging emotional support within the work-group. Should one of the press operators arrive at work looking forlorn, Jimbo would say to another press operator: "Buddy up to _____ today. I think he could sure use some encouragement. He seems to be under the weather."

Support the Group. A time-tested managerial practice that helps bring a group closer to the managers is for them to defend their groups to higher management. Support of this nature can take many forms. Among the most important is for the manager to act as an intermediary in bringing demands made by the group to higher management. Assume that a group of production workers thought the company should provide protective clothing because of a corrosive new chemical now used in the department. However, these workers realize that in the past no employees were issued protective clothing unless it was required by legislation. If the supervisor negotiated successfully with management for protective clothing for this group, this action would solidify future relationships with the department. The supervisor who supports the group often receives support in return.

Encourage Cooperative Behavior. An obvious but often overlooked method of building teamwork is to encourage cooperation rather than intense competition within the group.[5] One method of encouraging cooperation would be for the manager to praise employees for having collaborated on joint projects. Another would be to assign tasks that require input from several people in order to be completed. One manager of a chemical department encouraged cooperation by sending out two chemists on troubleshooting assignments from time to time. They were asked to present a joint recommendation for overcoming the problem.

Practice Equality. A team leader does not have to like all team members equally well. But leaders should try to make assignments on the basis of merit, otherwise they run the risk of being accused of favoritism. Equality thus means that each department member has an equal chance of obtaining whatever rewards the leader or manager has to offer providing that person performs well. Playing favorites detracts from teamwork because most people do not wish to cooperate with a selected one or two employees who receive undeserved rewards.

Be Open to Encourage Trust. Groups in which distrust and suspicion exist are often counterproductive. Only when groups achieve mutual trust and confidence are they more effective than individuals in solving problems and making decisions.[6] A good starting point in encouraging trust between the team leader and subordinates is for the leader to be as open and honest as the situation will allow. One civil service executive does this by distributing all his mail—except that classified as confidential or secret—to his subordinate managers. This practice has contributed to trust, but few subordinates bother to look at much of the executive's mail any longer.

Follow Through on Commitments. Managers who are negligent in following through on commitments to their subordinates may lose support of the group. In addition, the group may become demoralized and teamwork may consequently suffer. Commitments to employees include major and minor matters, such as conducting performance reviews on time, ordering supplies for the department, helping employees process benefit forms such as medical claims, and inquiring about job transfer or promotion possibilities. Following through on commitments also contributes to teamwork because it enhances a feeling of trust between the subordinates and the manager.

Select the Right-Size Group for the Task. Group effectiveness is bolstered when the right number of people are working on an assigned task.

A neighborhood bakery was operated by the owner and six employees. As business volume increased, three more people were hired. Customer service suffered a setback. Employees began to physically get in each other's way. The close-working conditions led to much conflict among employees. Too many employees spoiled the bakery.

A general guideline is that from five to seven people are the desired maximum when considerable interaction among the people in the group is needed. When people are not highly dependent upon one another, the group size may be increased without worrying about a loss of teamwork—and, therefore, effectiveness.

Choose the Right Mix of People. In some situations, a group of people with similar backgrounds is best suited to accomplishing the group goals. This is particularly true when cooperation among members is important. In group situations where a high degree of creativity and problem-solving ability is called for, a heterogeneous group is generally the most effective. People with different backgrounds (such as educational specialities or cultural values) help bring fresh perspectives to the problem.

A new product committee was used quite successfully by a national food manufacturer. People were invited to serve on the committee on a rotating basis. Members were carefully chosen from a diversity of educational and ethnic backgrounds. Among the new products successfully marketed by the company were a line of dog food treats and a soft food for senior citizens with denture problems.

Use Group Incentives. A key strategy in encouraging teamwork is to reward the group as a whole when such rewards are deserved. Assume a manager receives a compliment from higher management that he or she has done an outstanding job. The manager in question would share this praise with the group since most accomplishments of a manager reflect group effort. A popular form of group incentive is to reward good group performance with an organization-paid banquet. One company threw a roast beef and beer party to celebrate making a record shipment of industrial pumps.

Encourage Competition with Another Group. One of the best-known ways to encourage teamwork is to rally the support of the group against a real or imagined threat from the outside.[7] Beating the competition makes more sense when the competition is outside your own organization. When the enemy is within, the team spirit developed may become detrimental to the overall organization.

A plant manger told his supervisors: "Our sister plant in Montreal is way ahead of us in preventing lost-time accidents. We don't have to take this challenge lying down. Let's wish them the best of luck in reducing accidents, but let's create even better luck for our own plant."

By the end of the year the Ontario plant *did* reduce accidents a trifle more than did the Montreal plant.

Keep Communication Channels Open. Many minor problems between the manager and subordinates fester into major problems. The major problems, in turn, adversely affect team spirit and productivity. Early intervention in these problems could have prevented them from becoming a disruptive force. In order to work through little problems, the group leader should keep open channels of communication with the group.

One supervisor made it a practice to have lunch once a month with seven subordinates. It was called the "anything goes" lunch. One problem the group brought up was that the supervisor was being negligent in ordering office supplies for them. This simple problem was resolved before it escalated into ill will between the supervisor and the group thus hampering teamwork.

Minimize Personal Friction. A common sense strategy of merit for promoting teamwork is to have friends work together and enemies work apart. Assigning people to tasks according to their social preferences is only feasible when group members are arranged into small subteams. A potential disadvantage is that overly friendly workers may socialize too much on the job. But as magazine publisher Peter Diamandis puts it, "I have a hiring policy that's revolutionary. It took me 48 years to figure this out. I only hire people I like. Up until recently I hired experts; I hired people with great reputations. I hired all sorts of people who were sent to me for different reasons, and a lot of them didn't work out. So I decided to go back to basics and hire only the people I like, figuring that at the very least we'd all have a lot of fun. And it's turned out very well. Everybody takes on a lot of responsibility and does very well."[8]

Practice Job Rotation. Giving people an opportunity to try out different jobs contributes to teamwork because it encourages identification with the team as a whole rather than with individual jobs.[9] Such rotation promotes cooperation and teamwork in another subtle way. Workers come to appreciate the problems faced by other workers within the department as they perform each others' jobs.

Allow for Close Location among Members. Group cohesiveness, and therefore teamwork, is enhanced when team members are located close together and can interact frequently and easily. A management authority offers this explanation: "This may be due to the ability of the members to maintain eye contact if they are located close together. Eye movement, direction of gaze, and mutual eye contact are important nonverbal interactions that influence group effectiveness.[10] Whether or not this eye-contact explanation is valid, sharing a location seems important for group cohesiveness.

Reach Out to Isolates. In many human groups, at least one member is friendless and therefore lonely. If the manager can involve such individuals in group social interaction, the team productivity will sometimes increase. If the isolate is adamant about not getting involved with others, and the others do not want the isolate, intervention may backfire. One supervisor skillfully facilitated a loner becoming involved in the group. She asked that individual to be acting department head on a day that supervisors were asked to hand out good news about a cost-of-living adjustment. Being a bearer of good news helped ease the isolated employee into a position of group acceptance.

Orient New Members. New workers should be carefully introduced to the group to give them a chance to become psychologically part of the work unit. Many companies use a big-brother or big-sister program whereby experienced workers help assimilate new workers to the formal requirements of the job and the informal mores of the group. Improved teamwork is often the result.[11]

The Argument For and Against Autonomous Work Groups

Two arguments can be advanced for the team approach to work restructuring. Of prime importance, companies using autonomous work groups report substantial improvements in employee motivation, and these improvements can be directly linked to the achievement of financial goals. Work teams also improve productivity by giving production systems greater flexibility in meeting dynamic market demands.[12]

Volvo's relatively new Tuve truck assembly plant in Sweden provides specific data about how autonomous work groups lead to productivity increases. As reported by Paul Bernstein, Tuve was designed as a single-product (trucks) workshop of 25 blue-collar and 25 white-collar employees. Although comparisons between the team-oriented production process at Tuve versus other Volvo plants are difficult, a comparison with an older truck facility seven kilometers away showed Tuve to be 16 percent more efficient. For example, absenteeism averaged 16.5 percent at Tuve, compared to 20 percent at the truck facility with a more traditional assembly-line manufacturing process.[13]

Autonomous work groups enhance the quality of work life. Identification with the team and its product increase motivation and commitment, simultaneously improving job satisfaction and morale.

Despite these advantages, autonomous work groups are not suited to improving productivity and satisfaction in every work situation. Major arguments against the team approach to work restructuring include:

1. You need a relatively high-quality workforce for the team concept to be effective. To work effectively as team members, employees have to be mentally flexible, alert, and possess at least average interpersonal skills. In many plant and office locations, such employees are not available. Or if they are available, the employer may not be able to offer high enough wages to attract them.

2. The cost of introducing autonomous work groups can be prohibitive. A European specialist in industrial management notes that in plants where machines of the same type, such as lathes or drilling machines, are laid out together, they must be rearranged so different kinds of machines are grouped together. Furthermore, "If the work groups produce a large range of components or complete products, they may all need almost the same configuration of equipment. This means tooling and machinery surpluses. Buffer stocks are also needed so that each work group can work at a different pace. Placing buffer stocks between work groups may neutralize a classical advantage of the production line—the small quantities of material in work in progress.[14]

   Thus, the cost of converting an existing facility to work teams might be so high that the only feasible approach is to select a new location for the conversion.

3. Autonomous work groups might be limited in their effectiveness to that portion of the workforce who seek the type of stimulation found in team arrangements. A sizable portion of the workforce—perhaps as high as 70 percent—prefer to perform repetitive tasks independently.

4. When labor unions are present, designing jobs into teams could result in complicated, difficult-to-resolve labor-management issues. Among them are: Which employees will be denied membership in the new work groups? How do you establish wage rates for employees who can perform six different jobs? Is the employee who interacts directly with a supervisor from another department required to be a member of the bargaining unit?

5. Autonomous work groups are poorly suited to situations in which one department is dependent upon another for getting work accomplished. Since each unit operates independently, they are not attuned to adhering to each other's production schedules.

The Argument For and Against Building Teamwork

The informal methods of building teamwork described in this chapter have enormous payoffs in terms of organizational effectiveness. Work groups are the basic building blocks of the larger organization. To the extent that work groups are effective, the organization as a whole prospers. One of the underlying behavioral reasons that Japanese industry has been so successful is the high level of cooperation and teamwork among employees at all levels from production worker to the executive.[15]

On the other hand, maybe we are concerned too much about getting people to work together and to like each other. Too much cohesion has some undesirable consequences such as overconformity and groupthink—the end point of consensus whereby group members begin to think alike. In order to be creative, many organizations need more boat rocking, more mavericks, and less mutual admiration. Organizations move forward via the individual ingenuity of a relatively few pioneers. If we rely excessively upon teamwork and cooperation, these people may hold back from making their contributions.

GUIDELINES FOR ACTION AND SKILL DEVELOPMENT

To properly house a team operation, an organization must be redesigned thoroughly and a systems point of view maintained. First, attention must be paid to the design and layout of the physical setting. Building space must allow for the product flow and for the interaction of people necessary to perform teamwork. Second, it is usually necessary to create a relatively flat organization structure whereby team members are in control of a significant amount of their work.

Autonomous work groups are the most effective when the status barriers between management and employees are broken down. Doing so permits the establishment of an atmosphere of trust and open communication.[16]

Employees must be carefully chosen who show pride in their work and enjoy working in cooperative effort with others. Self-nomination or asking for volunteers for the autonomous work groups will decrease selection errors.

To avoid the ambiguity (and therefore, stress) often associated with the unpredictable income of pay systems based on group performance, pay plans for autonomous work group members should combine a fixed income with a group bonus. Experience suggests that the fixed portion of the wage should be based on job evaluation data and the skills of the employee. Typically, between 70 and 90 percent of an employee's wages are fixed. The group bonus is then divided equally among the team members.[17]

The optimal number of employees for the team normally is between 10 and 15. When the work teams are larger, job satisfaction and productivity cease to improve, owing perhaps to a lack of cohesiveness and interaction among members. An experience-based guideline for selecting the optimal size is as follows: "The ideal-sized group is one in which the smallest number of members can perform a whole task and still satisfy their social and psychological needs."[18]

Be prepared to transfer employees who do not make it as team members or team leaders to more tradiltional jobs. Some people are not suited to team arrangements even though they might nominate themselves for such assignments.

Questions and Activities

1. What similarities do you see between autonomous work groups and the teams used in project management?
2. Identify one or two clerical operations you think could be adapted well to autonomous work groups. Explain why.
3. What is the mechanism (the underlying process) by which autonomous work groups lead to improvements in product quality?
4. What method can a manager use to identify the informal leader among his or her subordinates?
5. What is your evaluation of Diamandis's strategy of hiring only people he likes?
6. Using concepts mentioned in this chapter, analyze why a work group familiar to you is either effective or ineffective.
7. Interview two people who have worked for a long period of time performing small parts of a task (such as an assembly worker, or a clerk performing similar work in an office). Obtain their perception of the desirability of autonomous work groups.
8. Interview two leaders from any type of organization to obtain their opinion on how to develop pride among group members.

Notes

[1]Daniel C. Feldman, "The Development and Enforcement of Group Norms," *Academy of Management Review,* January 1984, p. 47.

[2]Hank Nuwer, "Team Builder," *Success,* October 1983, p. 24.

[3]"Team Building," CRM/McGraw-Hill film, 1983.

[4]Alan C. Filley, Robert J. House, and Steven Kerr, *Managerial Process and Organizational Behavior,* 2nd. ed. (Glenview, Ill.: Scott, Foresman, 1976) p. 157.

[5]Analysis by Ed Lahniers, cited in Priscilla Petty, "Successful Teamwork Depends on Cooperation, Communication Style," Rochester *Democrat and Chronicle,* July 26, 1983, p. 8D.

[6]Edgar H. Schein, *Organizational Psychology,* 3d ed. (Englewood Cliffs, N.J.: Prentice-Hall, 1980) p. 151.

[7]Thomas J. Atchison and Winston W. Hill, *Management Today: Managing Work in Organizations* (Orlando, Fl.: Harcourt Brace Jovanovich, 1978) p. 251.

[8]"Magazine Publisher Diamandis," *MBA Executive*, April/May '80, p. 9.

[9]An early exposition of this point is made in George Strauss and Leonard R. Sayles, *Personnel: The Human Problems of Management*, 2d ed. (Englewood Cliffs, N.J.: Prentice-Hall, 1967) p. 199.

[10]William F. Glueck, *Management* (Hinsdale, Ill.: Dryden Press, 1977) p. 164.

[11]Strauss and Sayles, *Personnel*, p. 200.

[12]Panagiotis N. Fotilas, "Semi-Autonomous Work Groups: An Alternative in Organizing Production Work?" *Management Review*, July 1981, p. 52.

[13]Paul Bernstein, "Efficiency is Up and Absenteeism Down at New Volvo Plant," *World Wide Report*, December 1983, p. 94.

[14]Fotilas, "Semi-autonomous Work Groups," p. 51.

[15]Linda S. Dillon, "Adopting Japanese Management: Some Cultural Stumbling Blocks," *Personnel*, July-August 1983, pp. 73–77.

[16]Ernesto J. Poza and M. Lynne Markus, "Success Story: The Team Approach to Work Restructuring," *Organizational Dynamics*, Winter 1980, p. 24.

[17]Fotilas, "Semi-autonomous Work Groups," p. 53.

[18]Ibid, p. 52.

Some Additional References

Alber, Antone and Melvin Blumberg. "Team vs. Individual Approaches to Job Enrichment Programs." *Personnel*. January-February 1981, pp. 63–75.

Bernstein, Paul. "Using the Soft Approach for Hard Results." *Business*, April-June 1983, pp. 13–21.

Blumberg, Melvin. "Job Switching in Autonomous Work Groups: An Exploratory Study in a Pennsylvania Coal Mine." *Academy of Management Journal*, June 1980, pp. 287–306.

Bradford, Leland P., ed. *Group Development*, 2nd ed. San Diego, Calif.: University Associates, 1984.

Melohn, Thomas H. "How to Build Employee Trust and Productivity." *Harvard Business Review*, January-February 1983, pp. 56–57, 60–61.

Vancil, Richard E. and Charles H. Green. "How CEOs Use Top Management Committees," *Harvard Business Review*, January-February 1984, pp. 65–73.

Appendix to Chapter 10

The Effective Work Group Checklist*

The purpose of this checklist is to serve as an informal guide for diagnosing the effectiveness of a given work group. Both the leaders and group members should complete the checklist.[16] The answers will serve as discussion points for improving teamwork and effectiveness. The larger the number of statements answered yes, the more likely the group is productive and the members are satisfied.

	Mostly Yes	Mostly No
1. The atmosphere is relaxed and comfortable.	_____	_____
2. Group discussion is frequent, and it is usually pertinent to the task at hand.	_____	_____
3. Group members understand what they are trying to accomplish.	_____	_____
4. People listen to each others' suggestions and ideas.	_____	_____
5. Disagreements are tolerated and an attempt is made to resolve them.	_____	_____
6. There is general agreement on most courses of action taken.	_____	_____
7. The group welcomes frank criticism from inside and outside sources.	_____	_____
8. When the group takes action, clear assignments are made and accepted.	_____	_____
9. There is a well-established, relaxed working relationship among the members.	_____	_____
10. There is a high degree of trust and confidence among the leader and subordinates.	_____	_____

---

* This checklist is based on the observations of two theorists of group behavior in organizations: Douglas McGregor, *The Human Side of Enterprise* (New York: McGraw-Hill, 1960); and Rensis Likert, *New Patterns of Management* (New York: McGraw-Hill, 1961). The statements included in this checklist are those the present author believes are still valid today.

	Mostly Yes	*Mostly No*
11. The group members strive hard to help the group achieve its goal.	_____	_____
12. Suggestions and criticisms are offered and received with a helpful spirit.	_____	_____
13. There is a cooperative rather than a competitive relationship among group members.	_____	_____
14. The group goals are set high but not so high as to create anxieties or fear of failure.	_____	_____
15. The leaders and members hold a high opinion of the group's capabilities.	_____	_____
16. Creativity is stimulated within the group.	_____	_____
17. There is ample communication within the group on topics relevant to getting the work accomplished.	_____	_____
18. Group members feel confident in making decisions.	_____	_____
19. People are kept busy but not overloaded.	_____	_____
20. The leader of the group is well suited for the job.	_____	_____

Chapter 11

Quality Circles

The lawnmower division of a manufacturing company was experiencing a high number of customer complaints about its product. In response to these quality problems, division management decided to implement a program of quality circles—a small group (about 10) of employees performing similar work who voluntarily meet regularly to identify quality and production-related problems in their area, analyze the causes of the problems, recommend solutions, and monitor the results.

Biff, final assembly supervisor at the Sterling Company lawnmower division, felt proud yet apprehensive as he walked into the conference room located on the second floor of the plant. He purposely arrived five minutes after the hour in order to be the last member of the quality circle to enter the conference room. Smiling, Biff began with these comments:

It looks like everybody is here. That's a good sign. The way we planned this quality circle, none of you are in my department. Yet, I still recognize all your faces and I know now who you are. We're not that big a plant. Management thought it would be better to have a supervisor run the QC who wasn't your regular supervisor. That way none of you will be shy about making a point that could be interpreted as a personal criticism of the boss.

You may have heard that the QC idea is now being used by General Electric, Lockheed, and many other U.S. companies. You guessed it. The idea came originally from the United States and was then developed by Japanese industry. Those folks sure try hard to squeeze all the bugs out of a product. At Sterling Mowers, we're going to have our own quality control circles. Since all of you are volunteers, I'd like you to tell each other and me why you volunteered. Let's start with you Luther, since you're a respected old-timer.

Luther: Careful now Biff, I'm not that much older than you. [*Laughter.*] The way I see it, I hate to see Sterling Mowers run down hill. We once had a dandy mower. Now, too many of them are getting out into the hands of the consumer in poor shape. I want to do something about the problem.

Ruby: I guess it's my turn. I'm younger than most of the workers in this plant. I'm interested in working my way up a bit. Maybe getting promoted to supervisor or better. I look upon the QC as a way of being noticed for some of my good ideas.

Alfie: Couldn't have expressed it better myself. I want a piece of the same action.

Hank: Guess I have a different reason for joining the circle. I figured a bull session like this for an hour or so every two weeks would put a little more fun in my job. By now I can almost put on those mulching blades blindfolded.

Georgia: I'm with you. I'm looking forward to stretching my mind a little bit during working hours.

Biff: Now that we know why we're here, let's dig right in. Just to get us started, what are the quality problems with Sterling Mowers that you think we can do something about? If any solution to the problem comes to mind, you might mention it now. But we'll do most of the problem solving at later meetings. We're just trying to identify some important problems today.

I'd like to begin with a tip from my neighbor. He bought a Sterling mulching model early last spring. He had it home but two weeks, and the darn thing wouldn't shut off unless he pulled out the wire that connects to the spark plug. He went back to the dealer, and they had to put in a new switch. By the time he got his mower back from the dealer, his grass was seven inches high. He told me to tell the company president that Sterling owed him a good mowing. Can't say I blame him.

Ruby: Biff, we'd had that problem before. My opinion is that either we make our own switches from now on or buy them from a more reliable supplier. Those switches are shoddy merchandise.

Georgia: The way I hear it, we've been shocking too many people. They're fool enough to touch the spark plug when they pull off the connector. Our written warning doesn't work. We've got to invest 30 cents a mower and put a rubber insulator over the connector and plug. Some other brands have that kind of a safety gismo.

Luther: Here's a quality suggestion that stems from my conservative nature. I like to keep things for a long time, including my Sterling Mower. Unfortunately, the wheels run out of tread long before the motor conks out. Lucky for me I know where to get inexpensive replacements [*laughter*]. But other folks aren't so lucky. Those treadless wheels get mighty slippery on wet grass. We certainly don't want to see any users hurt by a sliding mower.

Hank: I'm not rich enough to have a yard. Nor do my folks have one. But I do see a quality problem that has created a lot of unhappy customers and dealers. The main blade falls off on too many of our mowers. I think we could use a better nut for connecting the blade to the drive shaft. The one we use right now is about the same kind our bike division uses to hold seats on tricycles.

Mike: Let me run one by you mechanical marvels. The advertising department has those fancy advertisements telling people they can use our mulching model to pulverize leaves in the fall. "With a Sterling Mulcher, you can throw your rake away." says the ad. But there's one rub. An uncle of mine has a mild case of arthritis. He tells me it's about impossible for him to pull start the mower once the weather gets cool. One cold fall day I asked him why he was out raking leaves when he had a Sterling mulcher in the garage. He told me his rake at least starts in cold weather.

Biff: I see we've already put enough problems out on the table to last us a year. Our plan is to put these problems and suggestions for their solution into a neat little package. We can even get fancy and try the charting technique used by the folks in industrial engineering. Then we bring all this information to plant management. If what we have to say makes sense to them, we'll be given the authority to make changes. Any business has to run this way. Suggestions are nice, but some of them might be too costly for management to pursue.

Here are some 5 by 8 cards. Just write down any suggestions you might have for tackling one of the problems we've mentioned so far. Or if another problem comes to mind, write that one down. At our next meeting, we'll refine all these suggestions. After that, we'll be doing some statistical analysis to help prevent us from being too subjective in our recommendations.

After 15 minutes are allowed for suggestion writing, Biff collects the cards. After reading them silently, he addresses the group:

Let me now read out these suggestions so everybody can hear them. Again, what we have here today is not necessarily the final solution. We may have to call in specialists from the quality control and product engineering departments to help us with the fine points. Here's the list:

Anybody working on the design of a lawnmower component must first be assigned to 10 hours of hard labor at mowing lawns. I really think some of the designs in our product were made by designers and engineers who never mowed a lawn.

Let's put an almost foolproof lockwasher between the nut and the drive shaft bolt. Our blades shouldn't fall off while the mower is in operation.

As I already told the group, how about finding a new source of supply for those switches that are used to turn the mower on and off?

Maybe we should be using polyurethane wheels instead of rubber ones. Then our mowers wouldn't lose traction before the motors wear out.

Starting right away, let's put an inexpensive insulator around the spark plug and connector cord.

Let's lean on engineering to help us figure out a way to build an easier starting motor—one that starts up with pull when the weather gets down to around 45 degrees F.

I'm going to jot these down on the chalkboard here. Then we can decide which should be our top priority item. My first thoughts are that the biggest technical problem would be making an easier starting mower. What I intend to do is plug this problem into a Pareto chart to help us identify our most serious problem. You may have heard of the 80–20 principle before, that is the heart of the Pareto diagrams. It refers to the fact that 20 percent of the problems cause 80 percent of the major mistakes. I'll bet that 80 percent of our customer complaints are in reference to starting the mower. What do you folks think?

The group then agreed that the other complaints were relatively minor in comparison to the slow cold-weather start problem. Biff then closed the meeting with these comments: "It seems that our top priority will be dealing with the slow start problem. Much of that is out of our hands. We'll try to get the head of product engineering to join us in our meeting two weeks from now. I'll ask him tactfully if he's ever mowed a lawn."

May I make a comment before we all leave?" asked Ruby. "I think I'm going to enjoy being part of the quality control circle. But I have a family to help support. I hope we don't tell management to make such a high-priced mower that most people won't want it. I hear that most of our customers take such bad care of their mowers that they have to be thrown away after a couple of years. We can't build in too much quality."

The group pondered Ruby's comment as they left the conference room.

A LOOK AT SOME OF THE EVIDENCE

Quality control circles, on balance, appear to be making a positive contribution to product quality, profits, morale, and even improved employee attendance.[1] The widespread attention QCs have received in recent years has led logically to their evaluation by both businesspeople and researchers. Here we will rely on several types of evaluations methods, sampling first the positive evidence, followed by negative.

Favorable Outcomes with QCs

Honeywell, the high-technology electronics firm, has become a pioneer in the application of QCs in North America. Currently they are operating several hundred QCs domestically. Typically about a half dozen assembly workers are brought together every two weeks by a first-level supervisor or team leader. "We feel that this type of participatory management program not only increases productivity," says Joseph Riordan, director of Honeywell's Corporate Productivity Services, "but it also upgrades the quality of work life for employees. Line workers feel that they are more a part of the action. As a result, we find that quality of work improves and absenteeism is reduced. With this kind of involvement, we have, in many cases, been able to increase the capacity of a line without the addition of tooling or extra shifts."

Honeywell used the quality control circle method to manage the problem of winning a renewal bid for a government contract. Other firms were making the same piece of electronic apparatus at competitive prices. "Here was a situation," Riodan relates, "where we already had cut our rejects down, where all of the learning had effectively gone out of the process." The problem was assigned to the quality circle representing that particular work area. "They came up with a suggestion for further automating the process that enabled us to improve our competitive position by about 20 percent and win the contract."[2]

In an attempt to determine the appropriateness of QCs to North American firms, a team of researchers set up a one-year field experiment at a metal fabricating facility of an electronics firm.[3] The subcomponents made by this facility are used by other divisions in the manufacture of electronic instrumentation products. Management of the facility was receptive to improving product quality and morale since both were seen as being below satisfactory levels.

Eleven quality circles, averaging nine production employees each, were established. A control group, consisting of employees doing comparable work, but not assigned to QCs, also was established. The research question formulated by Justin Y. Shimada, Kenneth M. Jenkins, and Lewis N.Goslin was, "Do employees who have received circle training and started a viable circle process have higher performance and better attitudes on the job than employees in the control group?" The researchers also wanted to investigate whether the quality control program was cost effective.

Performance was measured by a computerized monitoring system created out of the company's existing employee performance reporting system. Both quantity and quality measurements were taken. Employee attitudes were assessed by the Hackman-Oldham Job Diagnostic Survey, which measures employee attitudes about the specific work task they perform. Five job characteristics were combined into a single index called the Motivating Potential Score (MPS). The time period for the measurement process was one year, including the baseline data period.

The major result of the circle program was its positive impact on reject rate, as shown in the top half of Figure 11-1. Per capita reject rates for quality circle participants dropped by one-third to one-half of the former rate by the time the program had run three months. The reject rates for the control group surprisingly increased during the same period.

An explanation offered by the researchers for these results is that circle members tackled the issues of internal communication as a top priority item. For example, one of the initial projects implemented by the QCs was improving training manuals and procedures, including translating materials into a worker's native language, if the workers desired. Careful attention to better training in fundamentals prevented many errors.

Circle members made fewer errors. In addition, those errors the circle members did make tended to be less expensive to scrap or rework into usable parts. The explanation given for these results is that circle training instructs employees how to prioritize problems on the basis of dollar impact on the company. The cost savings generated by the lower reject rate represented a 300 percent return on investment in the cost of the program. However, the QC program did not increase those production rates which were more dependent upon orders and production technology than on quality. The researchers emphasized that the focus in this experiment was on quality, resulting in an increase in the net usable quantity produced.

To assess the impact of quality control circles on employee attitudes, two separate measures were taken of both the experimental and control groups. Prior to training about the QC method, both groups took the Job Diagnostic Survey. As anticipated, no significant difference was found between the two groups. Six months later, the JDS was readministered. By this time, the QC participants had been trained, were meeting regularly, and were solving operational problems with the circles.

The second testing indicated that the Motivating Potential Score for the circle participants increased, while the control group showed a decrease (see Figure 11-1, bottom). No other changes were present in the work environment that would impact the experimental group differently than the control group. The researchers therefore concluded that the improvement in employee job attitudes could be attributed to the circle training program and the problem-solving activity. The job characteristic most influenced by the quality activity was skill variety—the extent to which the job requires a variety of different skills. According to Shimada, Jenkins, and Goslin, the QC process affects attitudes primarily because it becomes a recurring part of the job itself.[4]

Negative Outcomes with Quality Circles

Despite the favorable outcomes reported, many negative instances have been reported. A review of the results of the first surge of QC activity in the

Figure 11–1
Impact of Quality Circles on Employee Performance and Attitudes

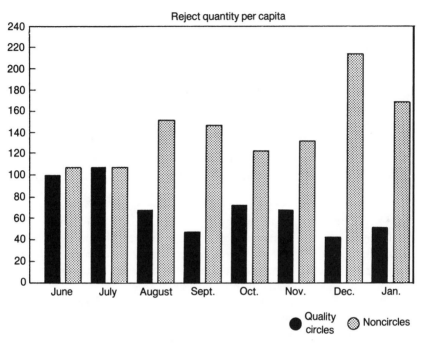

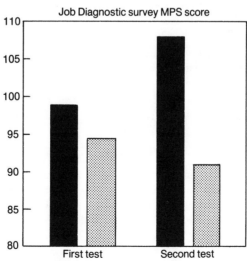

Source: Justin Y. Shimada, Kenneth M. Jenkins, and Lewis N. Goslin, "Quality Circles Meet the Challenge," *Business Forum,* Spring 1983, p. 20. Reprinted with permission.

United States revealed that as many as 75 percent of initially successful programs were no longer in operation after a few years. Even Lockheed, one of the American pioneers in this method, has decreased its involvement with quality circles.[5] Robert Cole, a recognized authority on the Japanese workforce, made these pessimistic remarks:

> The fact is that the circles do not work very well in many Japanese companies. Even in those plants recognized as having the best operating programs, management knows that perhaps only one-third of the circles are working well, with another third borderline and one-third simply making no contribution at all. For all of the rhetoric of voluntarism, in a number of companies, the workers clearly perceive circle activity as coercive. Japanese companies face a continuing struggle to revitalize circle activity to insure that it does not degenerate into ritualistic behavior.[6]

A study of quality circles in 29 companies conducted by Matthew Goodfellow found only eight of them to be cost effective in terms of gains in productivity. Management consultant Woodruff Imberman investigated the 21 unsuccessful QC efforts and found four major causes of failure. First, in many firms the employees intensely disliked management. Their antagonism carried over to the quality control circles which some employees perceived to be a management ploy to reduce overtime and trim down the workforce by increasing productivity. Second, most organizations did a poor job of selling the QCs. Instead of conducting individual discussions with employees, they relied on flip charts, booklets, and formal management presentations. The workers were left wondering, "What's in it for me?"

Third, the supervisors chosen to lead the circles received some training in human relations and group dynamics, but they felt that little of this information satisfied the specific needs of their own departments. Fourth, most of the 21 firms regarded the QC programs as merely a way of improving the efficiency of production techniques. They did not realize that QCs cannot succeed unless top management is willing to shift its philosophy toward emphasizing good human relations among employees themselves, and between management and employees.[7] This last point hints at the importance of establishing the conditions that allow a quality circle program to succeed.

KEY ELEMENTS OF A SUCCESSFUL PROGRAM

Quality control circle programs show some variation from company to company, whether these companies are engaged in manufacturing or service. Among the points of difference are how frequently they meet, how much authority is granted to the team leader or supervisor, whether they use a group facilitator in addition to a supervisor, and how much coordination there is with the already existing quality control department. Based on the judgments of several observers, the successful programs have certain elements in common. These key elements are closely tied in with systematic application of behavioral science knowledge, the use of quantitative problem-solving techniques (such as Pareto charts and histograms),and sound managerial judgment. A synthesis of these key elements is presented next.[8]

Quality circles work best in firms where good employee-management relations already exist. As noted by John D. Blair, Stanley L. Cohen, and Jerome V. Hurwitz, QCs are not likely to succeed in organizations suffering from acrimonious union-management conflict or high levels of distrust between employees and management.[9]

Top Management Is Committed to the Program. Without commitment from top management, the initiation of a QC program is inadvisable. Instead the director of the circle project should first prepare reports on other companies where QCs have been successful, and present them to top management.

Circle Leaders Use a Participative Leadership Style. Laurie Fitzgerald, a QC consultant, advocates the "leader-as-a-worker-for-the-members" concept. When the circle leader acts in a highly authoritarian role, the members are usually unresponsive.[10]

The Right People and the Right Area Are Selected. For quality circles to be effective, the program manager has to be enthusiastic, persistent, and hard-working. The facilitator or team leader must be energetic and cooperative. Also, another important step in getting the programs off the ground is to select an area of the company where one can expect cooperation and enthusiasm from participants.

Program Goals Are Stated Explicitly. Objectives should be made clear to avoid confusion or unreasonable expectations from the circle program. Among the goals of QC programs are improving product quality, increasing productivity, improving communications between workers and supervisors, decreasing product costs, improving the quality of work life, and preparing people for future supervisory assignments.

The Program Is Well Publicized throughout the Firm. Once the program is started, information about it should be disseminated widely throughout the company. Better communication results in less resistance and fewer negative rumors about the program. The content of the communication should be open and positive. As Sud Ingle notes, "Ups and downs always exist in this type of program, but one should keep a warm spirit and high aspirations."[11]

The Program Starts Slow and Grows Slowly. Slow and brief introduction of the program helps expose people to new concepts and helps reduce doubts about its intention and potential merit.

The QC Program Is Customized to Meet the Needs of the Firm. A subtle source of failure for some QC programs is the use of a canned set of procedures that do not pay attention to local circumstances. A QC participant whose work is data processing may have difficulty with the translation of a case from the aerospace industry. A workable compromise is to use standard training as a framework and build on it with the unique problems of the firm in question.

Quality Control Circles Are Used As a Method of Employee Development. A key purpose of these circles is to foster personal development of the participating workers. "If the QC is installed as a tool for selfish gain on the part of management, they would do better not to begin."[5]

Management Must Be Willing to Grant Recognition for Ideas Forthcoming from the Circles. If management attempts to manipulate the circle volunteers or try to take credit for improvements away from them, the program will most likely backfire. More will be lost than gained.

Membership Should Be Voluntary. As with job enrichment and all forms of participative management, employee preference is an influential factor. Employees who desire to contribute their ideas will generally perform better than employees who are arbitrarily assigned to the QC.

Quality Circles Are Group Efforts and Not Individual Efforts. Recognizing this factor decreases showboating and competition, and increases cooperation and the value of interdependence within the group or department. Quality circles, not individual employees, receive credit for innovations and suggestions for improvement.

Ample Training Is Provided. Program volunteers generally need some training in conference techniques or group dynamics. At a minimum, the circle leader will need skills in group participation methods. Otherwise, he or she will wind up conducting lectures about topics such as quality improvement and productivity improvement. Leaders and participants will also need training in the use of whatever statistical and problem-solving methods are to be used.Following are eight major problem-solving techniques and their purposes.[12]

1. Brainstorming is used to identify all problems, even those beyond the control of the circle members.
2. A check sheet is used to log problems within the circle's sphere of influence within a certain time frame.
3. A Pareto chart graphically demonstrates check sheet data to identify

the most serious problem, i.e., those 20 percent of the problems that cause 80 percent of the major mistakes.

4. A cause-and-effect diagram graphically demonstrates the cause of a particular problem.
5. Histograms or bar charts are graphed showing the frequency and magnitude of specific problems.
6. Scatter diagrams or "measle charts" identify major defect locations by having dots on the pictures of products, thus identifying dense dot clusters.
7. Graph and control charts monitor a production process and are compared with production samples.
8. Stratification, generally accomplished by inspecting the same products from differing production areas, randomizes the sampling process.

Creativity Is Encouraged. As illustrated in the opening case and mentioned above, brainstorming, or variations thereof, fit naturally into the quality circle method and philosophy. Maintaining an attitude of "anything goes" is particularly important, even if rough ideas are later refined. If half-processed ideas are shot down by the leader or other members, idea generation will extinguish quickly.

Projects Are Related to Members' Actual Job Responsibilities. Quality circles are not arenas for amateur speculation about other people's work. People make suggestions about improving the quality of work for which they are already responsible. Thus the mower manufacturers at Sterling are not plagued with sorting out suggestions from the quality circles at divisions engaged in the manufacture of something entirely different such as lawn chairs. (We are not taking the dogmatic position, however, that productive innovations in one field cannot come from people outside that field.)

Effectiveness Is Measured Using Baseline Data. The data shown in Figure 11-1 illustrate this principle. Before-and-after data should be collected for each QC project in order to measure the effectiveness of the QC suggestions. Based on results obtained with a quality circle they implemented in a medium technology firm, Robert J. Barbato and Richard E. Drexel suggest that it is important to measure and report success in terms directly related to productivity. Effectiveness can be tested using baseline measures such as the amount of rework, rate of absenteeism, rate of turnover, and attitude change.[13]

The Argument For and Against Quality Circles

A major argument for quality circles is that they represent a low cost, efficient vehicle for unleashing the creative potential of employees. In the process highly desirable ends are achieved such as quality improvement and improved quality of work life. Quality circles, in fact, are considered part of the quality of work life movement.

Another favorable feature of these circles is that they are perceived positively by management, workers, the union, and stockholders. A firm contemplating implementing such a program thus does not run the risk of internal or external opposition. (It is conceivable, however, that opposition will be forthcoming if management fails to develop a formal reward system for quality circle contributions.)

Quality circles contribute to organizational effectiveness in another important way. They have emerged as a useful method of developing present and future managers. An example of this oft-repeated phenomenon is furnished by C. Philip Alexander. He reports that a major computer manufacturing firm established a quality circle separate from the training department. After the program had been operating two years, the director of training observed that the supervisors who were quality circle leaders were significantly more self-confident, knowledgeable, and poised than other supervisors who were attending the regular training program. The director believed that the supervisors' involvement in the QC training programs and activities were the major contributor to this difference.[14]

One major criticism of quality circles is that many of them are not cost effective. Furthermore, even more pessimistic is the criticism offered by Blair, Cohen, and Hurwitz that the reported successes of QCs may be attributable to factors other than the actual quality circle program. One explanation is that the attention paid to employees by management may be the force behind the gains in productivity and morale (the well-known Hawthorne effect). Another possible explanation of the successes of quality circle programs is that the gains are due to improved group dynamics and problem-solving techniques.[15] Therefore, an entire QC program need not be conducted just to achieve these gains.

A discouraging argument has been advanced that quality circles may not be suited to the North American workers. Matsushita Electric, a leading user of the quality circle method in Japan, does not use circles in its U. S. plant (located in Chicago) because it does not consider the American worker suited to circle activities.[16] Perhaps Matsushita management believes that Americans are too self-oriented to be group oriented.

Quality circles may prove to be breeding grounds for friction and role confusion between the quality control department and the groups themselves. Unless management carefully defines the relationship of quality circles vis-á-vis the quality control department, much duplication of effort (and therefore waste of resources) will be inevitable.

Exclusive reliance upon volunteers for the circles may result in the loss of potentially valuable ideas. Many nonassertive people may shy away from participation in the circles, despite their having valid ideas for product improvement.

Some employees who volunteer to join quality control circles may be doing so for the wrong reasons. The circle may develop the reputation of being "a good way to get away from the line for awhile and enjoy a coffee break and a good bull session." (To counter such an abuse of the quality circle program, QC group members might monitor the quality of input from their own group members.)

GUIDELINES FOR ACTION AND SKILL DEVELOPMENT

An early strategic step in implementing a quality control circle is to clarify relationships between the circle and the formal quality control department. Otherwise, the quality control department may perceive the circle as a redundancy or threat. One effective arrangement is for the quality circle to complement the quality control department; the QC department thus does not become subject to the loss of authority.

Membership in the circle should be voluntary and on a rotating basis. In many instances a team member will soon run out of fresh ideas for quality improvement. Rotating membership will result in a wider sampling of ideas being generated.

Quality control circles should be implemented on a pilot basis. As the circle produces results and wins the acceptance of managers and employees alike, it can be expanded as the demand for its output increases.

Do not emphasize quick financial returns or productivity increases from the output of the quality circles. The program should be seen as a long-range program which will raise the quality consciousness of the organization. (Nevertheless, as noted in this chapter, immediate positive results are often forthcoming.)

Management must make good use of many of the suggestions forthcoming from the quality control circle, yet still define the limits of the power and authority of the circle. On the one hand, if none of the circle's suggestions are adopted, the circle will lose its effectiveness as an agent for change. Circle members will become discouraged because of their lack of clout. On the other hand, if the circle has too much power and authority, it will be seen as a governing body for technical change. Under the latter circumstances, it is also possible that people will use the circle for political purposes. A given individual who wants to get a technical modification authorized may try to influence a member of the quality circle to suggest that modification during a circle meeting.

To develop skill in conducting a quality circle, the leader should follow closely the above suggestions in addition to those offered in

---

the chapter section: Key Elements of a Successful Program. Training in group dynamics and methods of participative management will be particularly helpful. If the right structure is established for the circle, it will facilitate skill development. Experience suggests that it is best to begin with about nine members and a leader. It may also prove helpful at the outset to appoint a group facilitator (an internal or external consultant) who can help the group run more smoothly.

Questions and Activities

1. In your estimation, are the results achieved so far with quality circles too good to be true?

2. If you were the manager of the quality control department, what would be your attitude toward the quality circle?

3. What application do you see for quality circles in service organizations, such as the public assistance (welfare) department, hospitals, and banks?

4. What similarity and differences do you see between a suggestion system and a QC?

5. Typically the team leader of a QC is not the regular boss of the circle members. Why do you think things are arranged this way?

6. To what extend do you think it is realistic to expect production workers to learn the statistical and problem-solving techniques typically used in a quality circle?

7. Try and locate a person who has participated in a quality circle. Record that individual's description of the method and results of his or her quality circle experience.

Notes

[1]Mike Catiller, "Quality Circles—A New Beginning," BNA *Communicator,* Winter 1983, p. 13.

[2]This quote and the preceding ones are from Mike Michaelson, "The Decline of American Productivity," *Success,* October 1980, p. 28.

[3]The description of this experiment follows closely the information found in Justin Y. Shimada, Kenneth M. Jenkins, and Lewis N. Goslin, "Quality Circles Can Meet the Challenge," *Business Forum,* Spring 1983, pp. 18–21.

[4]Ibid., p. 21.

[5]John D. Blair, Stanley L. Cohen, and Jerome V. Hurwitz, "Quality Circles: Practical Considerations for Public Managers," *Public Productivity Review,* March/June 1982, p. 14.

[6]Robert E. Cole, "Will QC Circles Work in the U.S.?" *Quality Progress,* July 1980, p. 30.

[7]Information synthesized in Berkeley Rice,"Square Holes for Quality Circles," *Psychology Today,* February 1984, p.17.

[8]The following list is based on two primary sources: Ed Yager, "Examining the Quality Control Circle," *Personnel Journal*, October 1979, p. 684; Sud Ingle, "How to Avoid Quality Circle Failure in Your Company," *Training and Development Journal*, June 1982, pp. 57–59.

[9]Blair, Cohen, and Hurwitz, "Quality Circles," p. 16.

[10]Laurie Fitzgerald, "Quality Circles—Three More Obstacles,"*Training and Development Journal*, May 1982, p.7.

[11]Ingle, "How to Avoid Quality Circle Failure," p. 59.

[12]George Munchus, III, "Employer-Employee Based Quality Circles in Japan: Human Resource Policy Implications for American Firms," *Academy of Management Review*, April 1983, p. 257.

[13]Robert J. Barbato and Richard E.Dexel, "Americanizing Quality Circles," in M. Sang Lee and Gary Schwendiman, eds. *Management by Japanese Systems* (New York: Praeger, 1982), p. 494.

[14]C. Philip Alexander, "A Hidden Benefit of Quality Circles," *Personnel Journal*, February 1984, p. 54.

[15]Blair, Cohen, and Hurwitz, "Quality Circles," p. 12.

[16]Munchus, "Employer-Employee Based Quality Circles," p. 261.

Some Additional References

Barnes, Peggy L. "Attrition—and What It Does to a Quality Circle," *BNA Communicator*, Winter 1983, pp. 11, 12, 16.

Garvin, David A. "Quality on the Line." *Harvard Business Review*, September–October 1983, pp. 64–75.

Schonberger, Richard J. *Japanese Manufacturing Techniques: Nine Hidden Lessons in Simplicity.* New York: The Free Press, 1982.

Takeuchi, Hirotaka, and John A. Quelch. "Quality is More than Making a Good Product." *Harvard Business Review*, July–August 1983, pp. 139–145.

Thompson, Philip C. *Quality Circles: How to Make Them Work in America.* New York, AMACOM, 1982.

Part 4

Improving Productivity and Quality at the Organizational Level

In this part of the book, we examine four programs designed to improve productivity and product quality, while improving the quality of work life simultaneously. All four are generally used across the entire organization, or at least a substantial-size unit of the firm. Three of these programs (the Scanlon Plan, labor-management participation teams, and Japanese-style management) are typically installed in manufacturing environments, while modified work schedules have found their widest application in office environments.

The Scanlon Plan, described in Chapter 12, is based more on practice than management theory. Nevertheless, it is a well-researched and well-documented technique of improving the productivity of the firm and the individual worker. Tracing back to the 1930s, Scanlon Plans are now regarded as standard methods of improving plantwide productivity through profit sharing. Currently these plans have attracted much interest as manufacturing companies seek ways to improve productivity.

Chapter 13, Modified Work Schedules, describes a widely used method of giving employees a greater say in determining their own work schedules. This method is popular because so many workers are part of two-paycheck families and some flexibility is required in matching work to family demands. Modified work schedules have grown more out of practice than theory or research. Theoretical precedents can be found in some of the 1930s literature about the importance of rest breaks for improving productivity.

Chapter 14 describes labor-management committees composed of small groups of representatives from labor and management who attempt to improve quality and work life and/or productivity through joint problem solving. Also referred to as labor-management participation teams, they follow the logic and theory of participative decision making. Chapter 15 describes Japanese management practices and their application to the American firm. In addition, we look at some of the controversy surrounding the true merit of Japanese-style management. Although Japanese management has not received much attention in North America until the current decade, it too is based clearly on well-established concepts of participative management.

Quality circles (described in Part 3), Scanlon Plans, labor-management participation teams, and Japanese-style management have an important conceptual and applied element in common. All of them work best when incorporated into a corporate culture that espouses the value of high quality and productivity. To be successful, organization-wide programs of this nature should not be considered isolated programs or "hot topics," but as part of a total commitment to high quality and productivity. This philosophy of quality-conciousness has been popularized by the work of Phil Crosby and associates, as described in *Quality is Free* (Mentor Books, 1979).

Chapter 12

The Scanlon Plan

Rocky Mountain Data Systems is a speciality service firm providing diagnostic information to the dental profession based upon computerized analysis of X-rays. Total employment is about 30 people with annual sales of about $1.5 million. The firm was looking for a method of increasing worker productivity and the commitment. The president of the firm, Robert J. Schulof, explains below the specifics of why the plan was introduced. He also describes the firm's experiences with the plan and the results achieved.[1]

To explain the rationale behind productivity sharing, the company's version of the Scanlon Plan, it is necessary to explain why and how it started. As usual with a state-of-the art pioneering project, RMDS's growth in the first five years was steady, but profit was nil. Each new worker had to be taught skill-reading and recording data from X-rays using computer equipment. It takes a year to develop a really good technician and adding the usual 20 percent turnover to a 20 percent growth rate meant constant training and thus inefficiency.

I thought our workers were fairly productive. We had a merit review system which rewarded each worker according to his or her own total production and the quality of their work. Every six months, the work was reviewed and the employee received a raise proportionate to quantity and quality. Certainly we were doing all we could to provide incentive. . . . Since the company was breaking even, the workers were getting every dollar we could afford to pay them. As president, I had not had a raise in four years.

It is true of almost every successful business that the owner is the one who works hardest. He has the most to gain and the most to lose. Perhaps this was the answer. We set out to restructure our compensation package so that each worker would have the same zeal we (the two part-owners) did.

After years of experimentation with every new management fad published, we have found that for us, the principle that each worker should make as many decisions as possible about his or her work is quite feasible. Management should not try to do all the thinking. However, involving the employees "democratically" in the decision-making process tended to waste time and cause divisive factional splits. We found that running a business must be autocratic in a sense. Decisions cannot be made by committee; they must be made by the person who has the most information and is best qualified to make the decision. When that person is the worker, that is fine. But when it is the boss, we found that democracy didn't work for us.

So we had to do something new. *We accepted the objective to pay everyone working for us as much as we could, consistent with the individual's contribution and the company's ability to pay.*

After much experimentation, we hit on the following formula (a variation of a Scanlon Plan):

1. We took a base year which we considered to be adequate in terms of profits—not so high that it was achieved under fortuitous circumstances, but not so low that we could not exist if we could not better it. We chose a 12-month period in which we were basically scraping by with a 5 percent return on invested capital.

2. We calculated two figures : (a) the total gross receipts and (b) the total salary figures (all employees).

3. We divided our gross sales or receipts by the salaries paid in the past year. This gives us the productivity base.

4. Each month we divide the sales by the salaries paid to calculate the productivity ratio for the month. If the month's productivity ratio is greater than the productivity base, we pay a bonus that month to each employee equal to one-half of the increase; therefore, sharing the productivity gain between management and labor.

For example, in the base year salaries paid equaled 45 percent of the gross; therefore, the productivity base is 2.2. If, in a given month, the productivity ratio is 2.6, which is a 20 percent increase over the base, we would give each one of our employees a separate check at the end of the month for 10 percent of their salary, which is equal to the productivity increase. The productivity bonus has the following advantages over other methods of incentive:

1. *We can afford to pay it.* The people make more as we make more.
2. *It is paid monthly.* The reward is not far away, maximizing motivation. In addition, it has an advantage over straight salary in that the worker

cannot rest on his or her laurels. The employee must perform each
month to get the money.

3. *It is easy to calculate.* We do not need to do a complete accounting in
order to pay it. All we need to know are gross receipts and gross salaries.

4. *It is an incentive geared to the success of the whole team, not just one
individual trying to look like a hero.* It develops a positive attitude
toward the company.

5. *It solves the problem of employees who have reached the maximum in their
category.* They now have new hope to make more.

In addition, we offered a quarterly cash bonus equal to 10 percent of the
profits. This was done so that profit "became a dollar you put in your
pocket." The profit-sharing bonus had the (one) disadvantage of requiring an
extensive calculation.

What was the result of all this? The immediate result was, of course, an
enthusiastic reaction. Everyone seemed to respond well to the goal that we
shall all try to get rich together. After all, if we didn't want to become
wealthier, why were we working?

We noticed immediately that the cases began going out faster. People were
not only working harder, but smarter; since it was *their* business, they
wanted to make *their* customers happy. Even though business hadn't increased, the backlog decreased and service and quality improved. In addition,
discussions changed from, "Why haven't you repainted the bathrooms?" to
"Is there money in the budget to repaint the bathrooms, or should we wait?
We certainly don't want to cut into profits."

The result was a real cash bonus the first month of about 36 real dollars
(dollar figures in this section are all converted to 1985 dollars) per employee.
This really excited them and was likely a key element in the success of the
program. We hadn't set the goal too high and had shown them we were
serious about paying them real money. The lump sum of $30 meant a lot
more than a raise of $9 a week which would have been dribbled away.

In subsequent months, some strange things happened. The marginal
workers who were previously "ripping off the company" were now "rippng
off the workers." A few found the environment unfriendly, subsequently
quitting. It was no longer socially acceptable not to work to capacity.

Who were these people replaced by? Well, as each vacancy occurred, there
was a discussion as to whether or not the gap could be filled by current
employees. The employees were allowed to decide whether they could find a
way to take over the heavier load and thereby increase productivity (and their
take-home pay), or whether they needed help. In every case, they elected to
bear the burden.

After the marginal employees left, another phenomenon ensued. The real
performers, who had been holding back, became more motivated than ever!

Under the previous policy, they apparently had the attitude, "If they don't care, why should I?" We find that equality is a myth. In our work, people are very unequal, and a key to our success has been to have the most unequal people we can find.

Long-term Effects. After five years, what have we learned about the long term? The positive things include:

Profits.   Profits have been up for the last five years. Pretax net is now 11 percent on sales, 22 percent on assets.

Employee compensation.   Those employees who are still with us have seen their total pay go from an average of $13,572 per year to $26,100 per year—an increase of 14 percent per year compounded.

Customer satisfaction.   Sales have increased at the rate of 16 percent per year, with no price increases. New products have been added, but old products have held their price.

The peak-out phenomenon.   A major problem we had previously was employees advancing to the maximum salary for their particular job. Here we had a choice. We could either not increase the individual's salary once that person reaches the maximum assigned value of a particular job category or we could ignore maximums and continue to increase wages. In one case, we got a decrease in motivation and productivity since nothing to look forward to is not very motivating. In the other case, the company, in fact, paid more than the individual was really worth. Neither answer was beneficial to the company. Under productivity sharing and profit bonuses, there is no maximum for anyone. Everyone, by continuing to work harder and finding more efficient, more profitable ways of doing things, can continue to have a future and see their earnings increase, even if the nominal base salary is fixed at the maximum for their category.

Empire building.   In our company we had previously experienced the middle-management phenomenon of "empire building." The tendency was to reward middle management according to the amount of money they spend—not according to the profit they make. Generally speaking, the larger portion of the budget a department can command, the more people working for it, the more the manager justifies his or her salary. This is actually opposite to the company's benefit.

Under productivity sharing, we find middle managers making more money by finding ways to have their departments do the same amount of work with less people, not more.

The "it's not my department" syndrome.   There is nothing more frustrating than calling a service agency and being transferred from one place to another, because no one really cares. Under productivity and profit sharing, the employees have had the feeling that it was their company, not someone else's company. Therefore, everyone tends to take the same interest the proprietor would and customer service is not handled with a careless attitude.

Labor versus management. Generally, the classic picture is that management makes money by getting labor to do as much as possible and paying as little as possible. Labor, on the other hand, finding itself stifled, usually reacts just by doing less work. It is like a football team where the line and the backfield are on opposite sides.

Under productivity and profit sharing, the benefits are all coming out of the same pot. A fair way has been decided to divide up the pie and as the pie grows everyone is going to profit proportionately. Therefore, everyone is working in the same direction and the distinction between labor and management has more to do with degree rather than kind.

Acceptance of new methods. Generally speaking, new methods do not provide any benefit for the worker. If they involve a productivity increase, they require learning (a new sense of frustration for the worker), the possibility that his or her job will be phased out and little else. Therefore, all change is met with firm resistance.

Under productivity sharing, a new change is sold on the basis of how it will increase productivity and profits and therefore what it means to take-home compensation. Acceptance of change is never easy, but at least now we have a method for selling it. Leadership becomes just a matter of getting people to understand what we want done and how it will benefit them if they do it.

Turnover. Turnover has dropped over 70 percent, down to around 5 percent. This has been the main contributor to profits, since our previous problem was constant training.

Will the workers really invest in the future? Yes, but not for too long. Eight years ago we decided productivity and profits could be greatly improved by totally new methods. This possibility was greeted with enthusiasm for a while. However, productivity did not increase during the changeover period, which meant no increase in earnings during 1977, or a loss of 8 percent due to inflation, since we did not have COLA (cost-of-living adjustment).

One year later, we reaped the benefits of the investment. This was a good thing, because our people were well aware that their take-home earnings had lagged. They were willing to postpone the payoff, but *not forever.* If we would have seen no progress for a second year, we would have had the same morale problem as any other company that did not raise wages during an inflationary period.

Management is still under constant pressure to produce and to keep paying up.

The Negatives

If you think just because you're paying more money than the fellow down the block that everybody's happy—you're wrong. People will tend to forget the total amount of money they've earned in bonuses and to remember only what their base salary is when comparing themselves with their friends and neighbors. Therefore, it is important to continue a barrage of information showing what the average bonus has meant for the last year and what that means in terms of average salary per week. Otherwise, they may forget how good they have it.

Increased money doesn't solve all your problems. We have had a tendency, because of the good wages we were paying, to be a little lax on the other aspects of management. However, it doesn't work. A good communication program is still essential to keeping the employee morale and motivation up. The increased compensation and participation in profits does not solve your problems. All it does is open the door so that people are willing to listen to solutions, because they believe the employer intends to behave in a way that is to their benefit.

Fight to hire. In most situations, before productivity sharing, it was management's job to keep employment down. Middle management would constantly try to justify hiring more people, while top management would put them in the "hot seat" to provide justification. Now we have an opposite fight which is just as fierce, but possibly a little more healthy. If we feel a person is required in a department, management generally has to fight to get someone hired. We have shown a general tendency, if anything, to be understaffed rather than overstaffed. In some situations, this might be just as costly as the reverse mistake, so it is necessary to exercise caution.

Even though you are giving productivity and incentive bonuses, it is still necessary to upgrade the base salary structure to keep up with inflation. Otherwise, you may find that you cannot hire new people in. The promise of a bonus in the future, since it can't be guaranteed, is a relatively poor negotiating position. . . . Whereas people do like to gamble and one of the beautiful aspects of productivity sharing is "the sky is the limit," 20 percent is probably an optimum proportion of incentive compensation for most people.

It costs a lot. When you begin productivity sharing, you are paying a bonus that doesn't cost you anything until performance is improved. However, after several years when you look and see that bonus payments are equal to profits and you could have twice as much profit if you canceled the bonus payments, management begins to question the program. The fact is, we do find ourselves at times paying more than what the same person might be making in a different company. It is, therefore, necessary to always remember that, although you are paying more, by definition you are getting more, because the employees are more productive. We are still paying less per unit than formerly.

Group size. If your productivity bonus is spread over a company of 100 people, then the action of one person or a small group of people has a relatively little effect on the bonus. . . . For this reason we have found it advisable to attempt to control our productivity bonus according to the individual performance of the departments of approximately 20 people. The overall profit-sharing bonus can be for the whole company, but it does provide the greatest incentive if you can make the reward as close as possible to the effort for the productivity bonus.

Pay something fast. One of the affiliate companies tried a similar system which failed, whereas ours succeeded. One of the major differences was that they had set their goal so high that the bonus during the first few months was negligible. In our situation, we started the bonus in such a way that it would pay off immediately. I cannot overemphasize the importance of an immediate payoff, since otherwise people will not think you are serious about wanting to pay them more money.

Changing the formula. It is quite often difficult to arrive at a formula which will hold now and forever. An important concept is that both management and labor should be confident in the fact that management is implementing this bonus system as an attempt to pay fairly for effort. It may be necessary to adjust the bonus system in the future as product mixes change. For instance, many of our productivity improvements involve expenditures for new capital equipment. Therefore, it was necessary to incorporate some factor for the cost of the capital equipment into the bonus system.

Another problem is *value added*. Some products may be made totally from the ground up; others may be just adding a small increment of value to an expensive raw material. You may find that your product mix is indeed changing and that material cost becomes a greater or lesser portion of what is "produced." It might be, therefore, important to define your bonus in terms of value added rather than productivity as was stated previously. The important thing is that management attempts to keep things fair.

Sharing the wealth in order to create more has become the management philosophy and style of our company. It has been so successful that we added an additional 10 percent to our profit-sharing bonus this year. It is not the unique solution to all problems. However, we have found that all problems become more amenable to solution when everyone is benefiting by having the problems solved.

A GENERAL DESCRIPTION OF THE SCANLON PLAN

Rocky Mountain Data Systems's utilization of the Scanlon Plan (SP) tended to emphasize its financial arrangement rather than the participative management (or organization development) aspects. Prior to reviewing research about the Scanlon Plan, it is, therefore, important to present a general description of this organizationwide participation and incentive system.[3]

In a typical Scanlon Plan, each department of the company has a production committee composed of a supervisor and employee representatives chosen by the members or appointed by the labor union. The major function of the committee is to screen suggestions for improvements made by employees and management. If a suggestion is accepted, the cost saving is paid not only to the individual making the suggestion but to the work group as a whole. If the suggestion offered to the committee is questionable or if it has far-reaching impact (such as the purchase of automated equipment), it is forwarded to a screening committee (composed of management and employee representatives) for evaluation and possible implementation. Details about the Scanlon Plan production committee are supplied in Figure 12-1.

The screening committee also determines the level of bonus to be paid each time period. Both the company and the employees ultimately participate in the cost savings. In many companies, the management share is 25 percent of the savings; labor receives the other 75 percent. A number of steps are involved in computing the bonus. The basic idea is to determine what improvement in labor costs is attributable to the suggestion under consideration. Assume a technician eliminated the process of heat treating a particular part by allowing the part to solidify overnight without heating. The time saved might be translated into a 30 percent per part saving. If the normal labor cost of that part is $3.00, the elimination of heat treating would represent a 10 percent savings in labor cost. A representative method of preparing the bonus report is shown in Table 12-1.

The Scanlon Plan distributes bonuses based on savings in labor costs—something over which workers have control. The ratio of labor costs to total costs is called the *Scanlon Ratio*. However, there are many other ways of calculating labor savings. At Rocky Mountain, total gross receipts were divided by total salary figures to arrive at a monthly productivity ratio. This was then compared to productivity base for the previous year.

Research Evidence about the Scanlon Plan

On balance, the Scanlon Plan has been successful despite mixed results with the system. When the Scanlon Plan works, employees become quite active in submitting suggestions, they more readily accept the need for technological change, and a desire to conduct work efficiently often develops. A Michigan State University researcher, J. Kenneth White, set out to discover what factors caused or contributed to successful implementations of the plan.[4]

Data for the study came from 23 companies, all of which were currently using the SP or had used it in the past. Not every company was able to provide information about all the factors involved in the study. At the time the study was conducted, 12 of the companies had abandoned the SP, at least

Figure 12–1
Scanlon Plan Production Committee

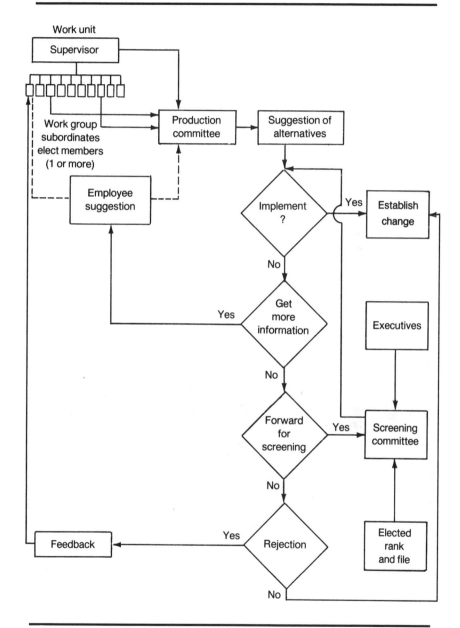

Source: John A. Fossum, *Labor Relations: Development, Structure, Process,* Revised Edition (Plano, Texas: Business Publications, Inc., 1982), p. 349.

Table 12–1
Bonus Report under the Scanlon Plan

a.	Scanlon ratio	0.40/1.00
b.	Value of production	$100,000
c.	Expected costs (a × b)	40,000
d.	Actual costs	30,000
e.	Bonus pool (c − d)	10,000
f.	Share to company—20% (e × .20)	2,000
g.	Share to employees—80% (adjusted pool) (g × .80)	8,000
h.	Share for future deficits—25% of adjusted pool (g × .25)	2,000
i.	Pool for immediate distribution (g − h)	6,000
j.	Bonus for each employee* as a percentage of pay for the production period (i/d)	20%

The June pay record might look like this for a typical employee:

Name	Monthly pay for June	Bonus percent
Ramon Santiago	$1500	20
Bonus		
$300	$1800	

*This example assumes that all employees are participating in the plan at the time this bonus is paid.

Source: Carl F. Frost, John H. Wakeley, and Robert A. Ruh, *The Scanlon Plan for Organization Development: Identity, Participation, and Equity* (East Lansing: Michigan State University Press, 1974), p. 15. Reprinted, adapted, and salary figures updated, with permission.

in practice if not formally. On the average, these 12 companies had used the plan for six years. Of the 11 companies who were currently using the SP, the earliest began in 1946, and the newest had been implemented less than one year at the time the study was conducted.

The companies ranged in size from 23 to 3,000 employees, with a median of 150. All were located in the Midwest and were engaged primarily in manufacturing. Eight of the companies were furniture manufacturers.

Two measures were used to classify a Scanlon Plan as successful or unsuccessful. One was whether the SP was subsequently abandoned or retained. The other was a rating of SP success based on three independent judges ratings of 13 companies' Scanlon Plans. Presumably not enough information was available for judges to rate all the SPs. Raters were asked to contrast the companies on "The extent to which the full effort, experience, creativity, and innovative ability of the entire workforce through the use of the Scanlon Plan are directed toward increasing the organization's total effectiveness."[5] Agreement among the raters was found to be quite high, statistically.

An attempt was made to obtain financial data and information about the number of suggestions generated under the SP. However, it was not possible to make company-to-company comparisons with these data.

Before presenting his conclusions, White is careful to note that there is no such thing as the Scanlon Plan—it is a process of organizational change that is unique in each of its applications. Thus no amount of research will enable one to specify precisely the circumstances in which the SP will or will not succeed. Given this limitation, the following conclusions and implications were drawn from the study.

- Employee participation, at least as perceived by the employees, is highly related to SP success. Therefore, a Scanlon Plan is unlikely to be successful unless a high degree of employee participation can be achieved.

- Company size does not seem to be a major factor in determining success of an SP. With perhaps up to 600 employees, the SP can be implemented without size imposing a limiting factor on the amount of success that can be achieved. (Previous research had suggested that the SP is best suited for a small company.)

- Managerial attitudes are strongly related to SP success. High expectations for the plan lead to good results; low expectations and skepticism lead to poor results. A positive attitude toward a modern approach to human resource management leads to good results; negative attitudes lead to poor results.

- Success of the SP is highly related to the number of years a company has stayed with the program. Therefore, patience seems to be in order for achieving high levels of success. Expectations in instant changes likely will be met with disappointment.

- Some tentative evidence sugggests that expectations may play a part in subsequent success. Therefore, when the plan is first considered, care should be taken that the employees develop favorable (but realistic) expectations. Also, employees and departments with initially high expectations should be selected to begin the program.

- The technology of the company does not seem to be related to success. A cursory examination of the technologies of successful and unsuccessful applications of the SP revealed no substantial differences.[6]

Strengths of the Scanlon Plan

The comments made by the president of Rocky Mountain Data Systems included a discussion of the strengths and weaknesses of the Scanlon Plan as used in his company. In this and the following section, we will make a few additional general statements about the same topic.

- In an era when declining productivity has become a dominant issue, Scanlon Plans are particularly timely. Few other methods of productivity improvement can claim a 50-year track record of so many successes.

- An important intangible benefit is the feeling employees have of actively participating in the management of the department, and sometimes the plant.

- A SP often contributes to desirable human resource management outcomes such as reduced turnover and increased ability to attract a better pool of employees. Most employees regard an SP as a favorable management practice.

- It gives the employee a carefully planned vehicle for submitting suggestions for productivity improvement. All suggestions are given consideration and cannot be squelched by a supervisor who chooses not to pay careful attention to employee suggestions.

- Scanlon Plans result in an increased number of suggestions from employees in comparison to organizations without such a plan. The plan encourages employees to unleash their talents for innovative thinking.

- A properly implemented SP helps develop employees at all levels and is useful in identifying employees with potential for supervisory responsibility. It also gives employees first hand experience with the need to justify capital and budget requests.

- Employees working under an SP become acutely aware of the cost of adding additional employees to the payroll. Featherbedding and the toleration of substandard performers is thus minimized.[7]

Weaknesses of the Scanlon Plan

Despite its contribution to labor-management relationships, the SP falls short of overcoming all worker suspicion toward management. One researcher reported that, "Several workers in one plant chortled that the company kept two sets of books and manipulated the bonus to exploit the workers. In that plant, and one other, some workers wanted to replace the incumbent union officials for cooperating in a speedup."[8]

The plan's bonus systems often engenders resistance because it places engineers and white-collar workers on a bonus and under the same plan as unionized production employees. A related problem occurs when one plant of a multiplant or multidivision company implements a Scanlon Plan. It is difficult to justify separate pay plans for employees at different locations.

The system is applicable mostly in situations where there is a combination of top management support and widespread worker acceptance for the plan. A correlated phenomenon is that the Scanlon Plan will not work well unless there is a healthy labor-management climate in the plant.[9]

GUIDELINES FOR ACTION AND SKILL DEVELOPMENT

Much of our discussion so far could be translated into guidelines for successfully implementing a Scanlon Plan. A few additional guidelines based on the experience of an SP consultant are presented in this section.

A delicate problem with an SP in a union plant is the role conflict faced by union leaders. During an SP meeting, the leader is supposed to cooperate fully with management in solving production problems. During a negotiating session, the leader is forced to work somewhat in opposition to management. To remove some of this role conflict, it is important for the same people not to deal with the same isssue in a Scanlon Plan meeting and a negotiating session. To help resolve such potential role conflict in one plant, the Scanlon Plan separated both the people and issues of problem-solving from the bargaining process.[10]

In unionized plants, it is essential to keep union matters out of Scanlon Plan problem-solving meetings. The SP consultant must keep all discussion of contract violations or safety out of the plan's committees. SP bonus payments should also be dispensed at a time distant from the expiration of the collective bargaining agreement. Should a strike be imminent, management would not be caught in the dilemma of making the bonus payment and thus supporting the workers during a strike, or withholding the bonus and undermining the plan.[11]

Like many methods of improving organizational effectiveness, the Scanlon Plan often experiences a quick plateauing of interest and results. Worthwhile suggestions about pressing problems are quickly used up. The antidote is to "feed the plan." Managers at all levels should be encouraged to submit the major production problems facing them to the attention of the Scanlon committees.[12]

Another major consideration when installing a Scanlon Plan is whether to use group or individual incentives, or a combination of the two. Typically group incentives are used, and they offer the advantage of being easy to administer. However, the link between an individual's effort and reward are somewhat weaker—a situation that can conceivably lead to a dimunition in motivation. The link between effort and pay is stronger under an individual incentive program, but unless the employees are involved in piece-work production, individual contribution is more difficult to measure. Another major drawback with individual incentives is that they may lead to a loss of interindividual and interdepartmental cooperation—precisely two of the problems an effective Scanlon Plan should help overcome.

It therefore seems advisable to follow the pattern of group incentives described in this chapter, while at the same time incorporating some small individual incentive into the total bonus program. Perhaps 5 to 10 percent of the bonus can be based on individual performance.

Questions and Activities

1. Currently, Scanlon Plans are operating in about 200 companies. Why not more?
2. To what extent is the Rocky Mountain Data Systems president justified in calling his incentive plan a Scanlon Plan?
3. What do you see as the critical difference between a conventional profit-sharing plan and the Scanlon Plan?
4. Suppose a company using an SP introduced high technology into the manufacturing process (such as cutting garments by a computerized machine). How might this effect the SP?
5. One negative feature of the SP at Rocky Mountain Data Systems was for middle management to want to run the company too lean. What is the long-term disadvantage of a company being understaffed?
6. How might an SP be used in a service business (such as a govenment agency or an insurance company) rather than a manufacturing company?
7. Interview a member of a labor union, explain to that person the basics of the Scanlon Plan, and then get his or her opinion about the fairness of the concept to employees.

Notes

[1] This first section of the chapter is reprinted from Robert J. Schulhof, "Five Years with a Scanlon Plan," *Personnel Administrator*, 30 Park Drive, Berea, OH 44017, June 1979, pp. 55-62, 92.

[2] Our policy is that the employee must have at least six month's service to be eligible for the bonus.

[3] John A. Fossum, *Labor Relations: Development, Structure, Process*, Revised Edition (Plano, Texas: Business Publications, 1982), pp. 348-351; Linda S. Tyler and Bob Fisher, "The Scanlon Concept: A Philosophy as Much as a System," *Personnel Administrator*, July 1983, pp. 33-35.

[4] This section of the chapter is based on J. Kenneth White, "The Scanlon Plan: Causes and Correlates of Success," *Academy of Management Review*, June 1979, pp. 292-312.

[5] Ibid., p. 295.

[6] Paraphrased from Ibid., pp. 310-11.

[7] All but the first item in this list is based somewhat on the review compiled by Fred A. Olsen, "Corporations Who Succeed through Communication—Three Case Studies," *Personnel Journal*, December 1979, pp. 864, 874.

[8] James W. Driscoll, "Working Creatively with a Union: Lessons from the Scanlon Plan," *Organizational Dynamics*, Summer 1979, p. 67.

[9] Ibid., pp. 75-76.

[10] Ibid., p. 68.

[11] Ibid., p. 74.

[12] Ibid., p. 73.

Some Additional References

Frost, Carl F. "The Scanlon Plan: Anyone for Free Enterprise?" *MSU Busines Topics*, January 1978, pp. 25–33.

Frost, Carl F.; John H. Wakeley; and Robert A. Ruh. *The Scanlon Plan for Organization Development: Identity, Participation, and Equity*. East Lansing: Michigan State University Press, 1974.

National Center for Productivity and Quality of Working Life. "A Plant-Wide Productivity Plan in Action: Three Years Experience with the Scanlon Plan." Washington, D.C.: NCPQWL, May 1975.

"Scanlon Plans in Operation: Recent Initiative in Labor-Management Cooperation." Washington, D.C.: NCPQWL, February 1976, pp. 43–50.

Moore, Brian E., and Timothy L. Ross. *The Scanlon Way to Improved Productivity: A Practical Guide*. New York: Wiley Interscience, 1979.

Sherman, George. "The Scanlon Concept: Its Capabilities for Productivity Improvement." *Personnel Administrator*, July 1976, pp. 17–21.

Chapter 13

Modified Work Schedules

The company described below was looking for a cost-effective method of reducing turnover and boosting morale. At the same, time, they were receptive to the idea of improving the quality of life for their employees. The vice president of administration believed that the large-scale adoption of modified work schedules would satisfy these purposes.

Zandau Corporation has experimented with deviations from the usual 9 to 5, 40-hour work week for a number of years. Currently they are convinced that a large-scale use of flextime and the judicious application of job sharing on a limited basis works best for them. The Zandau vice president of administration explained the basics of their modified work schedules to a case writer in approximately these words:

Zandau, as you know, is a multiplant, multidivision company. We have over 10,000 employees worldwide. Since our business is segmented into so many geographically separate plants and offices, we were in a good position to experiment with alternative work schedules. We had several goals in mind when we began the experiments. Since we are in business to make a profit, we wanted to reduce our biggest hidden cost of doing business— employee turnover. Plenty of evidence had accumulated that employees stay on the job longer when they have some say in choosing their own work hours. We also were looking for inexpensive yet effective ways to boosting morale.

On a more philosophical level, we wanted to do what we could to improve the quality of working life for our employees. If employees work at a decent job that also gives them a chance to take care of family demands with no big hassle, that's a real plus.

Before we get into the details of what is working for us, let me tell you about what did not work. We were too quick to jump on the bandwagon of the 4-day 10-hour workweek. They call it 4/40. Some employees liked it, but the program ran into substantial difficulties. Above all, it encouraged too much moonlighting. Many of our employees on 4/40 would use most of their three-day weekend to work another job. They came back to us on Monday generally fatigued and spent. Women with school-age children felt they could not properly take care of family demands after a 10- hour day. We got the same complaint from several concerned fathers.

Flextime, on the other hand, will probably become institutionalized at Zandau. The exact application of flextime varies from location to location, but its general scheme is the same. The employee has some leeway in choosing when to arrive and when to leave. Everybody has to be at work during the core time. It usually extends from 9:30 A.M. to 3:00 P.M. Aside from that, every employee must work a full eight hours and must take a half- hour lunch break. Flexibility takes place for a three-hour band in the morning and afternoon. Our employees on the program have the choice of coming to work anytime between 6:30 A.M. and 9:30 A.M. and leaving between 3:00 P.M. and 6:00 P.M.

The experts tell me that the term *job sharing* has several meanings. One aspect is *job splitting*, where two people divide up one job according to their skills. At Zandau, job sharing means that two people share one job. They each put in about 20 hours per week, but we are guaranteed full coverage. We usually insist that they spend about 15 to 30 minutes of overlap each working day. In that way they can properly coordinate what has to be done for the balance of the day. So far job sharing has had its biggest appeal to women who are highly skilled, but don't have room for a fulltime job in their schedules. Almost all of our job-sharers are women. The exceptions I can recall are a few male college students. Also, two male engineers with coronary bypasses share a job in our Wisconsin facility.

Next the management researcher interviewed a number of Zandau employees and supervisors to obtain a firsthand impression about how well modified work schedules are being received. The people interviewed were from a wide sampling of departments using modified work schedules.

The researcher spoke first to Gordon Jensen, director of communications at the home office, who said:

> You have come to the wrong person if you're trying to write a glowing report about flextime. The whole system lacks efficiency. I have to work about the same hours as I did before flextime. I'm accustomed to working from 8:30 A.M. to 5:00 P.M. On many days I need help in getting material together to respond to inquiries that arrive in the afternoon. But many of our employees choose to work early hours and that means they start getting ready by 3:00 to leave at 3:30.
>
> If you were here at 3:30, you'd see them marching out. It's trouble finding someone to do any work that I need done after that hour. Clerks ask me why I don't solve the problem by preparing materials for them to work on earlier in the day. My answer is that the event requiring attention didn't break then. I can't predict what is going to happen. A lot of work in the communications field involves responding to emergencies.

The researcher then spoke to two word-processing technicians who reacted favorably to the option of running errands during late afternoon instead of on the weekends or at night. One technician said:

> I used to go shopping at the supermarket on Saturday mornings or Friday evening. It was like a zoo. Now by shopping on Tuesday afternoons, I avoid the crowds. If I want to go department-store shopping, I take a long lunch break. I once tried shopping for groceries during a long lunch break. By the time I got home in the early evening, some of my food spoiled. I saved time but lost money.

The other technician chimed in:

> I like to sleep late on Saturdays, so I prefer not to use Saturday mornings for going to the dentist or post office. Instead I choose to take an occasional long lunch hour. That's when I now do the errands I used to do on Saturday morning.

Tony, a drafting technician, spoke to the researcher about his unique situation vis-a-vis flextime:

> A major reason I applied for a job at Zandau was because of flextime. A couple of years ago my wife and I split. For reasons that made sense to us, I was given custody of our daughter Tracy. Being a single parent is much more difficult than I thought. Tracy is only eight years old which complicates things. She often needs a parent during a normal working day. Once her school nurse called me at the office. Tracy had come down with the measles. I had to rush home from the office to take care of things.
>
> Then there's the inevitable school play. My daughter had a minor role but she would have been heartbroken if no parent came to see her. Because of flextime, I was able to juggle my schedule and see the play. Where I worked before, personal time off was strictly for things like house closings, divorces, or funerals.

A topic casually explored by the researcher was the use of flextime to adjust to the biological time clocks of people. Several office employees had comments to make about this topic: A programmer reported:

> I'm what you call a night person. I take care of a lot of household chores at night. Then I often go out, read, or watch late night TV. I just don't feel alert or much like working early in the morning. With our new time system, I can routinely start work at nine in the morning and leave at six. It's good for me and for the company. I can do more work when my mind is geared for work.

A secretary who considers herself to be a morning person contributed these comments:

> I'm at my best early in the morning. I get weaker as the day goes on. I like to fall asleep by nine or ten in the evening. Since flextime was put in our office, I chose the option of starting at 6:30 A.M. Being home by 4:00 P.M. is an added benefit. It's still early enough to go for a swim or wash the car.

A facilities manager gave the researcher his perspective about the impact of flextime on the use of company facilities:

From my standpoint, the new system is a mammoth contribution. Before flextime, our parking lots seemed like demolition derbies. So many people were rushing to get into or out of the same parking lots. Now it's much more staggered. Not many people are entering or exiting the lots at the same time. We've dramatically reduced the number of fender benders. It's also easier to provide assistance to a disabled vehicle when the lots are not so cluttered with cars.

We still have the same number of cars using the lots during core time. But that never presented a problem because the cars were not in motion. The roads leading to our plants and offices have also become less congested. Rush-hour traffic around our plants and offices is much less severe than it used to be. Without so many cars pouring in and pouring out at the same time, traffic conditions are more livable.

The value of flextime to working parents was highlighted in a conversation with an accountant. He noted:

Flexible working hours have helped Gwen and I mesh our schedules. I start work later than my wife. So it's my responsibility to get Jason up and ready in the morning. I then drop him off at the babysitter's on my way to work. Gwen then picks Jason up in the early afternoon on her way home from work. If we both worked the same hours, things wouldn't run as smoothly.

A woman who shared an administrative assistant position with a friend was eager to report her experiences to the researcher. She observed that the arrangement was beneficial to both women and the organization:

The best argument I can offer for our job sharing is that our boss is getting the best thinking of two assistants for the price of one. I usually work in the morning, and Gladys usually works in the afternoon. It doesn't fit either of our lifestyles to work more than about 20 hours per week. Parkinson's Law kind of works in the organization's favor. Each of us seems to get in close to a whole day's work in half a day. Because we are working only four hours, we take few breaks.

I have to admit there are a few problems of coordination. We hold briefing sessions at noon each working day to figure out what each person should be doing. But some things do fall between the chairs. It's inevitable that I sometimes say to Gladys, "I thought you were going to track down the answer to that request." She responds that she thought I had agreed to do it.

As part of his investigation into modified work schedules, the researcher also spoke to several supervisors. An in-plant printing foreman presented a favorable analysis:

So far the program looks good to me. But you have to understand our operation. We have mostly older, dependable workers. They've been around a long time. They like the company and they help supervise the few younger employees we have in the department.

Our oldtimers use flextime mostly to take care of legitimate problems that come up like medical appointments. If they borrow time from the company in the morning, you can be sure they will pay it back in the afternoon. They seem to like the flexibility so it's fine with me. It sure is a real boost to their morale around holiday time. Many of them like to shop when the stores aren't so crowded. Also if the weather is bad, they can go home early to avoid being hassled in traffic.

An inventory-control supervisor gave the researcher a less favorable impression of flextime:

I don't care if you pass my comments back to management. I've told my boss, and now I'm telling you. The new system creates a bag full of problems for the first-level supervisor. What else can you expect? It's us who have to live with the bright ideas brought into the company by top management.

Headache number one is all the checking up on people you have to do. How do you know they've put in a full day's work? We have some time-recording devices, but the employees can punch them for each other. Even if the time cards are honest, it still requires that the supervisor carefully study them. When you find that an employee hasn't put in a full day, and hasn't made it up that month, then you've got a problem. It's no fun reading the riot act to an employee over attendance.

Another problem is one that I predicted would happen. The new excuse around here is called *flex-out*. Once and awhile I need a particular employee in a hurry. If I can't find that person, I naturally ask another worker where he or she might be. More than half the time I get the answer that the guy or gal has flexed out. It used to be that if I couldn't find an inventory clerk, they would tell me the person was in the restroom. Flex out is a better excuse. You can be gone away from your work station longer.

From the supervisor's standpoint, there are even worse problems. The company policy doesn't state in black and white that a supervisor cannot work flexible hours. But it might as well. I know of no supervisor who takes personal advantage of the policy. We have the opposite of flextime. If we want to do an honest job of supervising our employees, we have to work longer hours. Maybe after awhile, this problem will be worked out. But for now it's the supervisor's biggest headache associated with this program.

The way I look at it, if you have complete trust in your employees, flextime works. If you have good reason not to trust them, the system only encourages goofing off at company expense.

After gathering the information revealed in the preceding interviews, the management researcher pondered what kind of conclusions could be reached about the value of modified work schedules.

RESEARCH ABOUT FLEXTIME IN BUSINESS AND GOVERNMENT

The burgeoning use of modified work schedule in organizations has sparked the interest of management researchers. Much of the attention has been focused on flexible working hours (also referred to as flextime or flexitime). Two reports of this nature, buttressed by other carefully conducted studies, provide the information used in this section of the chapter. Both reports synthesize information from a number of different flextime programs. One report, prepared by a management professor and arbitrator, is based in flextime results in 11 American firms including the U.S. Geological Survey. Altogether 3,426 employees and supervisors were involved.[1] The other report, prepared by a government personnel psychologist, is based on flextime programs in eight settings within the Social Security Administration (SSA). A valuable feature of the SSA study is that it closely follows the scientific method. For example, control or contrast groups are used, and before and after measures on topics were taken in all of the settings. Partially as a result of this study, 37,000 out of 78,000 SSA employees now work under flextime.[2]

Our summary combines the two large-scale reports and the findings of several smaller studies. Specific findings are organized by topic (or dependent variable) rather than by setting. Each topic is not necessarily covered in all the reports and studies.

Job Satisfaction and Morale. Whether in business, industry, or government, flextime programs have a dramatic effect in elevating job satisfaction or morale. Seven of the 11 firms (non-SSA) reported on this dimension: "Opinions in four of them ranged from a low of 79 percent (supervisors) to a high of 89 percent (employees) who felt that morale had improved because of flextime.[3]

At SSA, the reaction of personnel to the introduction of flextime was unusually enthusiastic and their satisfaction with the system grew. Supervisors were slightly less enthusiastic than employees. Of interest, "The impact of flextime on morale and job satisfaction was generally more pronounced in the operational settings than in those dealing with administrative or staff kinds of functions."[4]

Here are two examples of illustrative findings at SSA:

■ Prior to flextime, about 7 percent of employees at Disability Insurance Benefit Authorization had formally requested assignments to new jobs. After flextime, the figure dropped to 1 percent.
■ Before and after measures of job satisfaction showed that from 6 percent (General Administration, Equal Opportunity, and Clerical) of the study participants to 26 percent (Clerical, Filing, and Transcribing) of the study participants enjoyed their work more under flextime.

Employee Attitudes Toward Flextime. The increases in satisfaction and morale associated with flexible working hours indicate that employees enjoy flextime programs. Simultaneously, they have favorable attitudes toward the program itself. Most employees surveyed preferred not to return to fixed-hour schedules. Some evidence to the contrary was also found. One bank reported that 3 percent of its workforce preferred the old system. Another bank reported that support for flexible working hours dropped slightly over a 12-month period. Despite this negative minority, 75 to 97 percent of employees in these banks favored continuing along with flextime.

Another perspective on the relationship between flexible working hours and job satisfaction is that flextime does not enhance work satisfaction, per se, but it does make working a little easier. This conclusion was based on a study conducted with 200 employees in two firms in Ohio. No significant differences were found for the flextime groups compared with the fixed-hour groups on various work satisfaction measures. However, employees working under flextime did report certain other improvements, including easier travel and parking, a greater feeling of being in control of their work (an important issue to be discussed later), and more opportunities for leisure activities.[5]

Productivity, Efficiency, and Organizational Effectiveness. Flextime programs appear to have a mixed influence on productivity and performance. Nine of the 11 non-SSA firms provided information about the impact of flextime on productivity. Results were more often based on opinion and judgment rather than hard data. Of the firms using hard data, Mutual of New York (insurance) reported a 2.9 percent gain in productivity and Control Data showed a "slightly favorable trend."[6] In contrast, the State Street Bank found that efficiency decreased in two out of three departments. Companies in which attitudes about productivity were reported, showed similar mixed results. Representative findings include the following:

- At Control Data 66 percent of employees believed productivity had increased, while 11 percent perceived a decline.
- At Smith-Kline 93 percent of employees thought productivity had improved, while 32 percent of supervisors shared that opinion.
- Accounting employees at a medium-sized airline perceived that productivity was high.

At the various SSA settings studied, a sizeable proportion of workers under flextime perceived an increase in the quantity and quality of their work. Most attributed this improvement to the introduction of flexible work hours. Supervisory perceptions and objective productivity measures (such as median number of cards keypunched) were more conservative. The chief researcher reported, "There was little evidence to suggest that flextime adversely affected job performance and in four of the five settings having objective data the system was associated with varying degrees of improvement."[7]

Two of the research results in SSA settings are of particular interest to the public: (a) In the unit called Processing of Retirement and Survivors Insurance Claims, the average age of the pending backlog declined, and there was a 2.1 percent decrease in the actual volume of the backlog. (b) A reversal of expectation took place in the unit called Public Contact Claims. Less frequent gains in productivity were found in the experimental flextime offices than in the nonflextime control offices. Productivity measures included work backlog and average number of work units completed per employee.

A carefully controlled study conducted by Randall B. Dunham and Jon L. Pierce evaluated the impact of a flextime schedule on job satisfaction and customer service (both measured by questionnaires) in a public utility. As found in other studies, job satisfaction increased substantially. In addition, customer service showed a small but significant increase throughout the trial period.[8] An important feature of this study is that it incorporated a time-series analysis in its design, as shown in Figure 13-1.

Absenteeism. Flextime programs are helpful in reducing absenteeism; at worst, they do not worsen the situation. Most of the settings reported a decrease in absentee rates since the implementation of flextime. The Berol Corporation and the U.S. Geological Survey reported absenteeism reductions of 50 percent or greater. In two of the study sites in the SSA, flextime was associated with a slight reduction of annual and sick leave usage; in a third the program had a negligible effect. In the clerical, filing, and transcribing setting of SSA, annual leave usage decreased by an average of six hours per employee per six months under flextime; sick leave was down about two hours. Similar declines were observed in the unit called Process of Retirement and Survivors Insurance Claims.

Tardiness. Flextime significantly reduced tardiness in most firms and SSA settings and virtually eliminated it in the other settings. For example, it was reported that tardiness at the First National Bank in Boston was almost eliminated. Strikingly, nearly all of the supervisors in two SSA settings (Computer Programming, and Analytical and Staff Support Service) reported that flextime reduced tardiness to an "irreducible minimum."[9]

Turnover. Flextime had a less dramatic effect on turnover than tardiness. A bank found only a 0.1 percent decrease; a manufacturing firm reported that it noticed a "slightly" favorable trend. However, at the U.S. Geological Survey, the turnover rate was reported to be the lowest in five years (based on 2,230 employees and supervisors).

Overtime. Flextime programs appear to be helpful in reducing overtime. Only three organizations reported a decline in overtime, but in each instance the decline was substantial. At Smith Kline Corporation, overtime costs were down more than 20 percent; The State Street Bank of Boston found that overtime costs declined from $38,258 to $21,115 over the period studied. Supervisors at the Geological Survey reported "substantial" decreases in overtime.

Figure 13–1
The Impact of Flextime on Quality of Customer Service

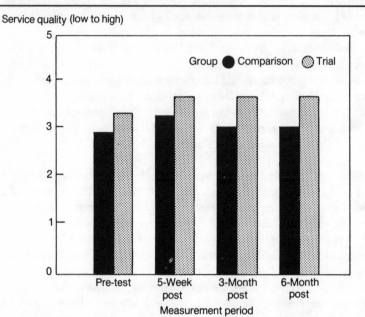

Service quality (low to high)

Source: Randall B. Dunham and Jon L. Pierce, "The Design and Evaluation of Alternative Work Schedules," *Personnel Administrator,* April 1983, p. 74.

Although it would appear that flexible working hours would have a positive impact on the personal lives of employees, this is not always true. A summary of modified work schedules prepared by Stanley D. Nollen concluded that flextime had a negligible effect on employees' home lives.[10] Nevertheless, there are probably subgroups of employees whose personal lives are enhanced by having greater flexibility to take care of personal matters during normal working hours.

Ease of Implementation and Patterns of Utilization. As studied in the SSA, no major operating problems surfaced. However, some settings had difficulty in providing full supervisory coverage throughout the flexible band (noncore) hours. Given the options available, employees generally chose to begin work earlier and had no strong feelings about having their time recorded by mechanical devices. An exception took place in the unit called General Administration, Equal Opportunity and Clerical. Supervisors and employees were generally dissatisfied with the use of mechanical timekeeping machines. Consequently, the machines were replaced by self-recording methods of tracking employee work hours.

The Case for and Against Modified Work Schedules

The strengths and weaknesses of both 4/40 and flexible working hours
follow a similar pattern: In general, they are more clearly related to improvement in attitudes than productivity. People tend to evaluate a modified work
schedule in terms of what it can do for them. A single parent who cannot find
suitable childcare arrangements to meet a 4/40 schedule will strongly resist
the program. Another individual who wants to work at the family restaurant
on weekends will quickly embrace the concept of 4/40 or 3/36. In this
section we will report observations made mostly about flextime because of its
ascendancy over 4/40 and job sharing. A current estimate is that 17 percent
of the American workforce has flexible hours.[11]

The most convincing case for modified work schedules is that they
contribute to both satisfaction and productivity in a variety of work settings.
Much of the research alluded to in this chapter has dealt with the advantages
of flextime. Although much less widely used, the 4–10 (four days a week, 10
hours a day) has also met with success. A county in Virginia implemented a
4–10 (also referred to as 4/40) schedule for its police division in response to
complaints expressed by officers about having to work seven consecutive
eight-hour days before getting time off. A serious morale problem existed
among the officers and the group manifested high turnover, excessive use of
sick time, and high absenteeism.

A committee assigned to the problem chose to adopt a 4–10 workweek,
with these modifications: "Each officer would work a rotating cycle of four
days on, three off; four days on, three off; and four days on, two off."[12] This
revamped schedule enabled officers to have up to 33 weekends off per year,
in contrast to the 12 alotted under the previous work schedule. After six
months of operation with the new work schedules, gains were found in both
satisfaction and productivity. Gains included (a) sick leave decreased 18.2
percent; (b) felony arrests by the police officers increased 42.5 percent,
misdemeanor arrests increased 69.5 percent, drunk driving arrests increased
75.4 percent, and other traffic-related arrests increased 38.9 percent.[13]

In the police officer example just described, the positive outcome may
have been achieved because the officers felt more relaxed and less fatigued. A
more general explanation of why modified work schedules lead to positive
outcomes is that employees gain more control over their work environments
(particularly with flexible working hours). John R. Turney and Stanley L.
Cohen observe that employees actively respond to their work environment
and are motivated toward higher productivity in relation to the extent to
which they feel they are in control of their work.[14] A person working under
a flextime system is likely to perceive such control.

A key advantage of flextime is that it can represent no change for a person
who wants to retain the same working hours. A sound business reason for
the continued growth of flextime programs is that they appear to motivate

employees toward worthwhile ends. Among the most impressive findings are increases in productivity, with simultaneous decreases in overtime, sick leave, and absenteeism. A major employee benefit derived from flextime is the employees' ability to schedule work to accommodate contingencies in their personal lives. Flextime also helps avoid traffic congestion. The power problem caused by so many people turning on home appliances and lights at the same time would also be alleviated.

Flextime also helps promote trust between superior and subordinate. Since most flexible work schedules allow employees to work before and/or after a supervisor is physically present, flextime gives supervisors daily experience in trusting subordinates.[15] Similarly, it gives employees the experience of being trusted to work without supervision.

A case can also be built against the widescale implementation of flextime programs. Many supervisors resist the program because flexible working hours make it difficult to supervise and even locate some employees. Communication with customers and other company employees often worsens, particularly when different units of the organization are located in different time zones. Adequate employee coverage can be a severe problem. Some employees will opt to flex out when they are needed most or when the workload promises to be the heaviest. Interdependent work—such as most assembly line operations or chemical processing—is usually unsuited to flextime. Other infeasible settings for the program are those requiring full staffing throughout or beyond the conventional workday. Examples include round-the-clock computer and security operations, health and safety personnel, and transportation services.[16]

The necessity for time-accounting systems can also create a problem in the use of a flexible work hour program. Many white-collar employees disliked time-accounting machines in the past when they were used more frequently. It is likely that such resistance will burgeon as flextime programs become more widespread.

GUIDELINES FOR ACTION AND SKILL DEVELOPMENT

A convenient way of introducing a modified work schedule to an organization is to begin with a pilot program in one substantial size organizational unit. If the program is well received, it can be expanded further. This gradual approach is also well suited to ironing out the potential bugs in the program.

Flexible work scheduling requires careful planning in order to reap its potential benefits. For example, if an employee arrives to work at 7 A.M. and the employee's superior who arrives at 9 A.M. has not planned any work for him or her during those two hours, productivity may decrease.[17]

A four-part model for selecting a work schedule should be given primary consideration. First, analyze the work demands of the organizational unit in question. Second, select an appropriate schedule. Third, analyze employee preferences. Fourth, if the selected schedule is compatible with employee preferences, use the schedule. If not, see if work demands or worker preferences can be altered by modifying service hours or by looking into a new applicant pool.[18]

Clear, appropriate objectives are needed when beginning a modified work schedule. The program is more likely to yield strong positive results if the objectives include such end conditions as increased morale and decreased commuting time.

Top management support, as with most new programs, is required for the successful implementation of modified work schedules. One company, for example, found that it is crucial to select a high-level executive with credibility and charisma to help sell the program to employees. That executive must also show full support for the program.

Modified work schedules with considerable flexibility tend to provide the maximum benefits. Among the areas requiring flexibility are amount of control transferred to workers, the amount of interdependence of jobs, and constraints on work hours set by law and collective agreements.[19]

Questions and Activities

1. Assume you are a manager and one of your subordinates always has the same excuse when you cannot locate him or her, claiming to be flexed out. How would you handle the situation?
2. To what extent should executives (managers in high-level positions) be included as participants in 4/40 or flextime?
3. How well would job sharing work for these positions: (a) marketing executive, (b) computer programmer, (c) pediatric nurse?
4. Firms using 4/40 have discovered that this work schedule encourages moonlighting. Should a company prohibit employees from moonlighting?
5. What do you see as the essential difference between flextime on the one hand and shift work and staggered hours on the other?
6. If you owned a small service firm such as an insurance agency or an advertising firm, would you authorize a program of flextime? Why or why not?
7. Take a poll in class about attitudes toward flexible working hours for oneself. If any negative votes are found, explore the reasons underlying the negative attitude toward flextime.

Notes

[1]Donald J. Petersen, "Flexitime in the United States: The Lessons of Experience," *Personnel*, January–February 1980, pp. 21–31.

[2]Cary B. Barad, "Flexitime under Scrutiny: Research on Work Adjustment and Organizational Performance," *Personnel Administrator*, May 1980, pp. 69–74.

[3]Petersen, "Flexitime in the United States," p. 26.

[4]Barad, "Flexitime under Scrutiny," p. 70.

[5]William D. Hicks and Richard J. Klimoski, "The Impact of Flexitime on Employee Attitudes," *Academy of Management Journal*, June 1981, p. 340.

[6]Petersen, "Flexitime in the United States," p. 27.

[7]Barad, "Flexitime under Scrutiny," p. 71.

[8]Randall B. Dunham and Jon L. Pierce, "The Design and Evaluation of Alternative Work Schedules," *Personnel Administrator*, April 1983, p. 75.

[9]Barad, "Flexitime under Scrutiny," p. 71.

[10]Stanley D. Nollen, *New Work Schedules in Practice* (New York: Van Nostrand Reinhold, 1982). Quoted in book review, *Personnel Psychology*, Autumn 1982, p. 709.

[11]Lois F. Copperman, "Alternative Work Policies in Private Firms," *Personnel Administrator*, October 1979, p. 41.

[12]Robert H. Crowder, Jr., "The Four-Day, Ten-Hour Workweek," *Personnel Journal*, January 1982, p. 26.

[13]Ibid., p. 28.

[14]John R. Turney and Stanley L. Cohen, "Alternative Work Schedules Increase Employee Satisfaction," *Personnel Journal*, March 1983, p. 202.

[15]Comment made in book review of Herman Gadon, *Alternative Work Schedules: Integrating Individual and Organizational Needs* (Reading, Mass.: Addison-Wesley, 1978) in *Personnel Psychology*, Summer 1979, p. 443.

[16]Barad, "Flexitime under Scrutiny," p. 74.

[17]Ann Fox, "Work When You Want," *Upstate*, January 29, 1979, p. 27. Review of *Alternative Work Schedules*, p. 444.

[18]The last three guidelines are from Petersen, "Flexitime under Scrutiny," pp. 29–30.

Some Additional References

Bogart, Agnes. "Part-time Employment Makes Retirees a Valuable Resource." *Personnel Administrator*, June 1983, pp. 35–39.

Frease, Michael, and Robert A. Zawacki. "Job Sharing: An Answer to Productivity Problems." *Personnel Administrator*, October 1979, pp. 35–38.

Gannon, Martin J., Douglas L. Norland, and Franklin E. Robeson. "Shift Work has Complex Effects on Lifestyles and Work Habits." *Personnel Administrator*, May 1983, pp. 93–97.

Rosow, Jerome M., and Robert Zager (directors). *New Work Schedules for a Changing Society.* Elmsford, N.Y.: Pergamon Press, 1981.

Teriet, Bernhard. "Flexiyear Schedules in Germany." *Personnel Journal*, June 1982, pp. 428–429.

Chapter 14

Labor-Management Committees

Like many large institutions for the retarded, Wrentham was the object of a court suit brought by the parents of the institution's residents. The Commonwealth of Massachusetts ended litigation by signing a consent decree which specified four major improvements related to caring for residents. A Parents' Organization affiliated with Wrentham helped the institution realize that improvements in the well-being of the residents was linked to improving the quality of work life (QWL) for employees. The labor-management committee formed to improve the quality of work life—and improve organizational effectiveness at the same time—is described below.[1]

The original idea for the Wrentham quality of work life (QWL) effort surfaced when two members of the staff development and training department and a manager of the institution attended workshops on employee involvement given by the Northeast Labor-Management Center. The workshops led to exploratory meetings and a six-month start-up contract that was later nullified by a state budget freeze. Then the Wrentham State School Parents' Organization stepped in and provided the local matching funds that were necessary to initiate the program.

The entry phase of the labor-management QWL project spanned a three-month period and included the following activities conducted with the help of two Northeast Labor-Management Consultants:

- Interviews with top management of Wrentham.
- A diagnosis of the organization—how it works, what and where the problems are.
- "Psychological contracting" with top management—making managers

aware of what the project would require of them and getting their commitment to the project.
- Four educational and planning workshops with top and middle management.
- Interviews and two educational planning workshops with union leaders.

Following the tradition of almost all joint labor-management quality of work life projects, a top-level steering committee was formed that provided the central policy-making forum for the project. The Wrentham Institutional Steering Committee was set up according to three criteria:

1. The committee should be representative of both labor and management.
2. It should include the major sources of power in the organization.
3. It should be kept to a workable size, not to exceed 12 members.

The consultants felt it was important to include all key management functions in the institution even though this would result in more management seats than union seats on the committee. But since the committee would use consensus decision-making and not voting, the issue of management outvoting the unions was avoided. Finally, the committee was composed of eight representatives from management and one representative from each of the four unions. The management side included the top administrators—the superintendent, the two assistant superintendents, and medical director and the director of labor relations. A section head, department head, and unit director rounded out the management group. The director of staff development and training, who took the lead in starting the QWL Program, was assigned to the institutional steering committee as a resource person. The same woman also became the facilitator for the committee.

During the first meeting of the steering committee, the members discussed their role in the project and how they would operate as a group. They established a timetable and worked through the union/management representation issue. By the end of the fourth meeting of the group, the committee had worked out a set of goals and principles. Moreover, two pilot sites were chosen, one of which was the institution's dietary department (described later).

The flavor and achievements of the labor-management start-up meetings are described in a progress report prepared by one of the members:

Relations between the labor and management representatives during their initial meetings were somewhat tense. Union leaders were apprehensive about the intention of management, and managers were not accustomed to collaborating with a group representing all of Wrentham's labor organizations. Turf issues between managers were evident at times during the early meetings.

Important to the early success of this group was the use of external facilitation, consensus decision-making, and individual consulting. The superintendent's increasing acceptance, support, and use of QWL process techniques has been a key factor in helping other top managers to stick with the process. The adoption of the QWL principle stating, "When problems arise, we won't retreat from using the QWL problem-solving approach," also helped the entire group stick together even though there was a lot of early conflict.

Selecting and training facilitators was an important part of the Wrentham program. Facilitators have several important functions. They handle the process aspects of a committee, making sure that different points of view are expressed, that conflicts are resolved openly and fully, and that the committee is kept aware of both its long-term goals and immediate tasks. The facilitators also carry a good deal of the responsibility for keeping the program moving after the consultant leaves the site. A facilitator must be adequately trained for the role, and also must have the necessary interpersonal skills.

The first facilitator training was a four-day, off-site training program for 38 staff members, including the members of the institutional steering committee, the two pilot site steering committees, and the work team facilitators from the two pilot sites. Trainees learned a variety of QWL skills including communication skills, group dynamics, leadership skills, and how to run work teams.

The dietary work teams were composed of individuals who represented the various functional components of the entire department. Such representative-type work teams have advantages but they can also create problems— for example, the teams would be making decisions that would require implementation by those who were not team members. This limits "ownership," and is contrary to the spirit of QWL.

The work teams were open to all staff members. Volunteers attended four, two-hour work team training sessions. By the end of the fourth session, the teams were ready to get down to business and address real problems.

QWL Activities in the Dietary Department

The dietary department has about 125 employees, with 75 of those involved in QWL activities. Dietary was chosen as a pilot site for three major reasons. First, as a Wrentham administrator put it:

They were always getting dumped on. They were heavily involved in Title XIX and were getting cited. Something had to be done. At first, the attitude around the department was, "Why us?" But this gave way to a more positive attitude on the part of the dietary staff because they now feel that because of the attention, we will have a better understanding of their problems.

The second reason for choosing dietary was that it provided a good test of whether or not QWL would work in a large public service institution. Third, the department contained the lowest paid employees of the organization. The dietary department was by no means the worst department. Yet there was a definite need for improvement and its performance affected the quality of life of the entire institution. If QWL made a difference here, people would know about it.

The dietary steering committee meets every week to review the progress of the work teams and set policy. But the work teams and the smaller *ad hoc* task forces are the "flesh and blood" of QWL. There are now three work teams in dietary and they are dealing with a broad range of important issues affecting the performance of the department.

One work team is trying to improve the performance of the 48 satellite kitchens that are scattered over the extensive grounds of the facility. Meals are prepared at the central kitchen and then transported by truck to each of the satellite kitchens. From there, meals are distributed to the residents. The complexity of the system makes for a logistical nightmare and it has created one especially serious problem: Meals sometimes arrive at the satellite kitchens at different temperatures. Everything the department does is closely monitored by the institution's own quality control staff and by the Massachusetts Department of Health. The latter has the responsibility for making sure that the terms of the Wrentham Consent Decree are being met. Inconsistent food temperatures can lead to a citation, considered to be a serious matter. But it is extremely difficult to deliver a few thousand meals in a day at the proper temperature given the variations in climate, staffing, and equipment.

The satellite kitchen work group has come up with several ideas for dealing with the problem. They have looked at the hot boxes—the large metal containers with internal heaters that are used to transfer meals from the trucks to the satellite kitchens. The hot boxes now in use are heavy, easily damaged, and expensive to repair. The work team is studying the feasibility of using lighter plastic boxes without an internal heat source. The boxes are cheaper and more durable. But will they work better? The work team is conducting comparison tests. As part of their research, four team members visited another state retardation facility in western Massachusetts to see how this institution dealt with a similar problem. The group included an administrative dietician, a supervisor, and two dietary aides. One team member noted:

> They were really surprised when we showed up with two dietary aides. It's unheard of to involve low-level staff members in such a trip. But they are part of the team and they have as much a say as anybody else. So they went.

The dietary work teams have also tackled other problems. A team did a study on using ground beef rather than stew beef. It did tests on fat content, studied the costs and nutrition factors, and recommended a better alternative that was supported by documentation and eventually accepted by the department of public health. Work teams have also dealt with problem areas such as procedures and training for drivers of the food trucks, alternative food delivery routes, and general communication issues within the department.

Normally, these kinds of problems are handled by management exclusively. Now much of the planning and brainstorming that goes into making basic changes in how the department runs is done by the QWL teams. Management is responding favorably to these changes. Mel Sheppard, the director of the dietary department, sums up his experience with the program in these words:

> The project takes time. It's often frustrating to schedule the work loads because the work teams use tremendous numbers of human hours to arrive at some of the answers that are already available. But the force of numbers adds to the power behind the decision. When I make a decision, it's one man's opinion. When the work team makes a decision, it means it's been gone over and over and it's going to be a long time before top management says no to it.
>
> I feel that it's definitely worth the time it is taking. There is a tremendous amount of good that is coming out of this.

EVIDENCE ABOUT THE EFFECTIVENESS OF LABOR-MANAGEMENT COMMITTEES

As the Wrentham case illustration indicates, labor-management committees are attempts to improve the quality of work life by giving employees a chance to play an important role in solving work problems. The typical goal of these QWL efforts is to improve labor-management relations with increases in productivity as a byproduct.[2] Labor-management committees (or labor-management participation teams) are now the most frequent formal activity included under the QWL label, and are therefore of considerable interest to the study of contemporary management. Their origins, however, trace back to World War II when they were used for patriotic reasons to spur productivity.[3]

The effectiveness of labor-management committees has been evaluated almost exclusively by testimony from company officials, and both internal and external consultants. They have not been evaluated more scientifically partly because labor-management committees tend to be much less structured than interventions such as quality circles and the Scanlon Plan. QWL encompasses so many different behaviors that evaluating the contributions of the committees becomes challenging.

As used in the present context, QWL is "an attempt to provide people at work (managers, supervisors, rank and file workers) with structured opportunities to become actively involved in a new interpersonal process of problem solving toward both a better way of working and a more effective work organization, the payoff from which includes the best interests of employees and employers in equal measure."[4]

Next, we will review the bulk of the current published evidence about the contribution of labor-management committees (LMCs) to both QWL and productivity.

General Motors Tarrytown. An historically important impetus to the current use of LMCs was the experience of General Motors in its Tarrytown, New York, plant. A QWL program was initiated at the plant in order to alleviate labor unrest and low productivity. Much of the effort involved worker participation teams (LMCs). Considerable improvements were attributed to the QWL activity. Absenteeism was reduced from 7.25 percent to about 2.5 percent. Employee turnover, breakage, disciplinary orders, and firings also decreased. Only 32 grievances were pending in December 1978 versus 2,000 grievances seven years earlier. In addition, many worker suggestions about technical matters were implemented that helped decrease dealer complaints about defective automobiles.[5]

The Jamestown Area Labor-Management Committee. The best-publicized, community-wide labor-management committee was established in Jamestown, New York. LMCs were formed to help revitalize a declining industrial base. The governing body of the Jamestown Area Labor-Management Committee (JALMC) included one union and one management co-chairperson, the mayor, the coordinator of the committee, and an equal number of labor and management representatives. The JALMC tackled many community-wide problems, and the LMCs formed under their jurisdiction helped the member companies solve a variety of production and personnel problems. Among their many contributions was helping in the redesign of an old foundry. An unfortunate consequence of this contribution was that several production jobs were eliminated. On balance, observers close to the scene believed that the LMCs had a positive impact on both productivity and the labor-management climate.[6]

Jones & Laughlin Steel Company. A productivity improvement program at this company led to the establishment of labor-management participation teams that were sanctioned by an agreement between U.S. Steel and the United Steelworkers Union. Similar to the Jamestown program, these labor-management committees were designed to both improve labor-management relations and productivity. Teams of 10 to 15 workers and supervisors were formed at the department level to solve problems within the plants that were not addressed in the traditional union-management procedures.

Very favorable results were reported at the Aliquippa, Pennsylvania, plant where the teams were first implemented. One team, for example, developed an inventory control system and worked out a plan to insure quick tool availability. Company officials estimated the total savings to be $300,000 plus lower costs for new tools, repairs, and damage due to accidents. The program was so successful that worker-participation teams were later formed at other Jones & Laughlin plants.[7]

Fairchild PROFIT Program. Top management at the Fairchild Republic division of Fairchild Industries became interested in improving two-way communications between supervisors and employees. They saw this as a vehicle for involving employees in the planning of work and allowing them to make suggestions for improving efficiency. The QWL effort they developed was given the acronymn PROFIT whose meaning is as follows:

P —Production/quality/support.
R —Review/results/reputation.
O —Our place/on the floor relating.
F —Fairchild people helping people.
I —Items/effect of work.
T —Today/tomorrow.[8]

The pilot program involved 10 groups of unionized employees and their supervisors. Approximately 150 employees and supervisors were involved out of a total plant population of 3,000. The program was concentrated in the subassembly shops because of their receptivity to a QWL project.

Supervisors and employees in a given work unit meet twice a week, both at the beginning and end of a shift (on company time) for a total of four meetings per week. A typical meeting runs about 15 to 30 minutes. During morning meetings, the supervisors outline work schedules and priorities are established. Employees discuss any problems they are currently experiencing or foresee. At the end of the shift, the work group meets again to review the quality and quantity of production.

During the second session of the day, employees discuss accomplishments and barriers to accomplishment, and make recommendations for improvement. Jack Ferrara of Fairchild notes, "Employees also are encouraged to discuss topics ranging from future contracts and how they affect Fairchild, to home and plant health and safety."[9]

Problems surfacing at the PROFIT meetings are reviewed by an overseeing committee composed of union and management representatives. The committee reviews PROFIT discussions and assigns teams to investigate problems and implement solutions beyond the immediate work group.

Ferrara's impression of the Fairchild worker-participation teams (PROFIT) is that both supervisors and union stewards are enthusiastic about the program and believe it has increased the motivation of the participants. Furthermore, the program appears to be promoting teamwork. This comes about through the natural work group reviewing its goals and plans, reviewing accomplishments, and identifying problems.[10]

The CWA/AT&T QWL Agreement. A 1980 memorandum of understanding between the Communications Workers of America (CWA) and the American Telephone and Telegraph Company established the National Committee on Joint Working Conditions and Service Quality Improvement. The committee serves as the basic vehicle for improving quality of worklife.[11] It is composed of three high level union officials and three human resource executives from different operating companies. The group's first task was to formulate a statement of principles that was intended to serve as a guide for subsequent QWL activity. Among the key points reached after several months of intensive negotiations were these:

- Workers will not be laid off as a result of ideas which come from the QWL process.
- Participation is voluntary.
- The union will be involved in every step of the process from planning to implementation.
- The collective bargaining and grievance procedures will remain separate from and unaffected by the QWL process.
- The QWL process will not infringe on any existing Union or employee rights.

The local worksite (both before and after the creation of AT&T independent subsidiaries in 1984) is the heart of the QWL effort. At the core of the program is the workplace committee that identifies problems and suggests methods of change. Local steering committees, composed of local union officials and Company (the accepted term for AT&T) district level supervisors, provide the resources for implementing suggestions from the workplace groups. Aside from special research projects, QWL activities are normally carried out during regular working hours and employees receive their normal rate of pay. (A feature common to virtually all labor-management committees.)

Committees come about in several ways. Often a CWA local president will make a suggestion to a supervisor or an operations director. The two may meet and eventually work out a joint agreement to initiate a QWL effort that is consistent with the statement of principles described previously. The local group may then enlist the support of a higher-level steering committee. Frequently, the latter assumes the responsibility for providing the necessary training and resource staff. Workplace committees are not required to follow any established agenda. Any issue can be tackled as long as it does not involve the labor-management contract.

Currently there are approximately 300 local workplace committees throughout the Bell System. Early experience suggests that environmental issues, such as lighting, desk placement, noise levels, the temperature of work areas, and provisions for privacy are often the first items for improvement suggested by the committee.

The QWL Review reports that after three years of operation there were no hard data assessments of the CWA/AT&T program, nor were there likely to be soon. The strategy is to allow local committees the freedom to explore without imposing demands on them for results. Nevertheless, union and management agree that QWL is already showing its worth. One indication is the rapid, spontaneous growth of local working committees, described by a CWA official as, "A real taste for participation out there." Another general result is a decrease in the number of grievances and an improvement in physical working conditions.

Based on the early promise of the program, in the future the QWL committees will become more involved in the planning aspects of managerial decisions. One example is joint technology change committees. These groups will give the union a voice in determining how new equipment is to be used and will allow the Bell System to accommodate the dual objectives of greater productivity and a better quality of work life for employees.

THE ARGUMENT FOR AND AGAINST LABOR-MANAGEMENT QWL COMMITTEES

The most convincing argument for a work organization adopting a program of labor-management committees, or worker-management participation teams, is that it often leads to an improvement in productivity and the quality of worklife. These dual ends are often accomplished because there is some relationship between a high quality of working life and labor productivity. N. Q. Herrick explains this connection in these terms:

> The concept, however, rests primarily on the belief that the actions which can reasonably be expected to insure labor productivity are the same actions which should be taken in any event to increase human fulfillment through work; that is, improving the conditions of security and equity and the opportunities for individuation and participation.[12]

Another valid argument in favor of LMCs is that even if they did not improve productivity or the quality of work life, they would still make a valuable contribution to the organization because the process fosters labor-management harmony. As workers and managers jointly solve problems they come to understand each others' problems and concerns, often leading to decreased intergroup conflict.

Although disadvantages to labor-management committees may be difficult to isolate, the process could be regarded as superfluous in firms where good communications between workers and supervisors already exist. The type of issues brought up in many worker-management participation teams (such as improving physical working conditions) are dealt with regularly in firms with good communication. A potential disadvantage of labor-management committee meetings is that they may waste considerable time while supervisors and employees conduct informal rap sessions about matters over which they have no control. Lowered productivity is the net result.

One negative feature of QWL programs is that they make difficult time demands on managers and employees because QWL emphasizes consensus decision making, similar to Japanese management systems.

Finally, as the Wrentham experience uncovered, a QWL program may work too well. The employees in the "experimental" organizational unit get the advantages of joint labor-management participation, while for other employees it is life as usual. This often engenders resentment and sometimes can destroy a program.[13]

GUIDELINES FOR ACTION AND SKILL DEVELOPMENT

The experience at Wrentham offers valuable lessons for managers and labor representatives in other organizations who are thinking about starting a QWL program. Although Wrentham is a third-sector (nongovernmental, not-for-profit) organization, their suggestions can be generalized to QWL organizations in private and public sector firms.

The first lesson is not to move too fast. QWL programs create difficult problems of timing and staging. If a pilot project is successful, the word gets around quickly and other sites want to get involved. At Wrentham, the initial pilot sites were developed in three weeks. Now, the proposed development cycle is two or three months.

Another lesson learned is to identify internal leaders as early as possible. The Wrentham work teams remained too dependent for too long on personnel from staff development and training. One way of dealing with this problem is to select employee involvement coordinators early on in the planning phase, get them involved, and define their responsibilities. The people selected, of course, should have the right skills and motivation to perform well.

Getting the word out about the program is also important. Publications such as a monthly QWL newsletter are an important means of providing information to people. A newsletter helps to disseminate good ideas and solutions to problems from a work team to other comparable teams throughout a facility. It has also been observed that seeing one's ideas in print is a form of recognition that helps build commitment to the program.[14]

Questions and Activities

1. What objections could labor unions conceivably have to labor-management committees?
2. LMCs were first used in the United States some 35 years ago, and then not much was heard about them until the late 1970s and early 1980s. What factors do you think accounted for their rebirth?
3. If you were a facilitator or leader of an LMC, how might you prevent it from becoming merely a bull session?
4. What advantages do you see of using an LMC or worker-participation team over simply using a suggestion system (in terms of generating ideas for improvement)?
5. Why are labor-management committees sometimes referred to as shop-floor democracy?
6. What contributions do you think a steering committee makes to the QWL programs described in this chapter?
7. Explain the concept of an LMC to any first-level supervisor you are able to find. Then get his or her opinion as to the impact of the LMC on a supervisor's power. Specifically, does it add to or take away power from the supervisor?

Notes

[1]The description of the Wrentham QWL program described throughout this chapter is paraphrased, adapted, and excerpted with permission from "Employee Involvement in Massachusetts: The Wrentham Story," *QWL Review*, September 1983, pp. 4–12, 18.

[2]John A. Fossum, *Labor Relations: Development, Structure, Process*, rev. ed. (Plano, Texas: Business Publications, 1982) p. 347.

[3]Herbert J. Chruden and Arthur W. Sherman, Jr., *Managing Human Resources*, 7th ed. (Cincinnati: South-Western Publishing, 1984) p. 366.

[4]Definition quoted in Thomas C. Tuttle, "Organizational Productivity: A Challenge for Psychologists," *American Psychologist*, April 1983, p. 482.

[5]Paul Bernstein, "Using the Soft Approach for Hard Results," *Business*, April-June 1983, p. 16; Robert H. Guest, "Quality of Work Life—Learning from Tarrytown," *Harvard Business Review*, July-August 1979, pp. 76–77.

[6]Martin D. Hanlon and John C. Williams, "Labor-Management Committee at Work," *QWL Review*, Summer 1982, pp. 2–8. (Publication of Civil Service Employee Association, New York State.)

[7]Bernstein, "Using the Soft Approach," p. 16; "J & L Leads New Trend in Cooperative Program," *Up Front*, July-August 1981, pp. 3 and 6. (Dallas, Texas: The LTV Corporation).

[8]Jack V. Ferrara, "Fairchild's QWL Program Improves Performance," *Personnel Administrator*, July 1983, p. 65. This section of the chapter is based on the Ferrara article.

[9]Ibid., p. 66.

[10]Ibid., p. 67.

[11]This section of the chapter is paraphrased and excerpted with permission from "QWL in the Bell System," *QWL Review*, March 1983, pp. 9–11.

[12]Quoted in Tuttle, "Organizational Productivity," p. 483.

[13]The last two disadvantages are from "Employee Involvement in Massachusetts," p. 12.

[14]Paraphrased with permission from ibid., p. 12.

Some Additional References

Bullock, R. J. *Improving Job Satisfaction*. Elmsford, N.Y.: Pergamon Press, 1984.

Greenberg, Paul D., and Edward M. Glaser. *Some Issues in Joint Union-Management Quality of Worklife Improvement Efforts*. Kalamazoo, Michigan: W. E. Upjohn Institute for Employment Research, 1980.

Lawler, Edward E. III. "Strategies for Improving the Quality of Worklife." *American Psychologist*, May 1982, pp. 486–493.

Schlesinger, Leonard A. *Quality of Work Life and the Supervisor*. New York: Praeger Publishers, 1982.

Weinberg, Edgar. *Labor-Management Cooperation for Productivity*. Elmsford, N.Y.: Pergamon Press, 1983.

Chapter 15

Japanese Management

Sanyo Manufacturing Corporation of Japan acquired an Arkansas television manufacturing plant about 10 years ago that had major management problems. Primarily because of a poor quality product, the company was close to bankruptcy. Its product had been bought by Sears, who asked Sanyo to buy the facility. Particularly because of concern about import restrictions on TV sets, Sanyo agreed to open a U.S. plant.[1]

Mr. Tanemichi Sohma, Vice President, Administration for Sanyo Manufacturing Corporation, described the first meeting between the new Japanese management and its Arkansas work force. This was a first move to "grow" employee involvement and morale:

> We inherited 500 people from Warwick, 350 union members, 150 salaried employees. This group was like a widow, and we are almost like a new husband, with Sears as the marriage broker. The love comes later. You know, the Japanese have been known for that kind of marriage for centuries, so we were not that afraid and we came in.
>
> The first day, the President spoke in English for the first time in public. He addressed all 500 employees in the warehouse—a very simple speech but a very powerful one. He said: "Let us work together in harmony and team work; let us make a quality product at a good price. Let everybody meet the customer and regain confidence from the customer. If we could do that, we are doing great. We can make money.
>
> So work started over coffee and donuts, and we had a little party. Sanyo brought transistor radios to each employee as an opening gift. And people loved it. They had never received that kind of warmth from management. So on the very first day they already began to like the new husband.

Before any other action, then, management gave priority attention to morale. The plant was "gloomy, dirty." Mr. Sohma said an effort to clean, "neaten up," and brighten the old plant began on the first day of operation. His description of the next morale boosting moves suggests a particular understanding of employee relations.

> The next thing is better communications with employees. We should not neglect any workers: As long as they are under our operation, they are Sanyo people. So let them know what we are going to do—what type of product is going to be produced; how we are going to move on to the next stage, and so forth. We informed them precisely.
>
> Soon, workers started thinking: "They are not hiding anything." The new husband is friendly. They smile, but there is still a big question mark in their minds. Many people came to me and asked: "Are you going to give us a bonus at the end of the year? Or profit sharing?" I replied: "This is a company we just started yesterday, and we cannot give you any promise. The former company promised you everything, but you did not get anything. So we would rather not promise." We knew, deep in our minds, that we would definitely give them a bonus—but we didn't mention that.

In three month's time, Sanyo had added 300 people. Before Warwick had started to fail, the plant had a payroll of 2,000, which had shrunk to 500 when Sanyo bought the company. In adding to its work force in the spring, Sanyo sought out former workers and rehired them. At this point, also, the Japanese-designed television set was introduced. The employees were used to a reject (defective) rate of 10 percent—a rate "unheard of in Japan," Mr. Sohma noted.

> Then, our reject rate became 3 percent, and next month 2 percent, and it is still coming down. Then the operators on the line started thinking: "We are the same people, the same hands, the same minds making a good TV product." Morale improved, of course, because we were producing a better product. Sears gave us more orders; money flowed in; a good cycle started.
>
> People say "the rich get richer"—and our place is just like that. The plant is getting noisier, busier; everybody starts smiling, and production becomes smooth. Toward the end of 1977, having started with 500 people, we had 1,500. And we moved up from making only 500 sets a day to 2,000 a day, then to 3,000. And all products passed inspection and went to the warehouse and then to Sears stores. So everybody was really happy. Although we had not promised, we paid a 7 percent annual wage bonus that year.

Personal involvement on the part of top management is apparently a major policy at Sanyo—as is the attention to detail suggested by this illustration:

> I walk around the factory everyday so that I get to know people and people get to know me. In the beginning, they thought that I was checking on them, that I thought the American work force may be slower than the Japanese. Actually, I was

not checking on them. I was looking around to see that they were working comfortably. If I saw something wrong, then I responded immediately and sent the maintenance man to cure the problem. Finally, they realized why I was so inquisitive.

I often go out of town for business; sometimes I have to go to Japan. When I come back, I go to the factory immediately. People say: "Where have you been? What did you do?" That reflects a very warm feeling and I enjoy it. Because people are now with me, and we are with them.

A similar policy theme is found in this description:

I open my office completely to anybody so that any question or any suggestion or complaint may be brought to me. I promised one thing—that I would listen to them. But I do not know how much I can take care of. Whatever the complaint, you listen and develop it the next day, or try to cure that situation *as soon as possible*. Then people notice that management is not sleeping. They are with us. You know bad news goes out in the factory in a few seconds. Good news goes slowly, but the idea penetrates day by day that the management is OK. That Osaka guys are not bad.

The plant that Sanyo acquired had been unionized by the International Union of Electrical Workers (IUE), though most of the employees were laid off by the time the takeover was accomplished. When it began to rebuild a work force, Sanyo sought out the former employees. It also sought out the union:

Our President always feels that Sanyo in Japan is a union company, and why should we be afraid of unionism? We should work with them and grow together. If we don't like what they are doing, we should be straightforward and tell them. And, if we want to change anything, there is no need for a surprise attack. So we should bring the people together beforehand, explain to them thoroughly, give them an understanding, and then we will have no problems. Sure enough, if we talk to them and give them enough time and preparation, they listen to us and notice how smoothly things run.

In other words, Sanyo deliberately included the existing union in its effort to create a spirit of cooperation. This involved making some changes in supervison—for Sanyo's reasons—that incidentally pleased the union as well:

Some of the general foremen are not really people-minded people, not really trying to improve the situation. Therefore, we removed those people to nonsupervisory assignments and brought in better people who could understand workers on the line. The union appreciated this effort.

Mr. Sohma mentioned a significant detail in the midst of discussing union relations that suggested volumes of standard labor relations text:

We brought in some Japanese workers, young, but with 6 to 10 years of experience in making television sets. Their English was limited, but I told them: "You don't need to teach them anything, just show them kindly. And if you have a problem, don't say a word. I will take care of it." I said this because in Japan it is very easy to say the words: "You're fired." It is said as a joke, because Japanese are not fired for the rest of their lives. But in Arkansas, if that kind of language would have been used by mistake, Americans would think that, ah, these youngsters are bosses, they are firing us. So I told them not to use that language—language that causes fear. So there was no conflict between Japanese engineers and technicians and U.S. workers.

They did a fantastic job and they got respect. After Americans saw these Japanese youngsters working very hard, preparing for tomorrow so that the production would become easier and better, they followed and they started learning together.

About two-and-a-half years after the Sanyo takeover, the union contract came up for renegotiation. Management made a substantial offer that the union rejected—but made no specific demands itself. Then, the union struck. Mr. Sohma thinks that the strike began as a test of the new management's strength, and also out of recognition that the plant was now making money.

During the course of the strike, Sanyo management in Japan learned about U.S. labor relations practice: "This is a different country: Business is business. A strike is business, not feelings." U.S. management sat tight—neither trying to operate during a strike nor following Japan's advice, which Mr. Sohma characterized thus: "After all, unions are human beings and you've got to go and kneel down and then they will listen to you."

In the seventh week of the strike, the union asked for talks, "and the strike was over." During the question period, Mr. Sohma noted that it was a negotiating year. He does not expect a strike. Sanyo has strengthened the personnel department to deal with the union. It also has "learned to do its homework" and to inform and negotiate "well in advance." Finally, the recession should dampen strike fire. Mr. Sohma described a very direct and open relationship with union officers over individual employee problems (or potential grievance cases):

> We are a unionized factory so we call the union's board of directors and tell them there is an employee behavior problem that we don't like. Openly and from the heart, we tell them off. You cannot manage our company, then you have to listen to us because we are thinking of people and these bad ones have to be corrected. From that point, we talk for many, many hours. Then, finally, they will understand our Japanese way of thinking and start changing. This happens quite often.
>
> But we have to be fair with them also. If they raise something that we are doing badly, then we immediately respond and change. Sometimes we have to pay the price of firing supervisors in order to accomplish a change. Because some of those salaried people are very strict and very hard on a worker. When that complaint comes, we watch carefully—if it is true, then we have to respect the union. But there is give and take. If we do something right, they have to do right also. That is the way we operate.

However, the anticipated negative reaction of the union has so far prevented Sanyo from introducing quality circles in its U.S. plant.

Japanese employees are said to identify with the company to the extent that they sing the company song, have company sports teams and company social engagements, even wear the company uniform. Mr. Sohma noted that company clothing would not be acceptable in the United States, or might be viewed as an imposition by management. On the other hand, Sanyo now has a company "olympics." There are many employee relations "tips" in his description of how they began:

The president of the corporation came after our strike and said: "Sohma, there is something missing. Maybe the human relationship is still weak. Why don't you, like our entire company, do some sports event like a small olympics?" I got the union people together and told them this. Not forcing, but from the heart, we want to do it together. The union officers said: "That's the best idea we ever heard. We want to do it."

Next day I called all the salaried people and asked them. They said, "No, it won't work in this country." So I said: "Salaried people are supposed to be with the corporation. That is why you are called white-collar workers. And what kind of attitude do you have? You better go back, cool your heads, and come back tomorrow morning." Sure enough, next morning everything changed. They said: "Let's do it, but we don't know how." I offered to bring them the materials from Japan and show them how to do it. From there on we worked and set up all the different committees: food committee, game committee, ground committee, security committee, everything that we could think of. We did a beautiful organization job and had a fantastic olympics.

The president of the entire corporation in Japan felt so happy about this thing that he gathered all the executives and their friends to fly in to see that olympics. I was worried because American people never had experienced that kind of sports event. I didn't know if this would work, because on a beautiful autumn day American people love to go fishing, hunting, and golfing. Why should they come to the factory with no pay and do something like that? I never prayed so hard in my life.

The next day was a beautiful day, and then the opening at 8:30. Many athletes were there—480, each team has 40 members, 12 different teams. They all wore different colored T-Shirts. And they were lining up. Then the people started coming—2,000 people. And this has become something of a tradition with Sanyo, Arkansas.

We worked for them: The captain of the team was a janitor, and we were vice presidents working under him. And he told us what to do: "You're running too slowly." This thing not only really amazed the people, but the people liked it. Then they came to us and said: "Let's do it again next year." The second time we did a much better one—and 4,000 people showed up.

This is the way Sanyo wants to work with people. No matter how old our company is, our equipment is old compared with some new companies that are coming in from Japan with automation and robots and so forth. We don't have any.

But we have a good human resource in Arkansas. So as long as we work with it. I think we can make the operation successful.

JAPANESE MANAGEMENT PHILOSOPHY AND STRATEGIES

The Sanyo experience provides a sample portrait of the nature of Japanese management. Nevertheless, in order to understand how Japanese management works, it is helpful to summarize its most frequently observed elements. Most recent analyses of Japanese management (including the ubiquitous explanations of Theory Z) are generalizations of the way in which a number of large, successful Japanese firms manage their human resources. Similarly, the concept of "American management" make the implicit assumption that most large, American firms have virtually identical philosophies and strategies in relation to dealing with employees. In reality, Japanese and American firms differ among themselves in their managerial philosophies and strategies.

These 16 philosophical and strategic concepts capture the essence of how the more successful Japanese firms manage their human resources.[2] Japanese management techniques, such as quality circles and *kan ban* (just-in-time inventory control) lie outside scope of this discussion.[3]

Personal Interest in Employees. The philosophical bedrock of Japanese management is the primary importance placed on human resources. Thus the traditional style of Japanese management emphasizes the importance of solid relationships between manager and subordinates and also among subordinates. Because employees are perceived to be key resources, the growth of the whole person rather than exclusively his or her job skills, is emphasized. One way in which the firm displays this *wholistic concern* is through substantial benefit packages and employee programs. The company olympics at Sanyo represents one such program.[4]

Long-Term Employment for Some Employees. Large Japanese firms have traditionally relied on an internal rather than an external labor market in matching the number of employees on board to the number of jobs that need to be filled. The strategy begins with hiring male employees upon graduation from high school or university with the expectation of keeping them permanently. The female workforce, however, is temporary, and many of the less desirable jobs are given to temporary workers or subcontracted outside the firm. As Nina Hatvany and Vladimir Pucik note, these practices give employers flexibility in adjusting the size of their workforce to present economic conditions while maintaining employment for full-time male workers.[5]

Unique Company Philosophy. Japanese chief executive officers typically articulate a company philosophy designed to give their firm uniqueness (a practice, of course similar to most large firms everywhere). Often these philosophies describe the firm as a family, distinct from any other firm. *Wa*, or harmony and teamwork, is incorporated into most company philosophies. Employees who "buy into" the firm's unique philosophy will presumably not be motivated to join another firm and thereby be forced to work under another philosophy.

Intensive Socialization of Employees. A major objective of Japanese human resource policies is to develop cohesiveness throughout the firm. To accomplish this end, as many workers as possible must fit naturally into the culture of the firm. A young person, for example, who balked at such ideas as singing company songs or socializing with co-workers after hours would not be invited to join the firm. The basic criteria for hiring new employees are moderate views and a personality capable of entering into harmonious relationships with other employees.

Perception of Employees as a Family. According to sociologist Jon P. Alston, a key principle of the Japanese managerial system is that all employees form a family (as stated in company philosophies). All employees develop a system of mutual obligations extending beyond what they are paid to do. Workers are supposed to be as loyal to the firm as they are to their families and villages. One consequence of this loyalty is that workers do whatever is needed for the corporation's benefit, including working overtime or taking evening courses in order to become more valuable employees.[6]

Emphasis on the Work Group. In the Japanese model of management, the group is more important than the individual. Correspondingly, the success of the work group is more important than the success of one individual. The importance of the group over the individual is so embedded in corporate policy that all pay raises and promotions for the first 20 years of employment are automatic. Pay increases and promotion are based on seniority rather than individual accomplishment. This practice minimizes competition and rivalry, while encouraging cooperation.[7]

A new analysis of individual versus group accomplishment suggests that Japanese managers, similar to their North American counterparts, are in fact imbued with a strong sense of individual achievement. However, in Japan, individual achievement is rewarded with acceptance from the group. The ambitious manager strives hard to excel in order to be seen as worthy by the group.[8] Presumably, a Japanese manager could function adequately in a Western organization if he (rarely she) learned to value individual rewards for individual achievement.

Individual Commitment to the Organization. Despite the emphasis on group responsibility, the individual also has obligations to the firm. As explained by Kae Chung and Margaret Ann Gray, "The chief responsibility is that of loyalty to the group due to long-term commitment between the firm and the individual. Duties include continual development of skills, improvement of quality control, maintenance of social harmony, service to the firm and interaction with its members outside of the normal working day. The Japanese systems will not function without such individual commitment to their organizations."[9]

Lengthy Orientation and Training. Japanese companies invest more time in orienting and training employees than do their American counterparts. In Japan, formal orientation to the company can take as long as two weeks, frequently conducted at an off-company site such as a resort. In a survey of 100 American employees in Japanese-owned companies, Richard G. Novotny found that these companies are not particularly strong on orientation and training. He offers this explanation for the difference:

> This lower level of orientation and training for U.S. employees is probably a result of the high turnover rates in this country (U.S.) compared with the Japanese practice of lifetime employment. The Japanese apparently feel that it does not pay for them to extensively orient and train Americans as they would Japanese, since the former may not stay with the company long enough for the orientation and training to be cost-effective.[10]

Information Sharing among All Employees. A pervasive theme of Japanese-managed firms is information sharing among all employees. It manifests itself, for example, in supervisors giving production workers almost any information they desire, such as the cost of materials, and profit margins on the product being manufactured. Information sharing is seen as a vehicle for involving employees in the work process and obtaining their commitment.[11]

Information sharing is fostered by the open communication system characteristic of Japanese offices and factories. Work spaces are open and crowded, allowing supervisors to be aware of what employees are doing and vice versa. It is rare even for high- ranking executives to have private offices. In factory environments, the supervisor and senior plant manager are constantly on the floor talking about problems, helping with units of work, conversing with outsiders, and instructing new employees.[12]

Collective Decision Making. It is widely acknowledged that Japanese managers involve subordinates in the decision-making process; there is some disagreement, however, as to the form and extent of this participation. According to Chung and Gray, the type of decision making characteristic of

Japanese business is best described by the word *nemawaski*, meaning root-binding. Each person has a sense of running the firm because almost nothing gets done until all the people involved agree. The Japanese believe that differences can best be resolved by gathering as much information as possible from as many sources as possible. Consequently all parties are well informed, everyone has time to adjust to the upcoming decision and all are committed to the implementation of the decision once consensus is reached.

Although this form of participative decision making can be agonizingly slow, the implementation phase proceeds swiftly because of the high level of commitment.[13]

Presence of Management Among the Workforce. Japanese firms have brought attention to the importance of "management by wandering around." Managers intermingle freely among workers on the shop floor, in the office, in meetings and discussions, and at informal social events. The managers who do the wandering around may be the emloyees' immediate supervisor, or a higher ranking manager.[14] Lower-ranking Japanese managers apparently are not concerned that their subordinates have the opportunity to communicate directly with higher levels of management.

Recognition of Employees as Experts. A key assumption of Japanese management is that workers, if motivated and sufficiently loyal, are intelligent enough to perform their duties without the need for extensive supervision and rules. The intelligent, well-motivated employee quickly becomes an expert in performing his or her specialized task. Therefore, the first step taken to improve productivity is to get the worker's opinion on how this might be achieved. This has sometimes taken the form of asking a production worker to help redesign the machine he or she operates regularly.[15] Quality circles, as described previously, are based on the principle of the "in-house expert."

Slow Promotion and Salary Advancement. A well-publicized feature of Japanese human resource management is heavy emphasis placed on seniority rather than merit for achieving organizational rewards. Employees of a given age group, particularly during the first several years of employment, receive comparable pay. Owing to the concept of long-term employment, Japanese workers learn to wait a long time for individual recognition in the form of promotion and salary increases. Bonuses are typically tied to the performance of the total firm. In some of the more prosperous firms, these bonuses may amount to as much as five month's pay.

Nonspecialized Careers. Long-term employment also makes it feasible for employees to rotate jobs throughout the firm. This extensive and prolonged training enables workers to learn different facets of the business and form a network of friendships. Once assigned to a more permanent position, individuals become generalists with an awareness of how the work of one department affects another, and how it affects the superordinate goals of the total organization.[16]

Evaluation of Attributes and Behavior. In recent years, most performance appraisal systems in North America have attempted to measure results instead of personal attributes and behavior (Management-by-objective is the best example). Japanese management, in contrast, believes strongly in measuring personal attributes (such as loyalty and enthusiasm) and behavior (such as creativity), as well as direct performance. In most Japanese firms, personality and behavior, rather than output are the key performance criteria. In this way, hard-working employees do not experience a sense of failure and frustration when productivity is low due to factors beyond their control.

Group performance is another factor frequently used in individual evaluation. Peer pressure is therefore placed on individuals to perform well, and this pressure functions as an organizational control. The use of group performance measures in evaluating individual contribution encourages the norm of cooperation so important to the Japanese management model.[17]

Implicit, Informal Control. Japanese managers rely heavily on unstated controls that are not part of a formal control system. These implicit controls focus on the long-term development of employees rather than on short-term performance. In this manner, a manager would be tolerant of a subordinate's mistakes if the manager thought they constituted a good learning experience. A short-term, performance-oriented viewpoint would be less tolerant of beginner's mistakes.

Group norms, developed slowly over a long period of time, are an important source of implicit control. Another informal control is exercised by differences in the way managers treat subordinates. The reason this type of control is so effective is because there is little room for manipulation of organizational rewards such as promotion and pay.[18]

The Evidence and Opinion in Favor of Japanese Management

Glowing pictures have been painted of Japanese management. A strong argument in favor of Japanese management is that Japanese companies have been very successful in competing with American and European companies. Japan has made notable inroads into many markets, with an array of products including:[19]

Automobiles, radios, binoculars, watches, textiles, trucks, steel, motorcycles, televisions, cameras, clocks, shoes, ships, castings, bicycles, tape recorders, telescopes, timers, hats, machine tools, printing presses, and the list appears to be growing.

The logic of this argument is that if Japanese companies are doing so well competively, the management systems guiding this growth must be meritorious. Furthermore, when Japanese firms take over American firms, productivity increases have been observed.[20]

Another compelling argument in favor of the Japanese model of management is that Japan is a country about the size of California, with few natural resources, yet it has become the third most powerful industrial nation. It has been outpaced industrially only by the United States and the Soviet Union. Japanese industry was more heavily hit by the oil crisis of the 1970s than were other countries, yet its productivity grew rapidly during this period. From early 1970s to the early 1980s, Japanese productivity grew at an annual rate of 8 percent while the productivity of American industries grew less than 2 percent. (However, by 1984 Japanese productivity increases had slowed down, and the rate of American productivity increases was around 4 percent. Many of the American gains were attributed to a tightening of controls and a push for productivity that took place in response to the recession of the early 1980s).

William Ouchi, whose book *Theory Z* helped popularize the North American adoption of Japanese management practices, provides much empirical evidence for its value. One of his supporting case histories involves the Buick Final Assembly plant, which at the time under study was beset with poor performance. Two years after introducing a Japanese style of participative management at all levels, the assembly plant ranked number one in GM with respect to productivity and quality.[21]

The Evidence and Opinion against Japanese Management

Despite the initial enthusiasm about Japanese management, a more balanced perspective emerged. We will summarize the reservations and concerns about both Japanese management itself, and the indiscriminate application of Japanese management practices of Western firms. We devote more attention to the negative than the positive because the arguments for Japanese management are already well publicized, and therefore well known.

American Productivity Exceeds Japanese Productivity. Although Japanese nonagricultural industry has achieved substantial gains in its rate of productivity, American productivity still remains much higher. A report by the Japanese Productivity Center published in 1983, compared U.S. levels of manufacturing sector labor productivity with Japan. Using an index of 100 to reflect Japanese productivity, the U.S. figures are as follows:

Iron & Steel, 66
Automobiles, 99
Electrical Machinery, 105

Chemical Industry, 112
Instruments, 116
General Machinery, 128
Textiles, 136
Leather Products, 200
Pulp & Paper Product, 209
Printing & Publishing, 217
Foods, 225
Apparels, 259
Manufacturing total (average), 138

According to these data, Japanese industry is more productive than American industry in iron and steel, and about the same in the production of automobiles. U.S. productivity is better in all other categories.[22] Comparable data are provided by George Odiorne. He reports that overall American productivity per worker is 1.57 times higher than Japanese—about $16,000 per U.S. worker versus $10,000 per Japanese worker. Odiorne also notes that the rate of productivity growth in Japan has followed a steady 10 year downward trend. Among the many nations with a faster rate of productivity growth than Japan are Taiwan, Korea, Thailand, and Great Britain.[23]

Japanese Management Is Best Suited to Imitation Rather Than Innovation. Japan remains a net importer of foreign technology because its technical workforce does better at imitation than innovation. The emphasis on work group harmony, obedience, and consensus curtail innovative thinking and behavior. Japanese industries thus concentrate on "core technologies" such as the 64K RAM (random-access memory) chips and robots. But they are forced to purchase most of the "peripheral technologies" needed for manufacturing and testing along with the product. According to Nicholas Valery, this means that "Never learning to make the really difficult part of their big systems, Japanese firms stay technologically 10 years behind their American rivals."[24]

The Success of Japanese Industry Is Due to Factors Other Than Management Style. The rapid growth of Japanese industry can be attributed to factors other than a superior style of human resource management. Among these key nonmanagerial factors are a supportive government policy, low-cost financing that facilitates capital expansion, friendly labor unions, and a workforce culturally conditioned to be obedient and cooperative. (Some American firms locate their manufacturing facilities in the rural south to achieve some of these advantages. The presence of a strong work ethic among rural people contributes to high productivity.) Some of the success of Japanese industries in worldwide markets can also be attributed to the heavy competition Japanese firms face domestically, particularly in electrical goods.

To survive and prosper at home, Japanese firms must turn out electronic equipment so low priced that it competes favorably overseas.

A report by the Highway Loss Data Institute indicates that the 11 car models with the best insurance claim experience were all American made; 12 of the 15 worst were Japanese made. American cars were found to be safer even when the comparison was made between compacts from both countries.[25]

The Most Effective Elements of Japanese Management Are American in Origin. The more publicized Japanese techniques of human resource management and manufacturing are based on ideas borrowed from the United States. American organizational psychologists pioneered in the development of participative leadership techniques as early as the 1950s. Quality control methods, including quality circles, were developed by Professor Deming around the same year, and later introduced to Japan. Furthermore, as Linda S. Dillon has observed,

> The real success of the Japanese approach lies in what they were able to learn from the United States in the early post-war years: The value of controlling costs, working hard, saving money, and giving customers value for their dollars. It was their ability to adapt those concepts to a Japanese culture that led to their productivity gains and subsequent worldwide envy.[26]

Cultural Differences Create Problems in Adopting Japanese Management. A number of managers and scholars have expressed concern about the transferability of Japanese human resource management to North American industry. One frequently expressed opinion is that Japanese management practices are best suited to a culturally homogeneous workforce. Since members of the homogeneous workforce share similar values, they are more likely to cooperate well with each other and be committed to the company. Workers do what is expected of them and do not block productivity improvements. The culturally diverse workforce in North America cooperate less well with each other and with the firm.

The survey of American employees working for Japanese-managed firms described previously, indicated that many employees perceived a major problem to be a lack of cultural understanding between Japanese managers and American workers. The language barrier constituted a major hurdle. Also, almost half the respondents believed that being able to understand Japanese was helpful in getting a promotion, and 20 percent said that knowledge of the language was necessary for an American to attain a top-management position.[27] These problems would not occur, however, if an American manager used Japanese management techniques.

Another reservation about the transferability of Japanese techniques is that collective decision making is less important in a culture with good written communication. Dillon believes that Japan's penchant for consensus decision making and quality circles are in part responses to the difficulties of the Japanese language. It is so complicated to prepare written documents that the Japanese rely on methods in the work place that favor oral communication. The typical office arrangement features employees in one work unit sharing a common office. Desks are arranged so that everyone is readily aware of what everybody else is doing.[28] Management by "wandering around" is another practice that decreases the necessity of preparing written reports and memos.

Another management practice better suited to Japan than North America is life-time employment. The approximately 30 percent of Japan's major corporations who do offer life-time employment do so to maintain a stable workforce in a competitive environment.[29] In our culture, it would be illegal and immoral to lay off women workers (and retain men) to adjust to the supply-and-demand cycle.

Japanese Firms Engage in Some Unsavory Personnel Practices. A scattering of evidence has surfaced that raises questions about the benevolence of Japanese firms. One complaint is that subcontractors are assigned dirty jobs and are poorly paid. The most outspoken indictment of Japanese firms was prepared by Satoshi Kamata, a journalist who took a job on a Toyota assembly line and kept a diary. According to his analysis, Toyota management had complete disregard for the physical and mental health of employees. Scheduled days off were routinely cancelled to attain production quotas, and equipment was outmoded and unsafe. In fear of being docked for lowered productivity, injured workers often covered up work accidents. Company security agents were authorized to snoop around employee dormitories.[30]

GUIDELINES FOR ACTION AND SKILL DEVELOPMENT

A major misinterpretation of Japanese management is that it is a straightforward system or technique to be installed, much like PERT. To work effectively, Japanese management must be incorporated into a philosophy of management that places primary value on human resources and internalizes the values behind consultative or participative management (such as every worker has the potential to   ntribute good ideas to the firm).

North American and other Western managers must carefully evaluate any Japanese management practices before adopting or adapting them. Jon Alston cautions that many Japanese practices are based on cultural principles too foreign for incorporation into other work forces.[31]

Firms in relatively stable and dominant market positions have a higher probability of successfuly adopting the Japanese model of

---

management than do firms in weak and unstable positions. Strong firms are less concerned about outside environmental forces and can therefore develop the internal climate necessary for Japanese management to work. Also, they can offer long-term employment and invest heavily in employee training.

Japanese management practices emphasizing consensual decision making and group harmony are best suited for firms (or units within a firm) engaged in stable and repetitive work. Firms, or organizational subunits, pursuing aggressive, risky, and unstable ventures in which innovation is required should look toward a style of management stressing individualistic performance.

The adoption of a Japanese management system requires the careful selection of employees who can function effectively under the new system, a major investment in continuing employee training and development, decentralization of decision making, and sharing with employees of the benefits stemming from productivity improvement. Also necessary is the development of a close partnership between management and any labor unions representing the company employees.[32]

Questions and Activities

1. What is your impression of the relative quality of comparably priced American and Japanese consumer products?
2. Which techniques described in the previous 14 chapters do you think fit the Japanese management model?
3. Why do you think IBM and GM are characterized by Ouchi as being Theory Z (Japanese-style) firms?
4. Are the values of today's stereotype of an MBA graduate compatible with the Japanese philosophy of management?
5. Japanese executives freely admit that many of their techniques were borrowed from behavioralists such as Argyris, McGregor, and Hertzberg. Why did it take American industry so long to pay careful attention to these ideas?
6. How well do you think Japanese employees would respond to American managers running their companies in Japan?
7. Among the many American firms described as using a Japanese style of management are IBM, GM, Hewlett Packard, and Rockwell International. Find somebody who works for, or has worked for, one of these firms. Interview the person to see if his or her description of the firm's management practices fits the description of Japanese management presented in this chapter.

Notes

[1] Case is reprinted with permission from "Japanese Management of U.S. Work Forces," The Conference Board Research Bulletin, Number 119, 1982. pp. 6–9.

[2] Based on a variety of sources as referenced below. However two major sources of this information are William G. Ouchi, *Theory Z: How American Business Can Meet the Japanese Challenge* (Reading, Mass.: Addison-Wesley, 1981); Nina Hatvany and Vladimir Pucik, "An Integrated Management Systems: Lessons from the Japanese Experience," *Academy of Management Review*, July 1981, pp. 469–480.

[3] For information on this topic, see Richard J. Schonberger, *Japanese Manufacturing Techniques: Nine Hidden Lessons in Simplicity* (New York: The Free Press, 1982).

[4] Kae H. Chung and Margaret Ann Gray, "Can We Adopt the Japanese Methods of Human Resources Management?" *Personnel Administrator*, May 1982, p. 43.

[5] Nina Hatvany and Vladimir Pucik, "An Integrated Management System: Lessons from the Japanese Experience," *Academy of Management Review*, July 1981, p. 471.

[6] Jon P. Alston, "Three Principles of Japanese Management," *Personnel Journal*, September 1983, p. 761.

[7] Ibid., p. 762.

[8] Ibid., p. 762.

[9] Chung and Gray, "Can We Adopt?" p. 43.

[10] Mary Zippo, "Working for the Japanese: Views of American Employees," *Personnel*, March–April 1982, p. 56.

[11] Audrey Freedman, "Learning from New U.S.—based Neighbors," *Conference Board Record*, July 1983, p. 32.

[12] Hatvany and Pucik, "An Integrated Management System," p. 473.

[13] Chung and Gray, "Can We Adopt?" p. 43.

[14] Freedman, "Learning from New U.S.—based," p. 32.

[15] Alston, "Three Principles," p. 758.

[16] Chung and Gray, "Can We Adopt?" p. 42.

[17] Hatvany and Pucik, "An Integrated Management System," p. 472.

[18] Chung and Gray, "Can We Adopt?" p. 43.

[19] "Lessons in Success," brochure from George Plossi Educational Services, Inc., Atlanta, Georgia, 1984.

[20] Several such cases are reported in "Japanese Management of U.S. Work Forces."

[21] Ouchi, *Theory Z*, p. 150.

[22] *Japan 1983: An International Comparison* (Japan: Keizai Koho Center, 1983), p. 65.

[23] George S. Odiorne, "The Trouble with Japanese Management Systems," *Business Horizons*, 1984 (In Press).

[24] Nicholas Valery, "The Fabled Giant's Might is Dwindling," *The Economist*, July 9, 1983.

[25] Odiorne, "The Trouble with Japanese."

[26] Linda S. Dillon, "Adopting Japanese Management: Some Cultural Stumbling Blocks," *Personnel*, July–August 1983, p. 77.

[27] Zippo, "Working for the Japanese," p. 58.

[28] Dillon, "Adopting Japanese Management," p. 75.

[29] Ibid., p. 74.

[30] Satoshi Kamata, *Japan in the Passing Lane* (New York: Pantheon, 1983). Information presented here is cited in book review, *Time*, February 14, 1983, p. 62.

[31] Alston, "Three Principles of Japanese," p. 763.

[32] The above three points are from Chung and Gray, "Can We Adopt?" p. 46.

Some Additional References

Joiner, Charles W. "One Manager's Story of How He Made the Z Concept Work." *Management Review*, May 1983, pp. 48–53.

Rehder, Robert R. "Education and Training: Have the Japanese Beaten Us Again?" *Personnel Journal*, January 1983, pp. 42–47.

Shetty, Y. Krishna, and Vernon M. Buehler. *Quality and Productivity Improvements: U.S. & Foreign Company Experiences.* New York: AMACOM, 1983.

Sullivan, Jeremiah J. "A Critique of Theory Z." *The Academy of Management Review*, January 1983, pp. 132–142.

Terutomo, Ozawa. *People and Productivity in Japan* (Work in America Institute Studies in Productivity No. 25.) Elmsford, N.Y.: Pergamon Press, 1982.

Part 5

Human Resource Management Programs

Human resource management (or personnel) departments today offer a variety of well-structured programs designed to enhance human potential or help troubled employees. The four chapters in this part of the book develop the central themes of enhancing potential or remedying problems. Chapter 16 presents an in-depth look at an exemplary career development program used at a large financial services firm. Chapter 17 described the operations of an assessment center used primarily for the purpose of assisting in management development. Assessment centers are generally thought of in terms of their role in the selection of higher-level employees.

Chapter 18 describes the operation of an employee assistance program, a widely accepted method for helping employees deal with personal problems such as alcoholism and drug addiction. Often these problems are triggered by job pressures but can stem from pressures at home. Whatever the cause, such problems result in lowered job performance.

Chapter 19 describes human resource accounting (HRA), an exploratory technique of contemporary applied management that has yet to achieve wide application. Accountants and human resource specialists have worked together to help gain acceptance for this technique in order to quantify the important role people play in making an organization function well. HRA fits in with the other management methods in Part 5 because it highlights the importance of taking good care of human resources. An organization that utilizes some of the techniques described throughout this book also might be interested in experimenting with human resource accounting.

Chapter 16

Career Development

The North American Insurance Group embarked upon a formal career development program for two primary reasons: to meet the present and future human resource requirements of its expanding business and to contribute to the well-being and personal growth of its key employees.

Virtually every employee of the North American Insurance Group has some opportunity to participate in the career development program. The focus of the program, however, is on a select group of individuals who are being groomed for higher level management positions. At a policyholder meeting, North American President M. Brewster Jones articulated the philosophy underlying the company's attempt to help people develop their careers:

> We at North American endeavor to serve both the public and our own employees to the best of our abilities, yet still maintain a competitive financial position within the insurance industry. One of the best ways we can serve our own employees is to give them the opportunity to work toward self-fulfillment in their careers. At the same time, we must optimize our investment in the career development of our employees. Toward this end, we have relied upon our own management wisdom and expert professional advice in the establishment of a formal career development program. The CDP, however, does not take the place of management development. Any program designed to improve the job performance of present or future managers is considered management development. Our CDP is but one aspect of management development.

Jones then introduced Graham Forbes, vice president of human resources, who explained the program in some depth to the policyholders. To supplement an oral description of the program, he used both transparencies and printed handouts. Forbes explained:

Our CDP consists of ten major segments, which I will describe shortly. The young woman next to me is a deaf interpreter who will translate my spoken words into manual language. Most of my key points will be displayed on the screen to my left. Please remember, that time only allows me to present the highlights of our career development program. After my 30-minute presentation, we will have about 10 minutes for questions and discussion.

Segment 1 is called human resource forecasting. Many career development programs in organizations fail because people are being developed for jobs and careers that may not exist in the future. The North American Insurance Group has developed into a full-line insurer plus a provider of a wide range of financial services. We now offer mutual funds and retirement plans in the form of IRAs, Keogh Plans, and tax-sheltered annuities. Recently we have entered into the promising field of real-estate investment trusts in which our customers can own small pieces of professionally managed, high-quality real estate. We make periodic forecasts of the types of managerial, professional, and technical skills we will be needing in the future.

We have carefully evaluated the potential impact of high technology in the office on the number of people needed to process the millions of pieces of paperwork that constitute the basic product of an insurance company. As we look down the road, we visualize decentralized financial centers whereby the public can come to us for insurance and financial counseling. The trend of recent regulation in most states and provinces is to allow insurance companies to compete favorably with banks and other financial institutions. We are no longer restricted to selling only insurance.

Another finding of our human resource forecasting is that we will be needing fewer first-level office supervisors in the future. The number of clerical help in proportion to our sales volume has steadily decreased in recent years. Advances in computer technology continue to shrink our need for clerks and supervisors. However, we see a growing need for managers to supervise people in such specialities as computer science and office systems analysis.

Segment 2 is the nomination of candidates for the CDP. You will recall that virtually all employees have some opportunity to participate in our program. But here we are talking about the identification of a very special group of employees— those supervisors and manages who appear to have substantial promise for future high-level management assignments. Nominations are welcome from all second-level managers and above. In addition, certain high-level staff personnel are also invited to nominate candidates for this elite group.

We inform our managers and staff people of the type of people we are looking for in this key group. Above all, they must have received outstanding ratings in three of their last four performance evaluations. In addition we look for those managers who to the best of their nominator's knowledge are exceptionally strong with respect to six sets of behavior: problem-solving ability, emotional stability, motivation, skills in dealing with people, insight into people and situations, and personal organization.

Yes, I have heard this cadre of people referred to as crown princes and princesses. Nevertheless, we are not deterred by such criticism. Nobody is promised a future top assignment because he or she is placed in this select group of people within the CDP. That person must continue to display outstanding job performance in order to qualify for further promotion. On-the-job accomplishment remains the number one vehicle for climbing the organizational ladder at North American.

We simply do not have the resources to place everybody in this key person group. As stated by Mr. Jones, we want to optimize our investment in the career development of employees. We, therefore, simply cannot place everybody in extensive and expensive management development programs.

Segment 3 is called career planning self-analysis. This segment is relatively straightforward. Every person in the key group is asked to complete a lengthy questionnaire designed to get them thinking about their own personal development in a systematic and provocative way. We call it the career planning inventory.[1] At the core of the CPI are some questions about goal setting. We want people to set goals that are more than wishful thinking. We encourage them to integrate their goal setting with a realistic view of the future of our organization. Participants in the program are required to discuss their goals with two levels of management above them. It is also possible to discuss these goals with a professional in the human resources department. These discussions are used as a form of reality testing.

Reality testing does not mean that we tell people they should not strive to reach the top. We do try to help people appreciate the odds they might be facing. Suppose a young person in the key group says that he or she can only be fulfilled by becoming a senior vice president. We can give that young person the constructive feedback that we anticipate only three openings for senior vice presidents in the next 20 years. Or let's assume another person says he or she would like to become manager of the automobile policy coding group in three years. We can tell that person that virtually all of the coding function will be computerized within three years. Therefore, we probably won't be needing another manager of the coding function.

Each goal established by the employee is subject to challenge by management. The purpose here is not to discourage our key people, but to help them establish realistic goals to which they are committed. If a manager can withstand a challenge to a goal, that manager may develop a stronger belief that the goal can be attained. Let's assume a 30-year-old key person says that she wants to become a product planner of new financial services to the public—a plum of an assignment. Her manager might say to her, "Why do you think you are uniquely qualified to attain such an assignment." She might respond that she has been preparing herself through a program of study in financial planning offered by the Institute of Insurance. Futhermore, she has already contributed several good marketing suggestions to the company. Then we know this person is serious about her goal formulation.

Segment 4 is called assessment and feedback. Each member of the key group is invited to spend several days in an assessment center. There the individual is put through a series of job-related exercises. His or her performance is carefully watched by a team of human behavior specialists and experienced managers. One important output of the assessment center is a confidential report which provides some additional data about the individual's promotability into higher management. The assessment center report also provides specific suggestions for the development of each person in the key group. Every participant receives a full report of the suggestions.

We also get data about the people based upon a further analysis of their career planning reports and assessments prepared by psychologists. You might be interested in knowing about the type of suggestions participants receive. After I attended the assessment center, the feedback counselor told me that I should develop better work habits. As you can see, that's why I use a careful outline for this talk, rather than speaking off the cuff. [*Laughter from the crowd*].

Some people have been counseled about ways to handle job-related stress. One young manager was so ambitious and hard driving that he would work himself into a frenzy. He was also beginning to irritate other people attending the assessment center. We can assume he behaved like that toward his subordinates. In any event, he was encouraged to attend biofeedback training sessions. There he learned to monitor his own excitement level. He acquired the necessary skill to calm himself down when he was becoming too tense.

A woman attending the sessions showed a tendency to be too deferential toward males she knew outranked her. After getting feedback on this tendency, she spent a few sessions with a career counselor of her own choosing. She now has that problem under control and is considered one of our more promising middle managers.

Segment 5 is on-the-job training. Our fundamental belief is that the best way to develop careers is to give people the right kind of job experience. We make a special effort to give our key people those kind of guided job experiences that will enable them to grow. On-the-job training can take a variety of forms. It could mean giving somebody an enriched job. One example would be to give a middle manager the added responsibility of doing some long-range planning for the vice president to whom he or she reports. We also try to rotate the jobs for key people frequently enough so they do not become stale or bored. Our key people are also prime candidates to serve on organization-wide committees or special venture teams. Recently we formed a special task force to study the feasibility of the North American Insurance Group acquiring a small mutual fund. Four of the seven members of that team were members of the key group.

Another important part of on-the-job training is the coaching given to the key people by their manager. Indeed, we encourage managers to provide adequate coaching to all of their subordinates—key group member or otherwise. Our basic assumption is that a person's boss is well situated to help subordinates improve. To illustrate, a boss might urge a subordinate manager to be more methodical in preparing budgets or taking care of paperwork in general.

However, we also realize that an immediate superior cannot take care of all the developmental needs of subordinates. For one reason, the boss may not have all that much contact with the subordinate. Another reason is the occasional jealousy that could surface. It has been known for a manager to resent a subordinate who is designated as a key person while the manager is not in that select group.

Segment 6 is management development programs. These programs are designed to supplement on-the-job training and coaching. We use a wide variety of formal management training and development programs. Some of our programs are conducted in-house; some are conducted by the American Insurance Institute; some others are conducted by universities or management consultants. About one half of our management development programs are directed at the key group member learning more about company policy and procedures. As you policyholders know, this is an era of constant flux for the insurance industry. Part of our philosophy is that anybody holding the rank of middle manager or above at North American should have a good working knowledge of the company and the insurance business in general. As our founder was fond of saying, "If you can't help your neighbor with an insurance problem, you have no business managing a part of our business."

Before we launch a management development program, we take a careful look at the kind of skills and knowledge we think our managers should have. We have an upcoming program called high technology in the office. Another one scheduled deals with measuring white collar productivity. Both programs speak to the rapid developments in making our operations increasingly cost effective.

We also conduct training sessions about such topics as evaluating employee performance, employee selection, maintaining motivation and morale, using a management information system, and budgeting. Once a person reaches a senior management position, development does not stop. However, the content of the management development programs shifts in emphasis. At that level the programs tend to emphasize concerns about the company and its external environment, or long-range strategy.

Segment 7 of the career development program is called performance appraisal counseling. Although we list it as seventh, this kind of development should take place at every performance evaluation. At North American, we expect the performance evaluation system to provide us useful data for administrative purposes. We use the evaluations as a basis for salary review and human resource forecasting. For instance, we might conclude from our study of the results of 500 performance appraisals that we are short on outstanding performers in the marketing end of our business. We would, therefore, need to step up our recruiting of high potential marketing personnel.

We also expect performance appraisals to be used for the coaching and development of manager and individual contributors. This aspect of performance appraisals is not much different than day-by-day coaching except that it is more formal and occurs at specific time intervals. After reviewing the subordinate's performance, the manager is supposed to make suggestions to that person for improvement and growth. A manager might suggest, for example, that a supervisor reporting to him or her should become more knowledgeable about variable annuities or should be more patient with average employees.

Performance appraisal counseling is the vehicle by which every employee at North American can participate in some form of career development counseling. An important part of our performance appraisal counseling is for the employee to make some comments about his or her future plans. The manager is supposed to react to these plans in some constructive manner. Each manager is instructed to provide some feedback on the future needs of the organization and how he or she sees that employee fitting in.

An employee is also free to request an interview with the next higher level of management to discuss career plans. I would say about one half of employees take advantage of this opportunity. Furthermore, some limited assistance in career counseling is offered by my department. Obviously if we offered every employee a full shot at career counseling, our premium rates would have to skyrocket.

Segment 8 is our management inventory chart. This is a highly confidential document. As you can see by the transparency (see Figure 16-1), the inventory chart is an organization chart with notations about the promotability of the people in the boxes. The chart we have reproduced here is hypothetical. In order to arrive at these judgments about people, we use all available information. The president and I

Figure 16–1
Management Inventory Chart

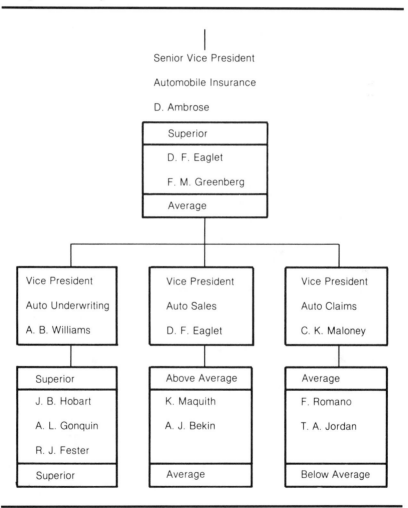

carefully scrutinize the performance appraisal results, the assessment center findings, and any other relevant information we have about the person. We make up a new chart every year, so nobody's evaluation is frozen. The management inventory chart helps us determine the strengths and weaknesses in our organization. It also helps us develop people's careers by pointing to likely paths or progression for them. For instance one manager might be in line to take over his or her boss's job because the boss is also on the way up the organization.

Our entire manager inventory chart covers every management position at North American. It is a living, breathing document that helps identify at a glance the promotable people in the organization. It also helps us spot which people need more development in order to qualify for promotion.

Performance

Superior: The unique, exceptional, top performer.

Above Average: Standards are usually exceeded. Does almost everything well.

Average: Does most things satisfactorily. Results are passable.

Below Average: Does several things unsatisfactorily. Achieves poor results. Job tenure doubtful.

Potential

Superior: Person of general management potential. Exceptional leadership qualities.

Above average: Promotable person. Should be able to advance one or two steps in the organization.

Average: Promotable, providing normal growth and development takes place.

Below average: Has achieved plateau. Considered unpromotable.

Segment 9 is a Career Development Information System (CDIS). As our career development program grew, it became apparent to our human resource specialists that we would need a sophisticated method of keeping track of both employees in the program and those that might be eligible for inclusion in the future. Another challenge we faced as the program grew was that our data base kept expanding. The logical answer was to computerize many aspects of our CDP. It is officially referred to now as the CDIS, meaning career development information system. It is a special- purpose human resource information system.

An important component of the information system we have developed for our career development program is the skills bank inventory. Our data base includes an updated listing of the unique skills and job experiences of all our employees, both those selected for the CDP and all other employees. When an attractive job opening develops that could be used for career development, we run a computer search to discover a fit between that opening and present employees. A good example is our newly formed real estate investment department. Growth in this aspect of our business created three new managerial positions. The skills inventory data base revealed 13 employees who had significant experience with large commercial real estate. Two of those people were already in our CDP, and the third person, a woman in her thirties, was invited into the program.

Segment 10 is evaluation of the CDP. I know that you policyholders evaluate the services we provide you. You look at our claims services; you carefully weigh our dividends versus those received by your friends who insure with other companies; you take careful note of the surplus funds we distribute to the automobile-policyholders among you. Similarly we evaluate any major expenditure on our part.

Our preliminary evaluation is that the CDP is a wise investment of our time, energy, and money. It appears that turnover among middle managers has decreased since the inception of CDP. They seem to feel that there is now more certain paths for advancement in our company in comparison to others. Going beneath the raw turnover statistics, it appears that we are keeping more of the corporate tigers and tigresses that we want to keep. I am referring to those outstanding young men and women who are destined to become leaders of the insurance industry. We would prefer that they choose to remain with North American. I think that our career development program is helping us achieve that end.

Another positive spinoff from the program is that we are making more precise identifications of people with potential. CDP has already been helpful in allowing us to make sound choices in filling vacancies in key jobs.

As a final note, the reaction to our career development program has been favorable. Even those employees who are not part of the key group have expressed positive attitudes toward the fact that career planning is now a formal part of the performance appraisal system.

Thank you so much for your attention. I think we have about 15 minutes left for questions.

Now that we have described one company's approach to career development, we will summarize general strategies of helping employees develop their careers.

CAREER DEVELOPMENT STRATEGIES FOR THE ORGANIZATION

North American Insurance Group's approach to career development provides an overview of how such a program might proceed in a well-managed organization. Although career development programs vary widely in nature, a set of general strategies can be delineated that are associated with effective career development in organizations. They include: utilize the career growth cycle; train and reward managers for career-planning skills; use human resource specialists as advisors; provide valid career opportunity information; use valid information in your data base; link training to career development; emphasize more than advancement; provide for different needs in different career stages; and integrate career development with management development.

Utilize the Career Growth Cycle. A basic theory of career growth says that success leads to more success. The whole process is triggered by a job that provides challenging, stretching goals. A person facing clearly defined, challenging goals will exert more effort. As effort increases so does good performance and its associated rewards. The person then feels successful. Since the feeling of success increases feelings of confidence and self-esteem, the person becomes increasingly involved in the job.[2]

The employer can capitalize on this growth cycle by first of all providing as many challenging enriched jobs as feasible. Goals should be clearly formulated and the person should receive frequent performance review and feedback about progress toward these goals. An employee's immediate supervisor is usually in the best position to provide such feedback. Insight into how a supervisor can make good use of the career growth cycle is provided by the situation of Frank, a minor league baseball coach:

> I joined the organization filled with enthusiasm. I knew I could win as a coach. My first coaching assignment was with the worst team in the league. By midseason I felt discouraged and burnt out. We had worked up to next to last in the league but that was hardly gratifying. By the end of the season, we were still next to last. I thought my career as a coach with the parent organization was over. But miraculously, they reassigned me the next year to a team with at least half a chance of winning some ball games. We got stronger every month, and I began to feel that I would have a future in big league coaching. If I hadn't been yanked from that first bad assignment, I think I would have quit baseball by now.

Train and Reward Managers for Career-Planning Skills. An effective career development program requires that managers throughout the organization be skilled in helping subordinates build their careers. These skills include such things as conducting performance evaluation sessions, assisting in goal-setting, and providing frequent feedback. Most skills of this nature can be acquired through training and practice. To reinforce training in career-planning skills, managers should be rewarded for their contribution to career planning.

A large Canadian computer company uses a dramatic approach to reward career-planning skills. Each manager is required to pick and develop a successor before the manager will be considered for promotion. In this way, the career development of subordinates is linked to the career progress of the managers.[3]

Use Human Resource Specialists as Advisors. As just implied, the major unit for career development is the employee and immediate manager. The personnel specialist should generally serve in the role of expert advisor who helps establish the program and serves as a consultant. If the human resource specialist becomes too heavily involved in the process, managers may be "taken off the hook." Another problem is that few organizations have the resources to provide individual counseling to all employees.[4]

Despite the general wisdom of this strategy, there are times when professional career counseling for individuals is the intervention of choice. Among the situations that call for professional counseling are career dilemmas caused by the mid-life crisis, cases of severe career dissatisfaction and modifying career plans to overcome stress disorders. As a result of professional career counseling, one manager came to realize that his stress symptoms were precipitated by the demands of his present job. He could no longer tolerate the daily confrontations with people. His stress symptoms subsided when he transferred to a position as a management information specialist.

Provide Valid Career Opportunity Information. Much of career planning is pure whimsy because it involves making plans for nonexistent opportunities. In one business machine company, hundreds of lower-ranking managers aspire to the position of machine-reconditioning center manager. They are enamored with the possibilities of being the general manager of an entire business operation. Unfortunately only five of these centers exist. To minimize such problems, a realistic picture of company opportunities should be presented to employees. Answers to questions such as these should be provided:

- What are the prospects for promotion or transfer from the present job?
- What percentage of employees reach a certain target level in this organization?
- What are the pay ranges at various job levels?
- Where is the fastest growth (and, therefore, the best promotion opportunity) in the company?
- If I have reached a dead end, what are paths for moving down so I can move up faster somewhere else?
- How do I go about requesting a transfer without alienating my boss?[5]
- How do I learn about opportunites in other divisions of the organization?

Use Valid Information in Your Data Base. An extension of the point just made is to have valid information in the data base underlying the company HRIS. The output in most human resource information systems is impressive on the surface— the reports appear to be scientific and valid because they are generated by a computer. However, the skills inventory and human resource forecasts contained in the system may contain many errors. Two career development specialists note that the majority of skills inventories actually contain information about education and experience—not skills.[6] It is also possible for the human resource forecasts to contain highly subjective estimates of future career opportunities in the firm. The basic input for these projections may be a hurried "guestimate" by a harried executive!

Alfred J. Walker, division manager—personnel data at American Telephone & Telegraph Co., points out that users of the HRIS should be informed about the currency of the information within the system.[7] In this way some misperceptions they may have about the validity of the data base can be minimized.

Link Training to Career Development. As implied by the case illustration at the beginning of this chapter, it is important to integrate training (and development programs in general) to career development. The individual should see the link between the training activity and his or her career plan. For example, if managers are required to attend a listening skills workshop, the relationship between listening acuity and managerial effectiveness should be explained. Career development consultant Beverly Kaye puts it in these words:

> Training programs that tie directly to the developmental needs of individuals will move those individuals toward their professional goals. As more time is spent in carefully planned and selected training events of all kinds instead of training "for its own sake" training will become more cost effective, and individuals, managers, and training professionals will reap the rewards.[8]

Emphasize More than Advancement. An unfortunate assumption made by many people about career planning is that it refers almost exclusively to upward mobility. Employees should also be encouraged to plan for growth and self-fulfillment within their present level of responsibility.[9] For many people psychological success comes from the kind of work they are presently performing. Many, if not most, sales representatives and technical specialists feel impelled to aspire toward administrative assignments. Once placed in these assignments, many of these people experience a decrease in job satisfaction and performance. Therefore, another fundamental reason that upward mobility should not be overemphasized in career planning; few employers have sufficient high level positions to satisfy all the aspirants. As one executive lamented to a consultant, "I wish you could help me identify a few good Indians. We already have too many chiefs."

Provide for Different Needs in Different Career Stages. Career development applies to all people at all stages of life.[10] An individual in early career has much more flexibility in terms of making choices. A person at midcareer might be concerned about such matters as integrating career plans with a spouse who has developed deep career commitments of his or her own. A person at late career might want to concentrate on retirement planning. A sophisticated career development program makes allowances for these different perspectives. One modern innovation in career development programs is to provide counseling and advice to couples facing the problems of a dual-career family. Another is to provide formal retirement counseling.

Integrate Career Development with Management Development. Career development is really only one major aspect of management development. People should be assigned to management development programs on the basis of both individual and organizational needs. For instance, it would be folly to send a manager to a three-month advanced management program at a university if that manager was seeking to get out of management. The North American Insurance Group, CDP is one example of how career development and management development might be integrated.

The assessment aspect of career development is well suited to helping achieve integration between career and management development. Formal assessment might reveal, for example, that manager A is deficient in oral communication skill. Manager A would then be assigned to an oral communication skill training program. During the assessment center, manager B might have proved to be an impulsive, haphazard decision-maker. Manager B might be assigned to a decision-making training program. (If that didn't work, he or she should be reassigned to a position with very little decision making.)

The Case for Career Development Programs

A convincing case can be made for the use of formal career development programs. Ideally, a properly planned and executed program serves the good of individuals, the organization, and society. Following are several of the potential benefits of an effectively conducted CDP.

Integration of Individual and Organizational Goals. Career development helps identify the link between attaining individual and organizational goals. As one Certified Public Accountant commented after a career-planning session with her boss, "I'm working for the right firm. If all goes according to plan, the firm will benefit from having its first woman partner, and I'll make enough money to buy what I want in life."

Communication of Concern for the Welfare of Individuals. An organization that helps employees plan their careers is demonstrating by its actions that it cares about the employee's welfare. The payoff to the organization is often a high degree of employee loyalty and commitment.

The Demonstration of Social Responsibility. Properly executed, career development programs are one way of contributing to the good of society. People with satisfying careers enjoy better mental health than their dissatisfied counterparts.

Implementation of Affirmative Action Programs. A career development program is a logical response to the charges that an organization is not fulfilling its responsibilities toward women, selected minorities, or ethnic groups. Without a solid program of career development, it is difficult for previously discriminated against groups to advance into higher-level positions.

Reduction of Turnover and Other Personnel Costs. Several studies demonstrated that when the enterprise makes a determined effort to help its employees plan their career, the result is lower turnover and personnel costs.[11]

Reduction of Mid-Career Problems. When employees properly plan their careers, they are less likely to fall victim to obsolescence and mid-career crisis. Burnout, too, can sometimes be minimized (see Chapter 4).

The Case against Career Development Programs

As with any other program or set of strategies described in this book, career development programs sometimes have negative side effects.

Most Career Planning Exercises Contain a Good Deal of Fantasy and Wishful Thinking. In the process of self- analysis, many individuals present a biased, unrealistic description of their personal strengths and goals. Almost everybody filling out a career development inventory lists "dealing with people" as a personal strength. Many people engage in goal setting so fanciful that their chances of success are less than 1 in 500. Despite the current trend toward pursuing a well-balanced, high quality life, an amusingly large number of people list as a career objective, "Chief executive officer of a major business corporation."[12]

Some Career Development Activities Are an Invasion of the Individual's Privacy. Career planning usually includes the individual divulging personal goals to a manager or staff specialist. The goals stated by many individuals are not particularly well integrated with or in the best interests of the organization. Many people plan to start a business of their own somewhat in competition with at least one product or service of their current employer. In the interests of candor, the person might reveal such a goal. To the disadvantage of the individual, he or she might now be perceived as disloyal and, therefore, out of consideration for major assignments in the future.

Career Development Programs Create an Elite Group of Crown Princes and Princesses. When a handful of people are designated as fast trackers, they become part of a self-fulfilling prophecy. Since they are known to be an elite group, their managers may tend to give them undeservingly high performance evaluations. Management's judgment in making them an elite group is, therefore, vindicated. Another problem with the crown prince and princesses effect is that other equally deserving employees may emerge who are not given equal consideration.

Resource limitations frequently preclude organization-wide implementation of a career development program. In these instances, efforts are targeted at those areas and people having the greatest potential payoff to the organization.[13] The people selected for the limited program are thus perceived as being crown princes and princesses.

Career Development Programs Often Give Rise to Disappointed Expectations. After participating in a CDP, many individuals believe that they should be receiving a promotion shortly. When the promotion does not materialize, they experience disappointment. Sometimes this disappointment translates into joining another organization that offers the person more responsibility. The underlying problem is that the CDP resulted in higher expectations for the employee.

Another way in which career development programs sometimes disappoint expectations is that they may train employees for opportunities that may never be available.[14] At the other extreme, some employees desire a secure, unchanging environment. Their expectations of being able to remain in such an environment are disrupted by a development program that emphasizes lateral moves and promotion.

GUIDELINES FOR ACTION AND SKILL DEVELOPMENT

If you are employed by an organization sponsoring a CDP, you should obviously follow the program and work within the system. However, you can help subordinates develop their careers without the benefit of a formal program. Among the informal actions you can take are encouraging subordinates to establish career goals, providing them feedback on where you think they need development, and sharing with them information about organizational opportunities.

Dealing with the career development of subordinates is a responsibility of major consequence. It is better to err on the side of being noncommittal than giving people negative information which could alter their lives. One example: "You are unsuited for a career in business." Similarly, when you do not feel you are qualified to handle a given employee concern (such as, "Would I be more successful if I went back to college?) seek professional assistance.

A formal career development program requires top management support in order to reach a high degree of effectiveness. If you are part of top management, give the CDP such support. If you are a lower-ranking manager or staff specialist, lobby for such support.

The presence of a career development program in your organization should not be interpreted as shifting responsibility for career planning and development from the individual to the organization (specifically the human resource department). As an individual, you still have the primary responsibility for managing your own career. And as a manager, you still have a heavy responsibility for helping subordinates develop their careers.[15]

When implementing a career development program, it is important to emphasize growth within a job, and horizontal growth, as well as vertical growth. The reason is that CDPs are generally interpreted as vehicles for moving upward in the organization. Counseling people about the reality that all growth cannot be vertical, can help minimize *some* discontent. One aspect of growth within a job appealing to many managers and professionals, is the development of new skills.

Questions and Activities

1. In recent years, career development programs have multiplied in number and received much publicity. What forces do you think have made CDPs so popular in recent years?
2. Where do people seeking help with career problems usually go for assistance?
3. What would be the advantages and disadvantages to an individual of going outside the organization for help with career planning (such as paying for the services of a career counselor)?
4. What do you think is the underlying reason that CDPs tend to reduce turnover?
5. Nevertheless, it is not unknown for a person to quit a firm after completing the early phases of a CDP. Why do you think this happens?
6. What facts about an individual do you think should be included in the company data base? Why?
7. What facts about an individual do you think should not be included in the company data base? Why?
8. Identify two other techniques described in another chapter in this book that you think are well suited to career development. Explain your choices.

Notes

[1] See the appendix to this chapter.

[2] Douglas T. Hall and Francine S. Hall, "What's New in Career Management?" *Organizational Dynamics*, Summer 1976, p. 29.

[3]Ibid., p. 30.

[4]Marilyn A. Morgan, Douglas T. Hall, and Alison Martier, "Career Development Strategies in Industry—Where Are We and Where Should We Be?" *Personnel*, March–April, 1979, p. 25.

[5]The first five questions in this list are quoted directly from ibid., p. 26.

[6]Elmer H. Burack and Robert D. Smith, *Personnel Management: A Human Resource System Approach* (New York: John Wiley, 1982), p. 455.

[7]Alfred J. Walker, "The Analytical Element is Important to an HRIS," *Personnel Administrator*, September 1983, p. 34.

[8]Beverly Kaye, "Career Development Puts Training in Its Place," *Personnel Journal*, February 1983, p. 137.

[9]Morgan, Hall, and Martier, p. 26.

[10]Ibid., p. 27.

[11]William F. Glueck, *Personnel: A Diagnostic Approach*, Third Edition (Plano, Texas: Business Publications, Inc., 1983).

[12]An excellent description of achieving realism in goal setting is Beverly L. Kaye, "How You Can Help Employees Formulate Their Career Goals," *Personnel Journal*, May 1980, pp. 368–372, 402.

[13]Comment made by W. J. Heisler in book review appearing in *Personnel Psychology* (Spring 1983), p. 166.

[14]Manuel London and Stephen A. Stumpf, *Managing Careers* (Reading, Mass.: Addison Wesley, 1982).

[15]Andrew F. Sikula and John F. McKenna, "Individuals Must Take Charge of Career Development," *Personnel Administrator* (October 1983), pp. 89–97.

Some Additional References

Collins, Eliza G. C. (Editor). *Executive Success: Making It in Management.* New York: John Wiley, 1983.

Dawson, Christopher M. "Will Career Plateauing Become a Bigger Problem?" *Personnel Journal*, January 1983, pp. 78–81.

Kennedy, Marilyn Moates, "Blueprint for Career Planning," *Business Week's Guide to Careers*, Fall/Winter 1983, pp. 60–61.

Montross, David H. and Christopher J. Shinkman, eds. *Career Development in the 1980s: Theory and Practice.* Springfield, Ill.: Charles C. Thomas, 1981.

Osipow, Samuel H. *Theories of Career Development* 3rd ed. Englewood Cliffs, N.J.: Prentice-Hall, 1983.

Walker, Alfred J. *HRIS Development: A Project Team Guide to Building an Effective Personnel Information System.* New York: Van Nostrand Reinhold, 1982.

Appendix to Chapter 16

The Career Development Inventory

Directions: Complete the following questionnaire for your personal use. You might wish to make up a worksheet before putting your answers in final form.

1. How would you describe yourself as a person?
2. What are you best at doing?
3. What are you worst at doing?
4. What are your two biggest accomplishments?
5. Write your own obituary as you would like it to appear at the termination of your life.
6. What would be the ideal job for you?
7. Why aren't you more rich and famous?
8. What career advice can you give yourself?
9. Describe the two peak experiences in your life.
10. What are your five most important values? (The things most important to you.)
11. What are my long-range work (professional) goals?
12. What are my intermediate-range work (professional) goals?
13. What are my short-range (professional) goals?
14. How realistic are those goals in terms of opportunities in my place of employment or in my field?
15. How well suited are my qualifications and skills for achieving those goals?
16. What personal improvements must I make to achieve my goals?
17. What do I want to achieve in my personal life?

Chapter 17

Assessment Centers for Management Development

Trans-National Corporation has been using the assessment center method for a number of years. Originally, the method was used to help select current employees with potential managerial positions. Soon it was discovered that the assessment center method could work equally well in developing managers. Assessments were used to identify particular developmental needs of individual managers. In this way, managers could be directed toward training and development programs suitable to their individual needs. Managers also gained valuable experience in going through the assessment center exercises.

The director of management development at Trans-National Corporation greeted the six assessment-center participants assigned to the conference room overlooking a large pond:

Welcome to the second day of the assessment and development program. You look alert and eager to proceed despite the rigors of the first day. So far you have all been evaluated by one of the staff psychologists through tests and interviews. Within one month after you leave tomorrow, you will have an in-depth discussion of the results of this assessment with one of our staff counselors. The sessions will take place back at your regular work locations. I know you were hoping to come back to our beautiful compound out here in the country for your feedback sessions [forced oohs and aahs from the six participants].

This afternoon you'll be put through a customer relations problem. More about that later. This morning's activity is called the leaderless group discussion. You will be evaluated by two Trans-National managers whom you probably have not met before. A third observer will be a staff psychologist who has not conducted your individual evaluation. As you can see, we strive for objectivity at every step of the assessment center method.

Unless there are a couple of pressing questions, seat yourselves comfortably around the circular conference table.

Quickly the three observors walk into the room, establishing no contact with the six participants—Burt, Mark, Judy, Phil, Derek, and Sandy. Each of these six people is then handed the same note simultaneously. It reads:

You six people are office supervisors. All members of upper management are away on a management conference. Your responsibility is to make a tight deadline on a shipment. If you are late on this order, your firm will lose $150,000 in penalties. You are a nonunion organization. An employee, who claims he is the spokeperson for all the factory employees, comes to you with an urgent message: "Either we all get a $50 bonus, or we all walk off the job this afternoon." You have a maximum of 60 minutes to decide what appropriate action to take.

All six participants remain silent for about three minutes before conversation begins. Following is a sampling of the deliberations of the six people under observation:

Phil: I don't know about you other five supervisors. But I don't even call this a problem. I'm not a person who threatens easily. I'd blast him right out the door. I'd tell him that no self-appointed straw boss is going to put the gun to my head. He can go back to work without the bonus or walk out the door. Nobody else will follow him out.

Judy: Aren't you being a little impetuous, Phil? You can't just fire people on the spot. In the 1980s people can protect themselves from capricious management actions. He could turn around and bring a lawsuit against our company. I'd sit him down and hear him out. Maybe if we got to the root of his problem, we would discover that money isn't the real issue.

Phil: I don't see what listening to him would do. He's already made up his mind. He's probably been plotting this strong-arm tactic for months.

Burt: Look gang, let's not forget we're supervisors. We have to be cautious in making major decisions. The information I have says that upper management is away on a management conference. It doesn't say they are out on a canoe in the middle of the Colorado River. Let's get on the phone and track them down. As a supervisor, I always touch base with my superiors before taking action. I'll bet we can get in touch with one of the executive groups within 20 minutes or so.

Derek: Do I hear some pussyfooting and evasiveness on your part Burt? This is our problem and we have to take care of it ourselves. Let's conduct a quick study. We'll go out on the factory floor and speak to a good sampling of the workers. Then we'll know if the workers are really pressing for a $50 bonus. Maybe two of us could go out right now. If all six of us storm the floor at the same time and start asking questions, it could upset morale. And we've got to get that shipment out on time.

Mark: So far the suggestion I like best is yours, Derek. But even there I see some problems. Are we going to ask employees, "Oh, by the way are you planning to extort $50 from us? [*The group laughs.*]

Derek: I was planning on being more subtle than that. We could just inquire about how well things are progressing toward making the shipments on time.

Sandy: Are we supervisors or mice? Or are we mathematical midgets? The way this announcement is slanted, it appears that top management cannot be involved in our decision making. I'm all for acting right now. We cannot afford to miss this shipment. Aside from losing $150,000, we stand the chance of losing an enormous amount of customer goodwill. Let's assume we have about 200 employees in the factory. We give them all their $50 bonus. That's $10,000 tax-deductible bucks. It's still a savings of $140,000. We'll look pretty astute in the eyes of top management if we just pay off the employees their $50 bonus for helping us get out this critical shipment.

Burt: I won't buy that. A supervisor doesn't have the authority to give 200 employees a $50 bonus. We'll all be fired for taking an action that big. I say let's call for a quick meeting with the spokesperson and about 12 other employees. We can then study the problem further. If we stall them, maybe the problem will go away. When management gets back, we can tell them what happened. Of course, I still think we should track down top management.

Phil: Since you people disagreed with my strong-arm tactics, let me suggest something a little less forceful. All six of us can go out to the shop floor together. I'll make a speech to the effect that anybody who is with us can stay. If the shipment goes out on time, we will warmly consider recommending them for a salary increase. Anybody who wants to hold us up for a quick $50 can walk out the door. The six of us can take over operator jobs. Besides, if we have to, we can get the maintenance employees to do production work. What I'm saying is that if we call their bluff, very few will actually walk off the job.

Mark: What I'm hearing you people say is that we should take some kind of action and do it right away. I'm all for summarizing the suggestions we have made so far. We can sort out the good from the bad and maybe come up with a composite solution. No use generating a bunch of alternatives that we don't act on. Everything that has been said so far has both good and bad points. After about 15 minutes of such an analysis, perhaps we could vote on the best solution.

Phil: Spoken like a true bureaucrat, Mark. You want us to come up with a compromise solution that probably will please nobody. I'm willing to go along with your plan as long as we don't eat up the whole clock before we decide on something. Okay, I'm willing to give it 15 minutes. But let's look at the alternatives I have proposed first.

While the six participants are interacting with each other in the leaderless group discussion (LGD), the three observers are making notations about them on the form shown in Figure 17-1. When the LGD session is completed, the observors spend about 20 minutes completing the ratings and comments. The comments made in the strengths and weaknesses columns are particularly useful for providing feedback to the participants during the follow-up sessions.

Irate Customer Exercise. In the afternoon session, the participants were put through the "irate customer exercise," designed to (*a*) assess how well they handle threats and pressure, and (*b*) give them experience in handling pressure and threats. Each participant is given 10 minutes to interact over the telephone with an assessor who plays the role of a highly upset customer. Each participant is told that he or she is the sales manager for a company that manufactures and sells electronic forklift trucks. Seated alone in a room, and placed at a desk, the participant is told to answer the phone should it ring. The phone does ring, and in an emotionally pitched voice, a "customer" (an assessment center staff member) bellows:

This is Johnson from Sheffield Industries. What in blazes are you people doing? We received shipment of 12 of your new forklift trucks designed for narrow aisles. Well, you shipped us 12 lemons—an industry record. Our material handling employees are going out of their minds. As soon as they load the lift with more than 200 pounds, the damn machines stall at mid-lift. You're ruining our production schedules. Get these forklifts off our premises, or we'll take legal action. I want an answer within the hour.

Next is a sampling of how each of the participants responded to Mr. Johnson:

Burt: I'm sorry to hear about your problems. I'll take your request up through channels, and I should be able to get you an answer quite soon. We should be able to do something about your problem.

Mark: It sounds to me like you are having technical problems with your forklift trucks. I will notify our customer service department immediately. They should be able to investigate your problem very soon. In the meantime, I will check and see if any other customer has had this problem. It does seem strange.

Judy: You certainly do have a problem, Mr. Johnson. And I can understand that you are in a rush for some action. But before we do

Figure 17–1
A Leaderless Group Discussion Observer Evaluation Form

Rater _____

Directions: Rate each participant on each of the six categories. Refer to the definition sheet before the evaluation session begins. Be sure to include a few comments about the strengths and weaknesses you observed for each candidate.

Names of participants

		Burt	Mark	Judy	Phil	Derek	Sandy
Oral communication skill	Excellent						
	Good						
	Fair						
	Poor						
Leadership	Excellent						
	Good						
	Fair						
	Poor						
Initiative	Excellent						
	Good						
	Fair						
	Poor						
Planning and organizing	Excellent						
	Good						
	Fair						
	Poor						
Judgment	Excellent						
	Good						
	Fair						
	Poor						
Management potential	Excellent						
	Good						
	Fair						
	Poor						

Figure 17-1 *(concluded)*

Comments and observations about each participant

	Strengths	Weaknesses
Participant A Burt		
Participant B Mark		
Participant C Judy		
Participant D Phil		
Participant E Derek		
Participant F Sandy		

Seating chart

(Seating chart: Sandy, Burt, Mark, Judy, Phil, Derek arranged in a circle)

DEFINITION OF ASSESSMENT DIMENSIONS

Use these definitions as a guide in rating the participants on the following dimensions of managerial behavior:

Oral communication skill—Effective expression of thoughts and ideas to other people which can include nonverbal communication such as gestures and eye contact. (Many positions require good speaking skills. Try to focus on the manner of presentation, not the content of what is said.)

Leadership—Use of appropriate interpersonal skills and methods in influencing people or groups toward achieving organizational goals.

(Many managerial and staff positions require leadership ability. The focus is not only on whether or not people are influenced, but the method chosen to influence them.)

Initiative—Active attempts to influence events to achieve goals; self-starting rather than starting only when prodded by others. Also, taking action to achieve goals beyond those required of you.

(Some jobs require people who will pick up on what needs to be done whether or not that action is part of their job description.)

Planning and organization—Similar to administrative ability; establishing a course of action for self and/or others to accomplish a goal. Also assigning personnel to appropriate tasks and allocating resources.

(Many managerial jobs require good planning and organizing ability. Typical activities of this nature include establishing goals, budgeting time, setting priorities, allocating proper amounts of time to activities.)

Judgment—Making decisions and selecting alternatives that are logically sound and show an understanding of how people are likely to respond to the decision.

Management potential—An overall aptitude or ability to assume additional managerial responsibility; promise for taking on more responsibility; an indication that this individual will continue to grow and develop.

(Some people are very effective employees yet they might very well be "in over their heads" if placed in a job with too many additional demands of a managerial nature.)

---

*The first five definitions are based on those presented in William C. Byham, "Starting an Assessment Center the Right Way," *The Personnel Administrator,* February 1980, p.31.

something drastic, I would like you to investigate all the alternatives. For instance, did your drivers receive proper training in the use of the forklifts? Are all the controls set properly? I want to personally visit one of your installations.

Phil: Good customer or not, Mr. Johnson, I want you to calm down before we conduct business any further. I don't take swearing from one of my customers. How do you know we are at fault. Before we get into a shooting match, let's get to the bottom of this problem.

Derek: Mr. Johnson, it sounds like you have every reason to be upset. It must be very frustrating for you to have our highly touted trucks fail when you need them most. If the shipment is defective, we will make good on every one of them. Give us a chance. I think we can help you with your problem by this afternoon. I'll be back to you in 45 minutes with a plan of action to help you. Please give me your telephone number.

Sandy: You do have a problem Mr. Johnson. I'm sorry to hear about it. The solution you suggest sounds very expensive. At this moment, I'm not sure about our policy on returns of defective machines. Maybe it would be less expensive for both of us, if we fixed whatever problem is causing the forklift trucks to stall. I'll consult with the right people today, and get back to you. In the meantime, please read the operator's manual for these machines.

Observer Comments. Next is a sampling of the comments made about the six participants (based on the LGD and irate customer exercise) by the three observors (two line managers and one psychologist):

Burt: Seems too cautious to me. I get the impression he will never be a take-charge guy. He's too concerned about touching base with top management before taking independent action. He definitely does not look like top management timber to me. He's too worried about being wrong. Strictly a clerical type. Does not have the tendency to run off half-cocked. Will deliberate before committing organizational resources.

Mark: Very low key guy. He talks almost in a whisper. Good committee worker. Let's other people do most of the work, then comes in and synthesizes what they have done. Good sense of timing. Know's when to convert thinking to action. Not much creativity of his own. Just acts on the thinking of the other people.

Judy: Kind of laid-back. Not much of a talker, but what she says makes sense. Very good at organizing her thoughts and formulating a constructive plan of action. Not too much initiative. Doesn't say much until she feels forced to.

Phil: Impulsive person who has an overwhelming need to take control. May jump ahead without giving proper thought to the implications of his decision. Forceful, take-charge manager. Won't stand for any tomfoolery. Boastful but effective. Suffers from a superiority complex. Has such a strong need to dominate that he doesn't listen to others.

Derek: Good analytical mind. Plans things out first before jumping in. Articulate and persuasive. Natural leadership qualities in a refined, gentlemanly way. Good teamworker. Good perceptiveness about people. Willing to give negative feedback to people.

Sandy: Creative problem solver. Displays good analytical skills. Good at financial manipulation but needs more business experience. Good personal charm. Backs it up with a keen analytical mind.

At the end of the day, the observors began the lengthy process of making sense of the wealth of data collected about the participants during the assessment process. The three assessors compose a panel which reviews each participant in depth. The strengths and weaknesses of each participant are carefully noted. (Data provided in Figure 17–1 are particularly useful here.) Examples of specific behavior displayed by a participant during any assessment center exercise are noted and discussed. A panel review usually takes about 90 to 120 minutes to complete.

The assessor who completed a background interview with the participant is responsible for preparing a complete developmental report.[1] It contains a full discussion of strengths and limitations as perceived by the observors. Each participant is then scheduled for a thorough follow-up session with a human resource specialist or psychologist. For instance, a follow-up session was scheduled with Phil in his office four weeks after he participated in the assessment center. A sample of his session proceeded in this manner:

Psychologist: What kind of impression do you think you made on others?

Phil: Since we were there mostly to be sized up for our leadership ability, I think I made a pretty good impression. If we were there to be evaluated as office politicians, I would not have done so well.

Psychologist: It sounds like you do have some concern that people might see you as a little heavy-handed.

Phil: For sure. I'm a little too tough for some people.

Psychologist: That's precisely the kind of feedback I have to give you. You did bring about a mixed reaction from the panel of observors, Some comments about you were quite positive. For example, one item of feedback I have here describes you as boastful, but effective. However, the general thrust is that, in your own words, you are too heavy-handed. You sometimes alienate people because you hit them over the head initially. It's good to be forceful, but you overdo it. Your comment about blasting the supervisor out the door is a case in point.

Phil: Maybe you're right. I attack too quickly. I've always been that way. I got suspended from my high school football team once for punching out a teammate. But I don't beat my wife or kids.

Psychologist: [*laughs*] I suspect you come on strong mostly in situations where you want to win.

Phil: How right you are. But where do we go from here?

Psychologist: The report provides a number of suggestions for improving your impulsive and heavy-handed approach to people. But above all, I think the process of change has already begun. Once you feel the need for change, it is within your power to change yourself. Only you can monitor your own behavior on a day-to day basis.

Phil: I guess I know what you mean. Before I blast out people, I should say to myself, "Am I being too harsh?" Or maybe I should count to 10.

Psychologist: Sounds good to me. I would also recommend that you read two books about assertiveness training [*Hands Phil a brief bibliography*]. But I think you should attend assertiveness training for the opposite reason 90 percent of people attend. I think you need to become less pushy and less domineering. We're trying to tame you down, make you less aggressive, not more emotionally expressive in your interactions with people. After reading, you might decide to attend assertiveness training. Maybe you would also benefit from attending an encounter group. You need more skill in gauging your impact on others.

Phil: Well, if you think these things can help me in my career, I'm willing to give them a try. I love a challenge.

Psychologist: With a positive attitude like that Phil, I'm confident that you can develop your skills in handling people.

The interaction between the psychologist and Phil should not be interpreted to mean that a miracle cure has been performed. While in his meeting with the psychologist, Phil is probably convinced that he will from now on be less heavy-handed and impulsive with people. Most likely, under pressure he will retreat to his typical behavior pattern. The significance of the counseling session, however, is that the seeds of change have been planted within Phil. He will give serious thought to his need for change as a result of the feedback. He now knows what direction he should be moving toward and should be able to bring about some of these changes over time.

What Is an Assessment Center?

The vignette illustrates the use of assessment centers in the development of present employees. However, the method has not yet been defined. In overview, an assessment center is an evaluation method that uses situational exercises and other measuring devices to identify promising job candidates and employees with potential for management.[2] More specifically, an assessment center consists of a standardized evaluation of behavior based on multiple sources of information (inputs). Several trained observors and different techniques are used. Judgments about behavior are made, in part, from specially developed assessment simulations (such as the leaderless group discussion). These judgments are pooled by the assessors at an evaluation meeting during which assessment data are reported and discussed. A consensus decision is usually reached about the evaluation of each individual. In order for a process to be considered a true assessment center the following elements are essential:

- Multiple assessment techniques must be used. At least one of these techniques must be a simulation of job behavior. Examples as simulations in addition to the leaderless group discussions include in-basket exercises, interview simulations, and fact-finding exercises.
- Multiple assessors must be used who receive thorough training prior to participating in a center.
- Judgments resulting in an outcome (such as recommendation for promotion, specific training, or development) must be based on pooling information from different assessors and techniques.
- An overall evaluation of behavior must be made by the assessors at a separate time from observation of behavior during the exercises.
- The dimensions, attributes, characteristics, qualities, skills, abilities, or knowledge evaluated by the assessment center are determined by an analysis of relevant job behaviors (job analysis).[3]

How Effective Are Assessment Centers?

Although we are concerned here primarily with the contribution of the assessment center method to management development, other research about the method is also relevant. Extensive research has been conducted on the ability of the assessment center to predict future job performance and behavior of employees. Assessment center predictions have been compared frequently to such measures of organizational advancement as salary increase, promotion, and job level attained. The results of these studies have been very positive. Over 20 studies have been published indicating that the ratings made of people in an assessment center (along the type of dimensions shown in Figure 17–1) are fairly good predictors of organizational advancement.[4]

Prediction of Progress into Management. A representative, thorough study of the predictive ability of the assessment center method was conducted at American Telephone and Telegraph Company.[5] The study compared the assessment center ratings received by 1,097 women with the level of management they had attained seven years later. A two-day management assessment center was used, staffed mostly by trained middle managers, about 40 percent of whom were women. The assessment techniques included in-basket exercises, two group exercises (similar to the one used at Trans-National), an interview, a written exercise, and two paper-and-pencil tests. An in-basket test and a written exercise of the type used in this study are shown in Figure 17-2.

Each woman was evaluated on 18 dimensions shown by past research to be related to management success. The evaluations were based on the reports prepared on performance in the assessment exercises. Additionally, an overall prediction of middle-management potential was made. A four-point scale was used that ranged from "more than acceptable" to "not acceptable." The women in the top two categories were then given additional financial compensation and career counseling to help prepare them for middle management. Local Bell telephone companies were not informed about the women who were rated in the bottom two categories.

In the study, the criterion of success chosen was the actual level of management attained by the woman at a specific point in time, which represented an average of seven years after the assessments. A sizeable correlation ($r = .42$) was found between overall predictions made by the assessment staff and subsequent progress seven years later. Many of the specific dimensions also showed a significant relationship to management job level. The seven most predictive dimensions were:

Leadership
Energy
Behavior flexibility
Inner work standards
Resistance to stress
Tolerance of uncertainty
Organizing and planning

Contribution to Management Development. As Virginia R. Boehm has noted, *management development* commonly refers to five different sets of activities:

1. The informal process of on-the-job learning.
2. Formal training and coursework.
3. Moving through an established sequence of positions.
4. Individualized career planning and career pathing.
5. Self-development and self-improvement.[6]

Assessment centers contribute to management development primarily in categories 4 and 5. The feedback portion of the method often gives

Figure 17-1
Samples of the In-Basket and Written Assessment Center Exercises

---

In-Basket

In the in-basket technique, the participant is required to sort through an assortment of mail, memos, reports and other information often found to come across a manager's desk. Participants must deal with each item and give instructions as to its proper handling. The ways in which the respondent deals with the items is said to provide clues to self-confidence, organizational planning abilities, decision-making, risk taking, and administrative skill (similar to the behaviors measured in the LGD.).* Following is a typical exercise:

> You have been working as company controller for a manufacturer of personal computers. The president of the company has been forced by the board of directors to vacate his post immediately because he has been charged with embezzlement. You are asked to assume the post of president, as of now. You report to your new office at 8:30 A.M. Monday, amidst considerable confusion and a sense of panic in the company.
>
> The former president's secretary brings you in a large cardboard box and says, "Here is what was on the president's desk before he left town late Thursday. The vice-presidents who worked with him are being interviewed by the board today and will be tied up until Wednesday. I have 10 phone calls for you to return, and the phone is ringing constantly."
>
> Before you begin to sort through the box of papers the secretary handed you, you open the top drawer to your new desk, you see a yellow tablet with "Urgent, action items," written on the first page. The first three items state:
>
> ■ Call George about borrowing money to cover next week's executive payroll.
> ■ Get the stockholder's meeting postponed.
> ■ Find way to inflate the accounts receivable list.
>
> It is now 9:01, and you must start taking action. Do something.

As with the LGD exercise, your performance will be observed and recorded by several trained observors.

Written Exercise

One type of written exercise used in an assessment center is the autobiographical essay. The instructions may take this form:

> Prepare a 900-word autobiography. Your sketch should tell us such things as: who you are, where you have been in your career, and where you are headed. Please include a detailed description of your strengths and areas of needed personal growth. Describe any obstacles you will have to overcome to reach your goals. And don't forget to develop some contingency plans in case your career does not go as you planned.

The team of assessors then carefully analyze each essay to arrive at judgments about the traits and behaviors of the individual related to managerial and professional success. Among the hundreds of possible variables measured by these autobiographical essays would be: strength of motivation, clarity of thinking, writing ability, organizing ability, creativity, time management, breadth of interests, self-insight, and self-confidence.

---

*Definition adapted from William E. Souder and Anna Mae Leksich, "Assessment Centers are Evolving Toward a Bright Future, " *Personnel Administrator,* November 1983, p. 81.

---

individuals tips they can use to plan their careers and make personal improvements (such as suggesting to an individual manager that he or she needs more skill in properly organizing work). The process of going through an assessment center either as a participant or an observor, can also contribute to one's development. The individual may become more perceptive in making observations about people, or may learn new skills for getting along better with others in a group effort.

Although the use of assessment centers for development has not been as rigorously evaluated as its use for selection, some scattered evidence has been gathered. A recent analysis of experience suggests that three major management development benefits can derive from an assessment center. First, the participants improve their interpersonal understandings. Second is the improved perceptiveness about people derived from assessor training and practice. And third, after their assessment center experience, managers often become more skilled in conducting performance appraisals and counseling subordinates about their careers.[7]

A study of participants' reactions to assessment centers provides some indirect—and highly subjective—evidence of their contribution to management development. Kenneth S. Teel and Henry DuBois interviewed 37 county and city employees who had participated in an assessment center used as a predictive device. Nineteen of these people received high scores at the center, while 18 received low scores. All were interviewed in depth about their experiences. Among their findings was that 95 percent of the high scorers and 61 percent of the low scorers agreed with the statement: "Information given me will be valuable in my personal development." Also, 95 percent of the high scorers and 44 percent of the low scorers agreed that "Developmental recommendations I received were worthwhile."[8]

The Argument for Assessment Centers

Assessment centers have become widely used for selection, management development, and career development (refer to Chapter 16). Today the federal government and over 3,000 companies in North America have assessment centers of their own or use the services of a centralized assessment center. They have reached an all-time popularity in their 80-year history. It could therefore be argued that any human resource management method this widely used by so many well-managed organizations must be of some value. A more compelling argument is that the assessment center method has proven cost effective.

One survey of assessment centers attempted to examine both cost and benefit. The average return on investment (ROI) for the method exceeds 300 percent, even though the average cost of evaluating a candidate is substantially higher when an assessment center procedure is used instead of a briefer method of individual evaluation.[9] The financial benefits include such things as (a) money not spent on hiring replacements for new hires who prove to be poor performers, and (b) reduced turnover because of the career development offered participants.

Above all, the assessment center method has proven itself as a valid selection device. Surveys indicate, assessment center evaluations do predict future performance in management positions. Repeated studies have demonstrated that those persons selected for managerial jobs by means of assessment centers, or promoted to higher-level jobs, perform as much as 50 percent better than individuals selected by traditional selection methods.[10]

The assessment center method is useful from top management's standpoint because it meets with user acceptance. As a case in point, the American Family Insurance Group surveyed the attitudes of 500 employees who had participated in the center, either as participants, assessors, or supervisors of assessors. The following results were obtained in response to the question "Taking everything into consideration, how do you feel about the assessment center?" Seventy-eight percent of the participants, 89.5 percent of the assessors, and 68.4 percent of the supervisors of assessors responded that they were either satisfied or very satisfied with the assessment center process.[11]

Finally, the assessment center method is an inherently fair method of evaluating people. One writer cogently observes:

> Assessment simulation supposedly provides a precise, objective, job-related test based on actual behavior rather than such tarnished standards as educational background, prior work record, seniority, or intelligence. Hence the method has gained a reputation as one of the only legally defensible approaches to management selection. Indeed, the Equal Employment Opportunity Commission itself now uses the method.[12]

The Argument against Assessment Centers

An often-heard argument against the assessment center method is that it tends to perpetuate sterotypes of the effective manager. People who receive high ratings in the assessment center simulation exercises tend to be bright, articulate, and well groomed. (On the other hand, one might argue that bright, articulate, and well-groomed people do make good managers.) A similar criticism can be made of the management development use of assessment centers. Participants often receive counseling and feedback that encourages them to behave in a sterotyped manner. As one emotional sales manager described his assessment center experience, "They tried to tame me into being a polite little bureaucrat. I was told my image was wrong for rising in the corporation."

Although the majority of assessment centers are conducted by professionals, some of them are run by people with no awareness of the need for such considerations as conducting a job analysis prior to making assessments of people. Additionally, some of these people have limited awareness of how much influence an invalid evaluation might have over the lives of the participants.

Assessment centers can sometimes be a focal point of resentment and complaint from those who receive poor evaluations in the exercise. "Many people believe that being evaluated unfavorably in an assessment center marks the end of their career, no matter how brilliant a record they may have compiled in their years on the job." Some candidates believe that success in the center depends more on a sparkling personality than on competence in performing managerial tasks.[13]

The Crown Prince or Princess argument advanced against career development programs (Chapter 16) also applies to the assessment center method. A handful of people who are rated highly in the assessment center are then sometimes placed in an elite group by management and singled out for choice assignments. Others who did not perform as well in the assessment center—but who are nevertheless good performers on the job—come to resent the "princes" and "princesses."

People who perform well in the assessment center exercises, yet who are not placed in a select group for choice assignments, create another problem. They sometimes suffer poor morale because they think their good performance at the assessment center earns them the right to rapid career progress.

A research-based concern about assessment centers is that the dimensions being measured may be less reliable than previously thought. Paul R. Sackett and George F. Dreher compared the ratings participants received on certain dimensions with the ratings they received on the same dimensions in other exercises. Assume that a manager was rated highly on the dimension of "planning and organizing ability" on the basis of his or her performance in a leaderless group discussion. That same manager should also be rated high on "planning and organizing ability" for his or her performance on an in-basket task. The researchers found the opposite to be true. In their words, "The lack of agreement among the various ratings of the same dimension (such as leadership or decision making) is the most striking finding of the study."[14]

The most telling criticism of assessment centers as selection devices is that they give a false impression of being valid. According to this line of reasoning, assessment center ratings predict how managers perceive performance, not performance itself. The same superficial characteristics about people lead to their high ratings within and outside the assessment center. Two management researchers note "perhaps the assessment center staff is evaluating candidates based on its familiarity with the preferences of the decision makers who will actually promote, thus merely duplicating already existing procedures."[15]

GUIDELINES FOR ACTION AND SKILL DEVELOPMENT

If you are being evaluated through the assessment center method, you should place yourself in a positive light, but try to utilize the characteristics and behaviors that you find natural. Some assessees falsely assume that they will receive high evaluations by acting in an aggressive, overbearing, dominating manner toward the other assessees and observors. In reality, such behavior will peg you as being insensitive to people and, therefore, as having relationship problems in an organizational environment.

For an assessment center to achieve useful outcomes such as improved selection and development of people, it must be conducted in a scientifically sound and professionally responsible manner. Three key elements must be given primary consideration[16]

1. Results of the assessment center method should be only one part of a total selection, promotion, or development system. The organization should combine other information about the individual (such as performance appraisal results) with the assessment center report before making any type of personnel decision. To achieve maximum utility, the assessment center should be part of a complete personnel decision-making system.
2. The assessment center exercises should be based upon a complete job analysis. Without such information, the dimensions used in the center will lack validity. For example, "oral presentation skill" should be included as a dimension of management ability only if good speaking ability has been revealed—through careful study—to be critical for success in a specific managerial job.
3. The exercise used in the center should reflect the job for which the person is being evaluated or developed. Such a "real world" relationship is referred to as content validity. The simulation exercise described earlier in this chapter concerned a group of supervisors who were forced to deal with the unforseen demands of production workers. Such an exercise should be used only if supervisors (and other managers) in the company were sometimes required to deal with emergency situations centering around employee demands. In contrast, a simulation exercise about interplanetary travel would not be content valid. In addition, the Equal Employment Opportunity Commission has been known to challenge exercises which appear totally unrelated to job performance!

Many administrative considerations also govern the effective implementation of assessment centers. First the center must have top management support and involvement.[17] Top management should set the major objectives for the center and establish the criteria for judging its effectiveness. Second, participants should be selected carefully, based on what the center hopes to achieve. Not everyone should participate in the center. However, it has been recommended that some superior performers and a variety of "problem children" be included among the participants. Such diversity can serve as a validity check on the procedures.

Assessment centers generate an enormous amount of paperwork. Sometimes up to 100 pages are genterd per assessee. It is therefore important to simplify paperwork, and to design a system that prevents the center from becoming bogged down in paperwork.[18]

Questions and Activities

1. Several years ago the Equal Employment Opportunity Commission strongly urged AT&T to put large numbers of women supervisors through their assessment center. (AT&T complied.) Why do you think the assessment center method was chosen as a way of creating improved job opportunities for women?

2. At some colleges and universities, assessment center techniques are used to help evaluate students for scholarships. What do you think of this practice?

3. Most of the actual evaluations of people in assessment centers are made by experienced managers rather than by human resource specialists or psychologists. What do you see as the potential advantages and disadvantages of this practice?

4. Which aspects of nonverbal behavior (review Chapter 10) do you think would be particularly critical for performing well in the leaderless group discussion exercise?

5. Should a person with a stutter or other speech impediment be sent to an assessment center? Why or why not?

6. In the assessment center method, evaluations of individuals reflect a consensus of the assessors' opinions. How might we guard against a few outspoken and domineering assessors making most of the decisions about the assessees?

7. Rate yourself on the dimensions of managerial behavior listed in Figure 17-1. On which of these dimensions do you need improvement in order to achieve your career goals?

Notes

[1]The sequence of events in the assessment center method are carefully described in James C. Quick et al., "Developing Administrative Personnel through the Assessment Center Technique," *Personnel Administrator*, February 1980, pp. 45–46.

[2]James L. Gibson, John M. Ivancevich, and James H. Donnelly, Jr., *Organizations: Behavior, Structure, Processes*, 4th ed. (Plano, Texas: Business Publications, Inc., 1982), p. 624.

[3]Above definition and description of an assessment center is paraphrased from Task Force on Assessment Center Standards, "Standards and Ethical Considerations for Assessment Center Operations," *The Personnel Administrator*, February 1980, pp. 35–36.

[4]Virginia R. Boehm, "Assessment Centers and Management Development," in Kendrith M. Rowland and Gerald R. Ferris, *Personnel Management* (Boston: Allyn and Bacon, 1982), p. 346.

[5]Richard J. Ritchie and Joseph L. Moses, "Assessment Center Correlates of Women's Advancement Into Middle Management: A 7- Year Longitudinal Analysis," *Journal of Applied Psychology*, May 1983, pp. 227–231.

[6]Boehm, "Assessment Centers and Management Development, " p. 349.

[7]William E. Souder and Anna Mae Leksich, "Assessment Centers are Evolving Toward a Bright Future," *Personnel Administrator*, November 1983, p. 86.

[8]Kenneth S. Teel and Henry DuBois, "Participants' Reactions to Assessment Centers," *Personnel Administrator*, March 1983, p. 87.

[9]S. L. Cohen et al., "Incorporating Assessment Center Techniques into Management Training and Development at Xerox," *Journal of Assessment Center Technology*, volume 2, 1979, pp. 1–5. As cited in Boehm, p. 356.

[10]Duane P. Schultz, *Psychology and Industry Today*, Second Edition (New York: Macmillan, 1978), p. 110.

[11]Treadway C. Parker, "Assessment Centers: A Statistical Study," *Personnel Administrator*, February 1980, pp. 65–67.

[12]Berkeley Rice, "Measuring Executive Muscle," *Psychology Today*, December 1978, p. 96.

[13]This criticism and quote from Schultz, *Psychology and Industry Today*, p. 109.

[14]Paul R. Sackett and George F. Dreher, "Constructs and Assessment Center Dimensions: Some Troubling Empirical Findings," *Journal of Applied Psychology*, August 1982, p. 409.

[15]Richard J. Klimoski and William J. Strickland, "Assessment Centers—Valid or Merely Prescient?" *Personnel Psychology*, Autumn 1977, p. 353.

[16]The following conditions are from William C. Byham, "Starting an Assessment Center the Correct Way," *Personnel Administrator*, February 1980, p. 27.

[17]Souder and Leksich, "Assessment Centers are Evolving Toward a Brighter Future," p. 86.

[18]Boehm, "Assessment Centers and Management Development," p. 342.

Some Additional References

Cohen, Stephen L. "The Bottom-Line on Assessment Center Technology." *Personnel Administrator*, February 1980, pp. 50–56.

Frank, Fredric D. and James R. Preston. "The Validity of the Assessment Center Approach and Related Issues." *Personnel Administrator*, June 1982, pp. 87–95.

Olivas, Louis. "Using Assessment Centers for Individual and Organization Development." *Personnel*, May-June 1980, pp. 63–67.

Thornton, George C. and William C. Byham. *Assessment Centers and Managerial Performance.* New York: Academic Press, 1982.

Tziner, Aharon, and Shimon Dolan. "Validity of an Assessment Center for Identifying Future Female Officers in the Military." *Journal of Applied Psychology*, December 1982, pp. 728–736.

Chapter 18

Employee Assistance Programs

Gates Rubber Company was looking for a way to help troubled employees and their families, and at the same time save the company some of the costs incurred when employee problems lower job performance. Edwin J. Busch Jr., director of corporate personnel services for this Denver, Colorado company explains the path they chose to achieve this end.[1]

About 10 years ago, Bob Dickson, our manager of training, convinced members of top management that an employee assistance program was not only worthwhile for the employees and their families, but was also a potential cost-saving vehicle for the company. Neither Dickson nor management could forsee the outstanding progress that was to take place in the first six years of the program. At that time, Gates had about 5,000 employees, about 60 percent of whom were union production employees, while the other 2,000 were managerial, professional, and technical employees.

Program Philosophy

The concept was simple and remains essentially unchanged to this day: An employee's personal problems are private *unless* they cause the employee's job performance to decline and deteriorate. When that happens, the personal problems become a matter of concern for the company. A trained employee is a valuable asset to be protected if possible.

The objective of the program then, as now, was to help troubled employees restore themselves to satisfactory job performance—or to prevent a troubled person's job performance from becoming unsatisfactory. The program's record of achievement is certain to warm the hearts of company controllers and social-minded executives alike because of solid savings in both people and money.

Getting Started

First, a single administrator-counselor was appointed to handle the program. Then, the program was launched with a series of meetings between office and factory supervisors and the program administrator, Bob Ellis. Ellis, a 25-year veteran with the company had spent 14 years as a volunteer helping others overcome alcoholism and drug abuse, and financial, marital, and emotional problems.

These meetings emphasized important factors in any successful employee assistance program. Among them were: self-referrals or supervisor referrals based on "documented, unacceptable" work performance; help with problems not directly work-related; job-security guarantees that careers and promotions would not be adversely affected by enrollment in the program; confidentiality procedures for maintaining information in files separate from personnel records; and coverage for employees' spouses and dependents.[2]

Supervisors were told that one out of every 12 employees might face personal problems which could adversely affect job performance, as a result of alcoholism, drug abuse, family, financial, or emotional difficulties. The supervisors were told what role they might be expected to play in the program, as illustrated in Figure 18–1.

At the same time, labor leaders in the plant were also briefed on ways in which the program could help union members with their personal problems and job performance. Confidentiality was repeatedly emphasized. No one beyond the program administrator and the referring supervisor would be aware of an employee's use of the program. Neither job security nor promotional chances would be jeopardized by participation in the program. If employees chose self-referral, not even the employees' supervisor need be aware of their participation in the program.

Both outside professionals and inside counselors have advantages in any employee assistance program. Gates chose inside counselors because of the expense factor and the rapport that could be developed between inside counselors and employees.

At the outset, it was obvious that we needed a counseling area that employees could visit without fear of being seen, since we had no idea how the use of such a self-help facility might be perceived by other employees. Later, as recognition of the success of the program spread, such anonymity was not needed. Yet, in the beginning, we chose a counseling area close to other heavily used employee services so employees could blend into the general traffic flow without being singled out.

Figure 18–1
A Model for an Employee Assistance Program

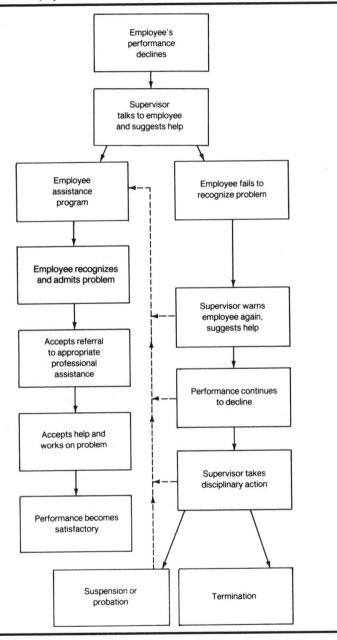

Costs and Benefits

Our initial proposal to management was based on a low-cost operation for the first year with the hope we could realize enough savings in employee absenteeism to offset program costs and possibly see some return on the corporate commitment to the program. One of the key factors in holding costs down while providing good service to employees, was the use of many public and private referral agencies. Most of these agencies specialized in some facet of the emotional-assistance spectrum at reasonable cost or without fee to the individual. These included such resources as consumer-credit counseling groups, community mental-health facilities, and alcohol and drug abuse counseling groups.

Just 55 employees used the service during the first few months. Yet even then we felt we had a winning combination since 23 of these "clients," reduced their absenteeism rate to less than one-half of what it has been for the same period of the previous year.

At the end of one year of program operation, we were able to report these figures to management:

1. 162 people, about 3 percent of our employee population participated;
2. Absenteeism totaled 4,106 hours versus 11,174 hours the previous year, an estimated savings of $56,000; and
3. Medical visits to the company clinic were reduced to 182 from 321 the previous year.

Based on an audit of the first year's savings and expenses, the company realized a return on its investment of more than three to one. In addition, we were able to retain 12 employees in their jobs when judges granted them probation to continue work under EAP supervision rather than being jailed for alcohol-related driving offenses.

Each succeeding year, the program has been more successful than the last. Almost without exception there have been continued reductions in the absenteeism rates of program clients. The number of employees who have improved their job performance after it had been affected by alcoholism, drugs, or marital or financial problems has also risen over these same six years.

Statistically, the reduction in absenteeism hours has improved more than 300 percent; medical visits to the company clinic were reduced more than 200 percent and avoidance of employee terminations has increased 10-fold in the six years of the programs.

Personal Endorsements

Testimonials for the program come from both participants and those working with the employee-clients. One employee wrote the company president, "The program has been the biggest motivator in my life during my 13 years of employment." After several years of operation, the president of the local United Rubber Workers commented: "Through this program, many people who would have gone down the drain are good, reliable employees of the company. Also, these same people are leading happy, useful lives. I cannot praise the results of the program enough. Its existence has been invaluable to the company, the union, and most of all to the employees."

Productivity gets a boost from the program as well. Tony Valdez, current administrator of the program, points out, "Employees who overcome drinking and emotional problems work harder, and an employee who receives help is a grateful employee and tends to work just that much better."

Current Status

The staff for the program remains small, with two full-time counselors and a licensed social worker. The staff has received special training, particularly in the field of alcoholism treatment. In addition, they take full advantage of the outstanding medical staff serving the company including the medical director, and a number of psychiatrists and other specialists. Outside referral sources include not only the many social-service agencies and community-service groups specializing in helping employees solve their personal problems, but also an attorney who provides both volunteer and paid legal services.

Most of the other major Gates' facilities now have their own employee-assistance programs, modeled after the original plan that was developed at corporate headquarters in Denver. Both the company and employees have benefited from the two most significant achievements of the program: improved human relationships—at home and work—and improved employee productivity.

GENERAL CHARACTERISTICS OF EMPLOYEE ASSISTANCE PROGRAMS

The description of the Gates Rubber Company EAP, including the model shown in Figure 3–1, provides good insight into the workings of a representative program of this kind. Since about 3,000 of these programs are in operation today, it is worthwhile to examine their general characteristics in detail. Our attempt to reach some generalizations about so many diverse programs is based on a synthesis of the philosophy, score, and operations of EAPs prepared by Professor John L. Tarver.[3]

Organizational Philosophy

The key ingredients to an employee assistance program are expressed in these propositions: "First, job performance must be the primary variable of concern in identifying troubled employees. However, it is important to recognize that almost all employee problems, whatever their nature or source, will ultimately have an impact on job performance. Supervisors must play an important part in EAPs because they are in the best position to observe and evaluate job performance."[4] Although supervisors must observe and report substandard performance, they are not expected to communicate a formal diagnosis to the employee, or even to make such a diagnosis. For example, the supervisor should not say to the employee who misses work because of financial problems, "Your problem is that you are a compulsive gambler."

Scope of Help Offered

There are three potential responses to dealing with human problems. The first is *prevention,* or keeping an anticipated problem from happening, such as lowering job pressures to help prevent some types of stress disorder. The second is *intervention* or stepping into a situation to affect its course, such as holding group discussions to discuss the management of ineffective performance. The third is *treatment,* the application of remedies to try to cure a problem. In practice, the term *intervention* is used to refer to activities that could be classified as either prevention or treatment.

EAPs frequently involve prevention; a few conduct educational programs about matters such as drug abuse. Most EAPs are concerned with intervention and treatment. An intervention takes place when a manager identifies a potential problem and then alerts the organization, for example, to the presence of an employee who appears to be distributing illegal drugs. The organization can then intervene to keep the problem from reaching fruition—in this case, eliminating a condition that could lead to employee drug abuse. Treatment, of course, refers to activities such as counseling an employee about a personal problem.

The Operation of an EAP

Figure 18-1 provides a general model of a representative EAP, but additional details are necessary to understand its complexity. EAPs can be organized in three different ways. They can be conducted (a) entirely by company specialists, (b) by an outside agency, or (c) by a combination of the two. The larger the organization, the more practical an in-house program. Tarver notes that externally run plans add more confidentiality to the program.[5]

Role of the Manager

The manager has a dual role in an employee assistance program. Of primary concern, the manager carries out the conventional managerial function of evaluating performance. When a subordinate's performance becomes substandard, the manager should make some determination as to whether the unacceptable performance stems from an organizational problem (poor equipment, limited resources) or a personal problem. A checklist for the type of behaviors usually associated with the problem of substance abuse is shown below.

Assuming the poor performance is most probably attributable to a personal problem, the subordinate must be confronted. Part of the confrontation process is tactfully to ask the subordinate to visit the EAP counselor. The boss should follow-up with the employee to see if he or she is progressing with the assistance program. Note carefully that this format does not require the superior to become embroiled in or delve into the specifics of the subordinate's personal problems.

In short, the manager detects the problem, confronts the subordinate, suggests a referral, and follows up on progress.

The Telltale Signs of Alcohol and Drug Abuse*

It is important for managers to recognize the physical symptoms and behavioral problems frequently associated with alcoholism and drug abuse on the job. The presence of more than one of these symptoms or problems indicates the need to confront the problem. Referral to the EAP counselor or outside resource is usually also indicated. The following is a list of telltale signs:

- Occasional and poorly explained lapses in fulfilling responsibilities.
- Unusual flare-ups or outbreaks of temper.
- Dramatic decreases in quality and quantity of work.
- More elaborate alibis for work deficiencies.
- Changes for the worse in physical appearance.
- Avoidance of boss and co-workers or becoming grandiose or belligerent.
- Swings in work pace become more pronounced and more frequent.
- Many work problems that previously had been partially hidden or ignored come to the surface.
- Attendance and punctuality become unreliable.
- Substantially longer lunch periods.
- Severe financial difficulties emerge.
- More frequent and more severe off-the-job accidents occur.

---

*Based in part on "Management Guide on Alcoholism and Other Behavioral Problems" (Long Grove, Ill.: Kemper Insurance Company), p. 10; Jordan M. Scher, ed., *Drug Abuse in Industry: Growing Corporate Dilemma* (Springfield, Ill.: Charles C. Thomas, 1973), p. 295.

■ Frequent use of breath purifiers to cover morning drinking during working hours.

■ Changing work patterns to assure occasions to sneak drinks during the day.

■ Increased nervousness, gastric upsets, and insomnia problems.

■ Frequent periods in which the person cannot concentrate on the work at hand.

■ Wearing sunglasses at inappropriate times to hide dilated pupils or bloodshot eyes.

■ Frequent reporting of unusually high expense account vouchers.

■ Finding employees in odd places during normal working hours, such as closets and storage rooms, and excessive time in lavatory.

Other Referral Sources

Immediate managers play a vital role in the EAP since they generate most of the referrals. Employees can also be referred to the EAP in several other ways. Self-referral is not uncommon when a program is widely trusted by employees. The employee's family also might alert the EAP coordinator to developing difficulties. Various units of the organization with employee contact (such as medical, personnel, and security) may spot employee problems. Finally, community agencies may be a source of referral. An employee convicted of driving while intoxicated might be ordered to participate in a company-sponsored alcoholism treatment program.

Whoever or whatever the referral source, the key point is that these potential sources of referral must recognize that confrontation and referral is preferable to allowing a problem to fester.

Role of the Coordinator

The EAP coordinator is the front-line person: he or she is the contact point for the troubled employee referred to the program. The coordinator must explain the nature of the program to the employee and motivate the employee to follow the program through to completion. Employees referred to the program enter with varying degrees of willingness to participate. Some even attend just to "get their supervisor off their back." After the initial interviews are completed, the in-house coordinator refers the employee to (a) the professional diagnostic and referral agent if the EAP is an external arrangement, or (b) to the in-house EAP staff.

The in-house coordinator has an important administrative task to perform. He or she must track and report on the impact of the assistance program in terms of trends in absenteeism, tardiness, accidents, and other areas where organizational performance can be affected by employee problems. The data collected can be used to measure the cost-effectiveness of the EAP. The EAP coordinator must maintain employee confidentiality while keeping track of the program.

Treatment Phase

Whether the EAP is contracted to an outside organization or conducted internally, the next step in the process involves diagnosis and treatment. The employee is diagnosed professionally, and a determination as to method of treatment is made. Next, the employee is directed to the appropriate helping resource in the referral network where the employee deals directly with his or her problem(s). Frequently the referral network will include community organizations with capabilities in the area of concern. Among them are Alcoholics Anonymous, Gambler's Anonymous, community mental health centers, family counseling agencies, and legal agencies.

Once the employee has been guided to the appropriate treatment program, the diagnostic and referral agent monitors progress and works with the internal EAP coordinator to help minimize conflicts between the job and treatment. For example, the employee may need to leave work early on occasion to attend treatment.

Employee Rights under the EAP

After the supervisor confronts an employee about declining or substandard performance and refers him or her to the assistance program, the employee has two choices. One is to recognize that he or she may have a treatable problem and voluntarily enter the EAP. The other choice is to continue on the job without seeking help. Either of these alternatives can ultimately lead to one of two outcomes: performance can be restored to an acceptable level or it can continue to decline. When the employee has willingly sought treatment, an effort is usually made to stay with the treatment program until a successful conclusion is reached. Nevertheless, if the employee's performance does not return to a satisfactory level despite the outside help, he or she may ultimately have to be dismissed. EAPs *cannot* save every employee.

Tarver notes that in the event the employee chooses to ignore the supervisor's initial referral, and his or her performance remains substandard, the matter must be handled through ordinary disciplinary means.[6] Under an EAP philosophy, supervisors are encouraged to provide advance warning and continue to encourage voluntary EAP participation.

THE CASE FOR AND AGAINST EMPLOYEE ASSISTANCE PROGRAMS

EAPs are now an established part of contemporary human resource management. Many small and medium-size firms which do not have a formal assistance program of their own follow a similar model of referring employees with personal problems to mental health facilities designed for that purpose. Since EAPs serve both economic and financial ends, not too much controversy surrounds their use. Nevertheless, it is important to examine the evidence for and against these programs.

The Evidence in Favor of EAPs

A compelling argument in favor of employee assistance programs is they are cost effective. There has been a growing realization of the costs associated with employee problems, such as alcohol and drug abuse, marital discord, mismanagement of personal finances, parent-child conflict, sexual disturbances, heart disease, and a host of other stress-related physical ailments. A sampling of these overall costs include the following:[7]

■ The National Association of Mental Health calculates an annual productivity loss of $17 billion due to employees' emotional problems, with the individual costing his or her firm $1,622 annually.
■ The United States Postal Service estimates a $168 million annual loss due to alcoholism.
■ Gulf Oil Canada Ltd., employing 11,000 workers, estimates its annual loss related to alcoholism at $400,000.
■ Alcoholism costs North American industry about $18 billion annually due to absenteeism and medical costs.
■ Troubled employees are said to cost their employers about 25 percent of their annual salaries in lost time, accidents, and increased insurance premiums.
■ Stress disorders, in general, cost organizations about $20 to $30 billion each year.
■ About 32 million workdays and $8.6 billion in wages are lost annually to heart-related diseases.

How Effective Have EAPs Been in Reducing Some of These Costs?

The rationale for establishing an EAP is clear. If you can help employees cope with their personal problems—before they get out of control—you will save the organization a substantial amount of money. The money saved includes direct costs of hospitalization, sick leave, and severance pay. Among the major indirect costs are lost productivity and managerial time spent disciplining and counseling employees plagued by personal problems. Some data show that the results achieved by assistance programs support this rationale.

The Human Ecology Institute reported the first comprehensive research about the effectiveness of EAPs. A general finding from a study of 11 large programs was that 57 percent of the cases referred for alcoholism were recovered or noticeably improved after treatment. Supervisory ratings and other means of performance assessment revealed that there was an associated positive change in work performance.[8]

Similar findings about the effectiveness of industry-based alcoholism programs have been noted. The New York Police Department reports a 75 percent recovery rate; DuPont 66 percent; Illinois Bell 57 percent; Eastman Kodak 75 percent; General Motors 80 percent; and Inland Steel 82 percent.[9]

An experimental study about the effectiveness of an EAP was conducted at the Oldsmobile Division of General Motors. Two researchers compared a group of workers who voluntarily entered GM's treatment program with a control group of 24 known drug abusers who chose not to participate. The two groups were comparable but not identical. For example, the fact that the control group declined treatment while the experimental group volunteered could have influenced the outcome of the study.

The "treatment" and "no treatment" groups were compared on a number of job-related variables. Among the findings were: (1) The treated employees lost $45,000 in wages during the year following their treatment, as opposed to a wage loss of $85,000 for the nontreated employees. (2) The treated group showed a decline in disciplinary incidents, absences, and sickness and accident benefits, while the untreated group showed an increase in these factors during the period of the study.

Although this program served 117 employees over a 24-month period, no new personnel had to be hired to administer the program, adding to its cost effectiveness.[10]

Control Data Corporation has furnished evidence of the cost-effectiveness of its EAP in reducing worker compensation costs. A study of four compensation cases projected a savings to the company of $705,000 through rehabilitation intervention. (The CDC assistance program included rehabilitation services.) The four employees involved had high seniority, and would have been off the job indefinitely had not the company set up a homework arrangement or created new jobs for them. A company official notes:

> The figures were compiled using a maximum pay-out to age 65 on the assumption that the individual would never return to full-time employment. Only work-time loss has been computed; therefore, the figures do not include medical expenses or permanency ratings.[11]

Evidence and Arguments against EAPs

No program or method of applied management receives all rave reviews. Along these lines, some negative evidence has been gathered about the effectiveness of EAPs, and some criticisms can be made of them. A survey of drug abuse in 75 organizations conducted by James W. Schreier seriously questions the effectiveness of assistance programs in dealing with employee drug abuse. The drugs studied included alcohol, marijuana, heroin, cocaine, and "other drugs." Data were collected in both 1976 and 1981, allowing comparisons over time. According to Schreier, the survey data showed an alarming failure of current educational and employee assistance efforts in controlling the drug problem. In 1981, more of the firms studied believed that the drug abuse and alcoholism problem in work organizations is equal to or more serious than it was in 1976, both in their own and in other firms.[12]

The argument can be advanced that employee assistance programs are too paternalistic. According to this line of reasoning, managers should tell substandard performers to shape up or ship out in a tactful manner, but the company should not provide the facilities for them to shape up. Overcoming personal problems that interfere with the employee's job effectiveness is the employee's exclusive responsibility. Perhaps there is a limit to how much the employer should be asked to do for the employee.

A similar criticism of EAPs is that the cost of overcoming personal problems should be borne directly by the troubled employee. Under an EAP, the treatment cost is considered a benefit. A relatively small number of employees, however, participate in this benefit. A large majority should not be asked to have some of their benefits shunted toward the rehabilitation of problem employees.

A potentially serious argument against EAPs is that most of the negative comments about them never surface into published reports because most written material about EAPs are by people who run such programs. A case in point is the amount of coercion many employees believe is used to get them to join the program—a perception that to this author's knowledge has not been reported. An orderly in a state mental hospital made this point: "Supervisors here put a lot of pressure on the employee with a drinking problem to enroll in the assistance program. You are told that if you don't join up, you'll be canned. So you get a lot of workers claiming how great the program is and how it's cured their problem."

Finally, the point can be made that EAPs border on meddling in the personal lives of employees. Despite the reassuring statements about the confidentiality of the program, who attends the program is hardly a secret. Attendees run the risk of being permanently labeled as problem emloyees.

GUIDELINES FOR ACTION AND SKILL DEVELOPMENT

The presence of an EAP does not mean that somebody else (the EAP counselor) is now taking care of your toughest personnel problems. As a manager, you still have to monitor performance and provide encouragement to the subordinate who is attempting to resolve personal problems which impair job performance. Once the problem is resolved, and the employee returns to satisfactory performance, it is still necessary to stay alert to new manifestations of the same problem and be alert to new problems.

Confronting subordinates with your observations that they are in need of outside help for their personal problems is a delicate task. Tips for conducting the confrontation session include:

1. As difficult as it may seem, attempt to relax.
2. Get to the central purpose of the meeting almost immediately. The gravity of the problem should be communicated during the first few minutes of the interview.
3. Avoid being apologetic or defensive about the need for the meeting. Every organization has a responsibility both to the outsiders it serves and to itself to insist on acceptable job performance.
4. Confrontations about unacceptable performance and behavior should be conducted in a private, quiet work area or office with no interruptions allowed.
5. Confrontations should be conducted with feeling (particularly sincerity) but not with hostility.
6. Confront job-related behavior, not personality traits. For instance, it is poor practice to say to a temperamental employee, "You're a hot-head and you had better shape up." It is better to say, "You argue so frequently with other employees that they are not giving you the cooperation you need to get your work done."

Dealing with problem employees and the problems of employees has become a managerial skill well worth practicing. A prediction has already been made that in the future, EAPs will be required by law.[13] And EAPs are gaining widespread acceptance in North American work organizations.

Employee assistance programs are not reserved for lower-ranking employees. Managerial, professional, and technical and sales personnel should feel free to use such assistance when the need arises.

Questions and Activities

1. Draw up a list of at least 12 problems you think could be potentially handled by an EAP.
2. Identify several personal problems you think should be off limits for an EAP. Explain your reasoning.

3. Related to the above, should an EAP be obliged to help an employee overcome the problem of stealing company supplies? Why or why not?

4. How much time should the organization allow an employee to correct a personal problem (that was impairing job performance) before he or she is terminated?

5. What is the relationship of an EAP to employee discipline?

6. Should employees be given time off with pay to attend treatment sessions for personal problems? Discuss.

7. During an annual meeting, a stockholder asked the company president, "How can you justify spending stockholder's money to rehabilitate junkies?" How might the president respond?

8. If you had a personal problem that was interfering with your job effectiveness, would you visit the EAP in your organization? Why or why not?

Notes

[1] The following case about Gates Rubber Company is paraphrased and excerpted from Edwin J. Busch Jr., "Developing an Employee Assistance Program," *Personnel Journal* (September 1981), pp. 708–711. Reprinted with permission.

[2] *Bulletin to Management*, Bureau of National Affairs (April 16, 1981), p. 8.

[3] Portions of this section of the chapter are based on and adapted from John L. Tarver, "Employee Assistance Programs: A New Concept in Human Resource Management," *The Alabama Business & Economic Journal* (April 1983), pp. 21–23.

[4] Bradley Googins, "Employee Assistance Programs," *Social Work* (November 1975), p. 465. Cited in Tarver, p. 21.

[5] Tarver, p. 22.

[6] Ibid., p. 23.

[7] Based on several sources, with some of the figures adjusted for the current value of the U.S. dollar. The sources include: Gopal C. Pati and John L. Adkins, Jr., "The Employer's Role in Alcoholism Assistance," *Personnel Journal* (July 1983), p. 569; William G. Wagner, "Assisting Employees with Personal Problems," *Personnel Administrator* (November 1982), p. 59; Robert Witte and Marsha Cannon, "Employee Assistance Programs: Getting Top Management's Support," *Personnel Administrator* (June 1979), p. 25.

[8] The Human Ecology Institute, "Characteristics of Selected Occupational Programs," (Raleigh, N.C., June 1976). Reported in McGaffey, "New Horizons," p. 29.

[9] Pati and Adkins, "The Employer's Role," p. 569.

[10] Ibid.

[11] David J. Reed, "One Approach to Employee Assistance," *Personnel Journal* (August 1983), p. 652.

[12] James W. Schreier, "A Survey of Drug Abuse in Organizations," *Personnel Journal* (June 1983), p. 483.

[13] Witte and Cannon, "Employee Assistance Programs," p. 24.

Some Additional References

Alpander, Guvenc G. "Training First-Line Supervisors to Criticize Constructively." *Personnel Journal*, March 1980, pp. 216–221.

Asherman, Ira G. "The Corrective Discipline Process." *Personnel Journal*. July 1982, pp. 528–531.

Bittel, Lester R., and Jackson E. Ramsey. "What to Do About Misfit Supervisors (Part II)." *Management Review*. March 1983, pp. 37–43.

Kuzmits, Frank E. and Henry E. Hammons, II. "Rehabilitating the Troubled Employee." *Personnel Journal*. April 1979, pp. 238–242, 250.

Whitney, Gary G. "When the News Is Bad: Leveling with Employees." *Personnel*. January–February 1983, pp. 37–45.

Stewart, Valerie and Andrew Stewart. *Managing the Poor Performer*. (Brookfield, Vermont: Gower Publishing Company, 1982).

Chapter 19

Human Resource Accounting

The American Accounting Association defines human resource accounting (HRA) as "the process of identifying and measuring the data about human resources and communicating this information to interested parties."[1] In this chapter, we present one conceptual example of the use of HRA, and one application within an accounting firm intent on managing its investment in personnel.

A DEMONSTRATION OF THE COST OF HUMAN RESOURCES

Since the use of human resource accounting concepts is still in the experimental stage, research about its contribution to the organization is limited. Nevertheless, a demonstration of a cost analysis of human resources will help illustrate its potential contribution. The Upjohn Company experience, described here, deals with the return on investment of human resources rather than their cost. We rely on accounting professor Clark E. Chastain for his analysis of the cost of human resources as reported in the *University of Michigan Business Review*.[2]

Just as conventional accounting continues to report most economic events and transactions in terms of cost, many human resource transactions can be presented in cost terms. Many decisions involving people may need to be based, at least in part, on approximate costs.

Cost is the sacrifice incurred to obtain an asset or a service. Human resource costs may be divided into direct and indirect. Direct costs refer to the amounts that can be traced directly to the resource. Indirect costs cannot be traced directly since they are incurred for general use in more than one activity, and they must be allocated among activities based on assumptions relating to benefits received. Opportunity cost, often quite important in HRA and in managerial decisions, is used to refer to either revenue, costs, or income forgone, or lost, when a decision is made. For example, to acquire and train a new manager might cost a company $6,000, while to promote a person internally might result in $5,000 familiarization and training costs. Once management makes the decision to hire the new person, actual costs of $6,000 are incurred, while the opportunity costs (those forgone) are $5,000.

Human resource costs may generally be broken into three major components—acquisition, learning, and separation. To illustrate each of those and some of their uses we have gone through a step-by-step breakdown in Exhibits 1, 2, and 3. The exhibits reflect the costs incurred in (1) acquiring John Savoy and (2) training him as production manager for production department number one in the Rayford Manufacturing Company. Separation costs are given in Exhibit 3.

Exhibit 1
Acquisition Costs

Name of employee: John Savoy, manager,
 production department No. 1, hired July 1, 1985

		Direct	Indirect
1.	Recruitment—Costs incurred to identify possible sources of personnel		
	Advertisement—newspaper	$ 40	
	College recruiting	–	
	Employment agency fee (one-half month salary)	2,000	
	Entertainment—dining at the country club	160	
	Travel—visit with the company	200	
	Administrative	200	
		$2,600	
2.	Selection—Determining which applicant is offered employment		
	Interviewing, testing, administrative costs for three applicants: Savoy, Law, and Durks (These costs tend to be higher for higher-level jobs.)	$1,000	
3.	Hiring and placing—Costs to bring Savoy aboard		
	Hiring, moving and travel allowance	$2,200	
	Placement—administrative costs to place Savoy on the job (company ID, placing his name on the payroll and department records, arranging for auto parking)	200	
		$2,400	
4.	Promotion or hiring within considered		
	Opportunity costs, alternative slection of Rex York, assistant manager in a different department; cost of moving him and acquiring a replacement		$7,000
		$6,000	$7,000

Exhibit 2
Learning Costs

John Savoy began work July 1, 1985

	Direct	Indirect
1. Formal training		
Two-week course		
Salary	$ 2,000	
School costs, books, and fees	400	
	$ 2,400	
2. On-the-job training		
Only 40 percent effective first three months on the job, costs of ineffectiveness equals 60 percent times $12,000 salary month	$ 7,200	
70 percent effective, second three months, cost equal 30 percent times $12,000	3,600	
	$10,800	
3. Cost of trainer's time		
Production superintendent, one-half month times his salary $6,000		$ 3,000
Production manager from Department No. 2, one-half month times his monthly salary $4,000		$ 5,000
4. Lost productivity by other people during the training period		
Production Department No. 1		$ 2,000
Production Department No. 2		1,600
Sales, administration		1,400
Total		$ 5,000
	$13,200	$10,000

Original human resource
cost, John Savoy

	Grand total	Direct	Indirect
Acquisition	$13,000	$ 6,000	$ 7,000
Learning	23,00	13,200	10,000
Total	$36,000	$19,200	$17,000

Some elaboration on the information in Exhibits 1, 2, and 3 will probably be helpful. The indirect costs, as mentioned earlier, cannot be traced directly to John Savoy, but must be allocated among the costs of human resources and other activities that are involved. The selection process for a new production manager involved three people: Savoy, Law, and Durks. The recruitment and selection costs for the two people not hired is treated as part of the costs of acquiring Savoy, since the total recruitment and selection costs were incurred to acquire one production manager.

The opportunity cost to transfer Rex York from another department to

Exhibit 3
Separation Costs

John Savoy, manager, production department No. 1
    resigned, effective December 31, 1985

	Direct	Indirect
1. Separation pay		
None given to John, who left within one year	0	
Cost due to reduced efficiency in other departments in December when Savoy decided to resign	$1,600	
	$1,600	
2. Loss of efficiency prior to separation		
Savoy did not concentrate well on his job in December		$ 1,000
3. Cost of vacant position, January 1986		
Cost in Department No. 1		$ 4,000
Related costs in other departments		2,000
		$ 6,000
Total separation cost	$1,600	$ 7,000

Replacement cost for production department No. 1 manager

	Grand total	Direct	Indirect
1. Acquisition	$13,000	$ 6,000	$ 7,000
2. Learning	13,200	13,200	10,000
3. Separation	8,600	1,600	7,000
Total	$44,800	$20,800	$24,000

Production Department No. 1 is $7,000, the cost of moving him and recruiting and hiring a replacement. This opportunity cost should be recorded in supplemental records, not only in support of the current decision, but because such data will likely be useful in future manpower acquisition decisions. The original cost of the human resource—for Production Manager Department No. 1—is $36,200, shown at the bottom of Exhibit 2. Under HRA, this amount should be capitalized, entered on the balance sheet, and amortized in future periods as John Savoy contributes to the revenues of the company. An HR ledger control account would contain total human resource costs for all personnel covered by the HR accounting system: subsidiary ledger records with supporting information should be kept for each appropriate individual member. The control account should be debited periodically for additions, replacements, development, and transfers in; and credited for amortization, turnover losses (voluntary and involuntary), obsolesence, and transfers out.

Value of Human Resources. The concept that people have value to an organization, derived from general economic value theory, relates to the expectation that they will contribute services to it in the future. Two meanings of value are that a resource commands purchasing power or has exchange value, while the second is termed *use value*. The theory of human resource value, based on the latter concept, relates to the expected future benefits, contributions, services, or utility of organizational personnel.

Measurement of value is a many faceted and difficult issue. Conventional accounting is struggling to report a form of value—under Accounting Series Release No. 190 of March 1976 of the U.S. Securities and Exchange Commission. Human resource accounting faces the more preponderable task of valuing the intangible associated with the potential services of personnel. The task may be broken down into three subtasks: (1) individual employees, (2) groups such as departments or responses to centers, and (3) for the total human organization.

The original cost of $36,200 for human resources at the bottom of Exhibit 2 is comparable to the total cost of inventory when it is placed on the shelf ready for sale where it incurred the invoice cost of the goods, transportation, receiving, unpacking costs and so on. Similarly a machine's total costs include those necessary for it to begin effective operations. The human resource is ready to fully function in the position or service state for which it has been hired.

The resignation of John Savoy on December 31, 1985, is designed to show the separation costs incurred when an employee leaves. The period of six months, while short, points up a problem many firms have of the costs of turnover.

The total replacement cost of $44,800 may be titled the gross cost of turnover. Identifying the cost of personnel turnover is a prime step involved in reducing it.

Standard costs may be developed for the acquisition and training of people to improve efficiency. Return on investment techniques are being applied, much in an exploratory stage yet, to evaluate the efficiency in utilizing human resources.[3]

Reporting only the cost or investment in human resources is often strongly criticized. The reason is that the present value of an employee's expected future contributions to the entity may differ greatly from cost. Therefore, HRA gives much attention to determining the value of human assets.

Furthermore, the measurement model described earlier of acquisition, training, and separation items does not report all costs that are important for human resource decisions. Future costs related to the expected services of an employee may be needed.[4]

A current example of the usefulness of human resource data to management comes from the Montreal office of the accounting firm of Touche Ross & Co. The firm manages its investment in personnel by monitoring the rate and cost of turnover, along with recruitment, selection, and training.[5] Touche Ross uses human resource accounting for several reasons. One is to account for outlay and opportunity costs. The firm's long-term survival depends largely on the development of younger members to replace senior professional staff. In addition, the diversion of the senior members' energies into training juniors represents an opportunity cost—the seniors could be performing billable work instead of conducting training. Also, turnover rates in public accounting are quite high. The measurement and control of both the cost of training and turnover led to the development of an accounting system featuring both outlay costs (out-of-pocket expenditures) and opportunity costs (billings to clients foregone).

To implement the system, time records were introduced that were kept regularly by the auditors to keep track of time spent on client work. A *cost-of-time analysis* report was then developed. It addressed three dimensions of professional staff time: chargeable time, investment time (time spent in the development of human assets), and maintenance time (an expense with no future service potential). The report also compared planned versus actual hours for activities under the category, *investment* (such as recruiting, orientation, counseling, and development; formal training programs; and research). According to a Touche Ross official, "Not only are human services monitored through this planning and control report, but personnel who are alerted to its existence may be motivated to improve their allocation of time by tasks."[6]

Another product of this approach to HRA was a *Summary of Human Resource Investment* that produced a total shown for investments in personnel during the year. This total was often compared with the planned investment under the corresponding category in the Cost-of-Time Analysis report. The summary listed both the outlay and opportunity costs components of the human resource investment. The end result was a tool for monitoring the efficiency and effectiveness of investment in human capital, thus permitting the firm to evaluate whether or not training and other objectives were met.

Another product of the system was the *Statement of Human Resource Flows*. It reported on changes in human capital inventory both in terms of physical quantities and monetary units. An inventory at the start of the year was augmented during the year by transfers from other offices and recruiting from outside the firm. The closing inventory reflected transfers out, departures, and amortization.

The reports described provided Touche Ross officials with information that should help them improve the management of their human resources, particularly in these areas: determining the proper staff mix, controlling professional turnover, hiring policies, and training expenditures.

Value of Individuals. Determining the value of individuals (certainly periodically) would be useful in evaluating individual performance, the performance of management, in business acquisitions and combinations, for appraising salaries and wages for promotions, for merit and other pay increases, for transferring employees and for layoffs and terminations. A number of monetary methods for valuing individuals have been suggested.

1. Discounting the amount of the future net contributions of an individual to the present.
2. Original cost.
3. Replacement cost.
4. Compensation.
5. Opportunity cost.

Items 2–5 are surrogate or substitute measures.

A model exists which discounts the net future services of individuals to the present. The movement of people from one service state (position) to another within the company is a stochastic (probabilistic) process. The future or potential net contribution from an individual accruing to the organization are discounted to the present. For example, if a partner in a CPA firm has 1,000 hours billable to clients in the current year at $50 per hour, the gross contribution is $50,000. Assume his or her compensation including fringe benefits for the year is $40,000. The net contribution of $10,000 is the reward to the firm.

The model requires that we determine:

1. The set of service states in the organization.
2. The net value of each state to the organization.
3. The person's expected tenure in the firm.
4. The mobility probability that the individual will occupy each service state.

To value this partner, let us assume he will retire at the end of one year. The probability of continuing to occupy his present position is 1.0 (service state). Money is worth 8 percent to the firm. We discount his net contribution of $10,000 times the discount factor 0.9259 (present value of $1 at 8 percent for 1 period) and find that the partner's value is $9,259.

Compensation has the advantage of being a concrete, realistic, readily available, objective figure and appears to be useful in the nonprofit organization and expense centers. It is weak in that it may not truly indicate an individual's contribution and it doesn't allow for contributions to profit in the profit-making concern.[7]

Nonmonetary measures of individual value include skills, inventories rating and ranking methods of performance evaluation, potential assessments, and attitude surveys.

Value of Groups. Measuring the value of groups may be important for evaluating management's performance, mergers and business combinations, insurance, liquidation, bankruptcy, and for evaluating stock prices and security issues. Methods for valuing a profit-oriented group of organizations include economic value, unpurchased goodwill, and the human organization behavioral approach. For the nonprofit organization or expense center, we may capitalize compensation or use replacement cost or original cost valuation. The difficult problem in the profit-oriented enterprise is how to allocate earnings between human and conventional assets. Some writers have advocated using the investment or unamortized cost for each to arrive at an allocation ratio.[8]

THE STRENGTHS AND WEAKNESSES OF HRA

Although HRA has been around since the 1960s, it is still an exploratory technique in contemporary applied management. It is now gaining some acceptance as an internal control device in managing human resources. Human resource accounting has gained much less acceptance as a method of presenting data about a firm to external people. Published descriptions of the strengths and weaknesses of HRA show consistency in both the management and accounting fields.

Looking first at strengths, despite the ticklish measurement problems associated with HRA, it is better than using no measurement at all.[9] Acceptance of a formal system of measuring the worth of employees is long overdue. In addition, measuring human assets enhances the value of people. Steven Robbins observes that a major advantage of human resource accounting is that it makes managers aware that attracting and retaining employees has long-term value to the firm. If managers were charged with the unamortized balance in an employee's account should that employee leave, they would be inclined to try to prevent turnover. Under an HRA system, executives would also be more hesitant to lay off employees to increase profits in the short-range. Robbins says this is true because, "The unamortized balance of the investment made in the employee would be charged against the manager's unit at the time of layoff."[10]

Measuring the return-on-investment in people would represent a major contribution to organizations. One specific application would be making sound decisions about the problems of overstaffing versus understaffing. Among them would be the issue of whether to retain senior (and therefore high paid) employees versus hiring inexperienced (and therefore low paid) employees.

Kenneth Sinclair observes that human resource accounting can enhance an organization's decision-making capabilities, both internally and externally in the following ways:

1. Individual projects can be compared from year to year, and so can the entire investment in acquisition or conservation of human resource by recognizing the investment alternatives and potential returns.
2. Assist in planning staff expenditures by highlighting the strengths and weaknesses in the entire work force.
3. Highlight any changes that might be needed in recruiting policies. For instance, the cost of hiring and training new employees might exceed the outlay required to retain an employee who is considered to be surplus at the time.
4. Improve corporate profitability through more enlightened and all-encompassing decision making. The result would be a more strongly motivated work force and management team.[11]

To date the perceived weaknesses of HRA have overshadowed its strengths. Of primary importance, HRA is not yet within the realm of generally accepted accounting principles. A basic difference is that, under HRA, employees are considered as assets, not costs. Under authoritative accounting rules, employees would have to be recorded as costs and amortized in the same manner as physical assets. Another clash with generally accepted accounting principles is that HRA reports employees' current values rather than historical (acquisition) costs, a controversial accounting practice.

HRA's underlying problem is that measures of the cost and value of human resources are not precise enough yet to enable managers to make the kinds of decisions they are able to make using traditional accounting data.[12]

Skepticism exists about whether or not accounting concepts can really reflect the value of persons to the organization. What is the true value of a competent hospital chief executive officer, manufacturing vice president, or hockey coach? Finally, subjective judgements are used in making estimates for HRA. For example, is a top-notch inventor worth five times as much as a top-notch sales representative? Or is the reverse true?

Finally, attaching financial values to individuals can create many other problems. It is conceivable that managers could use HRA as a means of manipulating employees. An employee's dollar worth might be deceased as a punishment. Managers might even transfer some people at the end of the year to make the department balance sheet look healthier. Employees could conceivably demand more money once they learned their dollar value had increased. The value attached to an individual could have a strong negative or positive impact on a person's career, even in situations where the value was inaccurate. (Much like having been erroneously branded as an overachiever or underachiever in school.) Another expressed concern is that the people who attached financial values to other people would be seen by many as wielding too much power over the lives of others.[13]

GUIDELINES FOR ACTION AND SKILL DEVELOPMENT

In terms of the method's current capabilities, human resource accounting must be conceptualized and practiced as Human Capital Budgeting—as a human investment management system providing internal information for management decision making.[14]

When using HRA, a method should be chosen which relates the value of a person to performance data. For example, an administrator with high performance ratings is theoretically more costly to replace than one with average ratings. The rationale is that exceptional performers are in short supply.

No one method of HRA is yet of demonstrated superiority to the others. It is, therefore, prudent to use multiple methods such as estimating costs attributed to acquisition, learning, and separation.

A meaningful approach to HRA should make some estimate of the economic value of the employee—the money equivalent of services rendered by the person. Some tentative suggestions along these lines have been formulated:

1. Estimate the total time in which the employee is expected to render services to the firm.
2. Identify the various service states (positions) that the employee could occupy during his or her time with the firm.
3. Measure the value derived by the firm from the employee's occupying various service states for specified periods.
4. Estimate the probability that the employee will occupy each state at the specified future time.

Questions and Activities

1. Defend the following statement: "Professional athletic teams have engaged in a form of HRA for many years."
2. Assume a professional model (female) claims a depreciation allowance on her federal income tax form, arguing that her economic value decreases with age. How would you respond to this deduction from an HRA perspective?
3. Bring a balance sheet from an annual report to class. Point out where estimates of the dollar value of human assets should be entered.

4. How does the concept of customer goodwill tie in with HRA?

5. Using concepts from HRA, explain how a given employee could prove to be a liability.

6. What objections might labor unions and employee associations have toward HRA?

7. Refer to a standard text in organizational behavior or management (see the Preface) and read the information about equity theory. How might managers and individuals use HRA to make more precise judgments with the equity theory of work motivation?

8. Calculate your replacement cost if you are currently employed. If not, calculate the replacement cost of somebody you know who is employed. Explain how you arrived at your figure.

Notes

[1] "Report of the Committee on Human Resource Accounting," *Accounting Review,* Supplement 1973, p. 169.

[2] This section of the chapter is excerpted from Clark E. Chastain, "The Evolution of Human Resource Accounting," *University of Michigan Business Review,* January 1979, pp. 16–23. All dollar amounts reported have been converted to current values.

[3] See Robert Rachlin, *Return on Investment: Strategies for Profit* (New York: Marr Publications, 1976), especially Chapter 11, "An ROI Approach to Manpower Education," pp. 83–95.

[4] Eric Flamholtz, *Human Resource Accounting* (Encino, Calif.: Pickenson Publishing, 1974), p. 15.

[5] Robert P. Radchuck, "Human Resource Accounting in Industry," *CAmagazine,* August 1981, pp. 116–117.

[6] Ibid., p. 117.

[7] Mohammad A. Sangeladji, "Human Resource Accounting: A Refined Measurement Model," *Management Accounting,* December 1977, pp.48–52.

[8] For further discussion of determining value, see Flamholtz, *Human Resource Accounting,* Chapters 5 and 6; Robert Rachlin, *Return On Investment,* Chapter 11; and, Rensis Likert and David G. Bowers, "Improving the Accuracy of P/L Reports by Estimating the Change in Dollar Value of the Human Organization," *Michigan Business Review,* March 1973, p. 21.

[9] Philip H. Mirvis and Barry A. Macy, "Human Resource Accounting: A Measurement Perspective," *Academy of Management Review,* April 1976, p. 76.

[10] Steven P. Robbins, *Management: Concepts and Applications* (Englewood Cliffs, N.J.: Prentice-Hall, 1984), p. 465.

[11] Kenneth Sinclair, "Human Asset Accounting as an Aid to Decision Making," *Accountancy,* March 1978, p. 97.

[12] Marc J. Wallace, Jr., N. Fredric Crandall, and Charles H. Fay, *Administering Human Resources: An Introduction to the Profession* (New York: Random House, 1982), p. 514.

[13] Sue A. Ebersberger, "Human Resources Accounting: Can We Afford It?" *Training and Development Journal,* August 1981, p. 40.

[14] Bruce G. Meyers and Hugh M. Shane, "Human Resource Accounting for Managerial Decisions: A Capital Budgeting Approach," *Personnel Administrator,* January 1984, p. 29.

Some Additional References

Craft, James and Jacob Bernberg. "Human Resource Accounting: Perspective and Prospects." *Industrial Relations*. February 1976, pp. 2–12.

Gillespie, Jackson, et. al. "A Human Resource Planning and Valuation Model." *Academy of Management Journal*. December 1976, pp. 650–656.

Mirvis, Philip H. and Edward E. Lawler, III. "Measuring the Financial Impact of Employee Attitudes." *Journal of Applied Psychology*. January 1977, pp. 1–8.

LaBau, Marilyn L. "Human Resource Accounting: Is Quality of Worklife Profitable?" *Management World*. January 1982, pp. 45–46.

Savich, Richard and Keith Ehrenreich. "Cost-Benefit Analysis of Human Resource Accounting Alternatives," *Human Resource Management*. Spring 1976, pp. 7–18.

Schneider, Katie R. *Human Resource Accounting: A Comprehensive Bibliography*. Greensboro, N.C.: Center for Creative Leadership, 1981.

Name Index

Wieder, Robert S., 33
Wiens, Arthur W., 106
Wieting, Gretchen K., 105, 106, 108
Williams,John C., 227
Winston, Stephanie, 20
Winter, Caryl, 106
Witte, Robert, 296

Y–Z

Yager, Ed, 185
Yukl, Gary A., 89
Zager, Robert, 216
Zaltman, Gerald, 3
Zawacki, Robert A., 216
Zippo, Mary, 244

Subject Index